PRIVATE PILOT—AIRPLANE

Private Pilot
Airplane

SARAH F. RAMBO

The Iowa State University Press / Ames

TO MY HUSBAND **LARRY,**

AND OUR CHILDREN, **LARRY, JAMES,** AND **LISA**

©1983 The Iowa State University Press. All rights reserved

Composed and printed by The Iowa State University Press, Ames, Iowa 50010

First edition, 1983

International Standard Book Number: 0–8138–1382–4

Library of Congress Cataloging in Publication Data

Rambo, Sarah F. (Sarah Frances), 1939–
   Private pilot airplane.

   Bibliography: p.
   Includes index.
   1. Private flying.   I. Title.
TL721.4.R34   1983   629.132′5217   82–21299
ISBN 0–8138–1382–4

CONTENTS

PREFACE   vii

ACRONYMS AND ABBREVIATIONS   viii

1. *Familiarization*   3

2. *Basic Air Work*   22

3. *Getting Ready for Solo*   49

4. *Local Solo Phase*   89

5. *Cross-Country Phase*   129

RECOMMENDED READING   180

INDEX   181

PREFACE

I did not start out planning a career in aviation. It sort of just grew, one flight at a time. Once you get hooked on airplanes, you find a way to keep on flying. Earning a flight instructor certificate was the way I found to stay aloft.

I didn't start out planning to write a book on flight training, either. It sort of grew the same way, one lesson at a time, written out in longhand for my own students to take home and review.

Although I have stuck with government publications as references throughout this book I owe a debt to the flight manuals by William K. Kershner.

I have tried to stay away from too many war stories (like the time a student reached down to adjust his seat and set off the fire extinguisher.) One thing I *have* taken the opportunity to do is to feature the "Mean Green Machine," Cessna N3567V. That little airplane and I went through a lot together, and it has since departed the fix. It is sorely missed. I also want to take this opportunity to thank a lot of wonderful people: My family, who have continued to support my obsession with airplanes even though it occasionally meant hardship, if not outright neglect; the flight instructors who have taught me and still continue to materialize over my shoulder when I need them; and most special thanks to each and every student pilot whose names and accomplishments will be forever in my logbook.

Sarah F. Rambo

Acronyms and Abbreviations

A & P	Airframe & Powerplant		**CAS**	Calibrated Airspeed
AD	Airworthiness Directives		**CAT**	Clear Air Turbulence
ADF	Automatic Direction Finder		**CDI**	Course Direction Indicator
AGL	Above Ground Level		**CFI**	Certificated Flight Instructor
AI	Attitude Indicator		**CG**	Center of Gravity
AI	Authorized Inspector		**Comm**	Communications
AIM	Airman's Information Manual		**CT**	Control Tower
AIRMET	Airmen's Meteorological Information		**DF**	Direction Finding (Steer)
ALT	Altitude		**DME**	Distance Measuring Equipment
ANDS	Accelerate North, Decelerate South		**EFAS**	En route Flight Advisory Service
ARROW	Airworthiness certificate, Radio station license, Registration certificate, Operating limitations, Weight and balance data		**EGT**	Exhaust Gas Temperature
			ELT	Emergency Locator Transmitter
ASEL	Airplane Single Engine Land		**ETA**	Estimated Time of Arrival
ASI	Airspeed Indicator		**ETE**	Estimated Time En route
ATA	Actual Time of Arrival		**FAA**	Federal Aviation Administration
ATC	Air Traffic Control			
ATIS	Automatic Terminal Information Service		**FARs**	Federal Aviation Regulations
			FBO	Fixed Base Operator
BFR	Biennial Flight Review		**FCC**	Federal Communications Commission
BKN	Broken ceiling			

fpm	feet per minute	**mi/min**	miles per minute
FSS	Flight Service Station	**MSL**	Mean Sea Level
		MVFR	Marginal VFR
G	Gravity		
GADO	General Aviation District Office	**NDB**	Non-Directional Beacon
		NORDO	No Radio
gph	gallons per hour	**NOTAMS**	Notices to Airmen
GS	Ground Speed		
GUMP	Gas, Undercarriage, Mixture, Props	**NTSB**	National Transportation Safety Board
Hg	Mercury		
HI	Heading Indicator	**OAT**	Outside Air Temperature
HSI	Horizontal Situation Indicator	**OBS**	Omnibearing Selector
		PATWAS	Pilot's Automatic Telephone Weather Answering Service
IAS	Indicated Airspeed		
IFR	Instrument Flight Rules	**PCA**	Positive Control Airspace
IMC	Instrument Meteorological Conditions	**PIC**	Pilot In Command
		PIREP	Pilot Weather Reports
kHz	Kilohertz		
		RVR	Runway Visual Range
MCA	Minimum Controllable Airspeed	**SBY**	Standby
MH	Magnetic Heading	**SIGMET**	Significant Meteorological Information
MHz	Megahertz		
MOA	Military Operations Area	**SWB**	Scheduled Weather Broadcasts

T	Terminal	**VHF**	Very High Frequency
TACAN	Tactical Air Navigation	V_{le}	Maximum landing gear extension speed
TAS	True Airspeed		
TCA	Terminal Control Area	V_{lo}	Normal lift-off speed
TH	True Heading	**VOR**	Very High Frequency Omnirange
TOC	Top Of Climb	**VORTAC**	Very High Frequency Omnirange Tactical Air Navigation
TRSA	Terminal Radar Service Area		
TST	Test	V_r	Rotation speed
TWEB	Transcribed Weather Broadcasts	**VSI**	Vertical Speed Indicator
		V_{so}	Power-off stall speed
Unicom	Aeronautical advisory station	**VVI**	Vertical Velocity Indicator
		V_x	Best angle of climb
V_a	Maneuvering speed	V_y	Best rate of climb
VAR	Variation	**WAC**	World Aeronautical Chart
VASI	Visual Approach Slope Indicator	**WCA**	Wind Correction Angle
VFR	Visual Flight Rules	**W/V**	Wind Velocity

PRIVATE PILOT—AIRPLANE

Familiarization

F O R whatever reason, you have become attracted to airplanes. Your motivation is between you and your ego; your justification may be between you and your bank! You have already investigated the process of private pilot certification to some extent, or you wouldn't be reading this book. Probably you have already signed up with a flight instructor and experienced your first dual flight.

Objectives

Compare the student who is flying out of a dirt strip with a part-time, freelance flight instructor with the one who is training in a highly organized, FAA-approved flight school at a busy, tower-controlled airport. Both students still share common objectives and most of the same problems. First let's state your objectives as a student pilot:

1. To obtain a private pilot certificate.
2. To meet and for safety's sake to exceed minimum acceptable standards of skill and experience.
3. To accomplish this in the minimum required time because flight training is very expensive.

The objectives of this book may be achieved by the solution of the following problems:

1. *How does a student pilot judge the quality of instruction he is receiving?* The part-time instructor met the same standards for certification as did the full-time instructor; many part-time instructors work during the weekends simply because they love instructing, and they do a superior job. Many full-

time instructors are only trying to build time in the air to improve their chances for employment by the airlines and are often bored with instructing.

Skilled and dedicated flight instructors may be found almost anywhere. Unfortunately, that is just as true of the not-so-dedicated, and you want to learn from the best. As a student, how are you supposed to know whether or not you are being properly and safely trained?

The first objective of this book is to make certain that the knowledge and skills you need at every stage of training are available. Do not hesitate to shop around for another flight school or another instructor if you feel that the training you are getting or the equipment you are flying is not meeting acceptable standards.

2. *How does a beginning student determine the amount of classroom work or home study involved in private pilot certification?* Students don't determine this, they must be directed. You came to fly, not to study, but you must also acquire a working knowledge of meteorology, aerodynamics, aircraft systems and instruments, radio communication, radio navigation, pilotage and dead reckoning, the national airspace structure, and the regulations governing pilot operations within the air traffic system.

You have a great many new habits to learn, many of them directly opposed to habits you now have. Pilot training demands close coordination between classroom and flight training because it can't all be done in the airplane. Studies have shown that an aircraft in flight is possibly the world's worst classroom. Of all new information initially presented to a student in flight, he is apt to retain a tiny 2%. Noise, tension, confusion, the inability to "freeze the action" for demonstration purposes, and other factors combine to distract the learning process.

We can never hope to make the home-study portion of your training as much fun as the flying part, but the training material doesn't have to read like an annual government report. The second objective of this book is to present the necessary information in such a manner that you are able to relate it to a flight situation. When that flight situation arises, you will remember what you need to know.

3. *How does a student earn a private pilot certificate in the minimum required flight hours?* A straight answer to this question is, he probably can't. Details of the rules governing student pilots may be found in Federal Aviation Regulations (FARs), Subpart C, and for private pilots in FAR 61, Subpart D. Private pilot certification requires a minimum of 40 hours flying time, broken down as follows: 20 hours dual with at least 3 hours cross-country, 3 hours at night, and 3 hours in preparation for flight check; 20 hours of solo, with at least 10 hours solo cross-country. It should be fairly obvious from this breakdown that a minimum of 40 hours for the private certificate is just that—a minimum. It takes an unusual student/instructor combination to achieve the performance standards in that limited time span. These particular minimums have been in effect for over 20 years, and during that time the aviation system has grown enormously. A student pilot must operate in the same system with the airlines and the military; obviously, there is more to cope with and to learn. I strongly recommend that you base your financial plans on a more realistic estimate of the time needed for certification—at least 55 hours of actual flight time. To accomplish this goal you will need to study many additional hours, formulating and practicing both ground and flight procedures. There is a free training aid readily available to help you reduce the expense of ground instruction and dual flight hours—the kitchen simulator.

To qualify for the private pilot certificate, you must meet the flight time requirements, pass a written exam, an oral exam, and a practical test (flight check). A formal ground school is an invaluable aid in gaining the knowledge necessary to pass the written exam, although home-study courses under the supervision of your flight instructor are also effective. The written test is given at your nearest GADO (General Aviation District Office) and may be taken free of charge during business hours. In many areas designated written test examiners are available, although they charge for their services. Their availability may be an advantage for large groups (an entire ground-school class) that prefer to be examined during evenings or weekends. The tests are sent to FAA headquarters in Oklahoma City and are graded by computer. You may take the test at any time during your training, but you should present a note from your flight instructor stating that you are ready. Without this statement you will be required to submit to an oral examination from a GADO inspector (by appointment) to determine your readiness. You will present your (passing) test results to your flight examiner at the time you take the oral exam and the flight check.

The ideal time to take the written exam is immediately following your first dual cross-country flight. At this point you have been exposed to everything in your flight training that will be covered on the written exam, yet there is still enough time for you to receive the results before your flight check. The score will take two weeks or more to come back from Oklahoma City. If you flunk it the first time, you must study, be certified by your flight instructor to retake it, and wait. During this delay you will require additional flight hours to maintain your proficiency for the flight check, so it is to your advantage to be prepared to pass the written test the first time. Besides, very soon after your dual cross-country flights you will be going solo cross-country. On these flights you are exercising all the privileges of a private pilot but one—carrying passengers. It stands to reason that by this time you should have the knowledge required of a private pilot firmly between your ears.

There are certain basic supplies and documents you will need to accomplish your training. As a student you must have at least a Class III medical certificate, which is valid for two years and also doubles as your student pilot certificate. Not all physicians may issue pilot medical certificates—only those who have been through the FAA special medical course—so get the name of a doctor through your flight school. You will need a Federal Communications Commission (FCC) radio permit. This is free and your flight school can supply you with the application form. Right now you also need a pilot logbook and your own copy of FARs, which will include National Transportation Safety Board (NTSB), Part 830. These are United States government publications, but they have been commercially reproduced to meet the needs of pilots. The copy of the regulations that you purchase may have additional parts, but you will be concerned with Parts 61 and 91, and NTSB, Part 830. You will also require your own copy of the *Airman's Information Manual* (AIM) entitled *Basic Flight Information and ATC Procedures*. This is another government publication, revised quarterly, so take care to get a current copy. Purchase also a local sectional chart and an aircraft owner's manual for your type of training aircraft. A little later in the program you will need a flight computer and a navigation plotter as well as copies of *Private Pilot—Airplane: Written Test Guide* (AC61-32B) and *Private Pilot—Airplane: Flight Test Guide* (AC61-54A).

Your flight instructor is well acquainted with all of this paraphernalia and will answer any questions that they raised. You are not only learning a new skill—you are learning a new vocabulary. A lot of pilot talk consists of acronyms, initialisms, and supercool slang. The most important piece of equipment you will use, you already have—your kitchen table.

Kitchen Simulator

If you try to do all of your flight training in an airplane, you are going to be a very "high-time" pilot before you earn your certificate. Flying an airplane is more a mental than a physical exercise, and flight training is largely a case of developing proper habit patterns. *Webster's Third International Dictionary* defines habit as "an acquired mode of behavior that has become nearly or completely involuntary." You can't expect to develop a whole set of solid, safe habits in a mere 40 hours.

Your kitchen table can serve very effectively as a flight simulator. Set aside time between dual flights—and *especially* prior to solo flights—to mentally review the maneuvers and procedures you expect to practice in the airplane. I have seen the first half-hour (or more) of a flight period completely wasted in bringing the student up to the point where he left off the last time. You can speed your progress immeasurably by mentally reviewing the maneuvers while they are fresh in your mind and by psyching yourself back up to speed prior to a flying lesson.

The military and the airlines have trained hundreds of thousands of highly proficient pilots, and their method of training involves MEMORIZING PROCEDURES. Those pilots sit in a stationary mock-up of the airplane and drill procedures until they can put their hands on every switch and lever blindfolded. They know every step to take to perform any maneuver. Certainly all emergency procedures are memorized in this manner. And this is done before they ever climb into the airplane. Flight simulator training continues as a requirement for both military aviators and airline pilots throughout their flying careers. If flight simulator training is good enough for an F-14 driver—and the lady in the left seat of a 747—then it is good enough for me.

Ground sessions with your flight instructor are just as valuable as flight time, and you probably pay for them at the same rate. Your flight instructor has a moral and legal responsibility to see that certain knowledge requirements as well as flying skills are met. It is foolish to pay him to read the book to you, but that is just about what he will be forced to do if you are not prepared.

Much of the material in this book is the sort of information that your flight instructor will be giving you during your preflight and postflight briefings. You probably won't remember all that he tells you—so hold your own extra briefing session with me in the kitchen simulator. When you come up with questions, prepare a list to ask your regular instructor during your next dual session.

I will also attempt to give you some dual fight instruction in your kitchen simulator. This is free (for the price of the book), and you are already cleared for solo. The kitchen simulator also burns considerably less fuel than the airplane.

Walk-Around Inspection

This section will make little or no sense if you have not yet flown dual. Dual means a *learning* flight and not a token familiarization ride. Even after several flights, you are probably still fairly foggy about what you are looking for during preflight inspection—and why! You are accustomed to jumping into your automobile and blasting off. If a car makes ominous noises, there are gas stations everywhere. With airplanes, you'd better get it right before you go. Spend some time in the kitchen simulator with your owner's manual and be sure you understand your machine before you kick the tires and light the fires. At first you feel that to accomplish the walk-around inspection safely would require at least the knowledge and ability to take the airplane apart and put it together again. This is not really necessary.

The owner's manual is an important part of the airplane's equipment, and a copy should be on board at all times. It contains the manufacturer's recommended procedures, such as aircraft limitations, emergency procedures, airspeeds, and performance data. Later you will learn to extract the needed information from the charts and graphs, and some of the information in the owner's manual you will commit to memory. For the present, read through the manual and become familiar with its format so that you can refer to it easily as questions arise.

The preflight check begins with the pilot's own mental and physical state. If you have personal troubles or business worries, push them aside or stop right now. The airplane will jealously demand your full attention. And are you healthy today? Altitude can do tricky things with many medications—even over-the-counter drugs you have used many times before. Beware of flying with symptoms masked by pills—even aspirin. If you don't feel well, fly another day. A stuffy nose can become a blocked sinus; this is called "pain."

With the body healthy and the head on right, you enter the cockpit. Stow loose equipment and remove the control lock, turn on the master switch, lower the flaps, check the fuel gauges, and turn the master off.

You are not going to rely on electric fuel gauges. Check the fuel quantity visually; at least you know the gauges are working and the battery is charged. Place the ignition key in a handy spot but never in the ignition. You will treat the propeller at all times as if it were a loaded shotgun and never go near it if the key is in the ignition or if the master switch is on. Your pocket is not a handy place for the key, and you will find out why the first time you put it there.

It is your responsibility to determine that the airplane is airworthy; namely that all the required maintenance inspections are current (FAR 91, Subpart C) and that the required aircraft documents are on board. Use the ARROW method to remember the required documents:

> **A**irworthiness Certificate
> **R**adio Station License
> **R**egistration Certificate
> **O**perating Limitations
> **W**eight and Balance Data

Walk around the airplane in any direction that feels right; continue around and take care of everything as you come to it. If you start running back and forth from one wing to another, you are apt to skip something (or wear yourself out). DON'T accept arbitrary instructions without asking WHY: If you know the reasons for them, you are less apt to forget them.

Starting from your door and walking toward the tail, you check the general condition of the airplane. Directly behind the tail is the best place from which to peer under the belly; check the safety wires on the rudder cables, nuts and bolts, and counterweights. Disconnect the tail chain and check the elevator for freedom of movement and security.

Proceed around the airplane looking for cracks, dents, and missing fasteners to the trailing edge of the wing. Wiggle the flap rods and look for worn roller tracks, etc. Raise the aileron and check hinges and cotter pins. Grasp the aileron firmly if the wind is gusty; many fingers have been severely pinched in these conditions. High-wing airplanes will also dump water in your face, so watch it.

Continuing around, when you come to a fuel sump, you will drain it. Water is heavier than avgas and will sink to the bottom of the tank. Because water doesn't burn well, it is best to remove any that may have accumulated. This can occur if the last fuel pump was contaminated. It is even more likely to occur from condensation of moist air in partially filled tanks. If the plane is fully refueled after each flight—and particularly after the last flight of the day— there is little likelihood of water contamination.

Avgas is color coded by octane; 80/87 is dyed red, 100/130 is green, and 100 low lead is blue. In a pinch you can use 100 octane instead of 80, but not the other way around. Use a higher octane than normal, if necessary, but never lower, and never use car gas. When you mix the red and green, it looks clear, like gin. Don't drink the whole tank. Memorize the following items concerning your fuel system: the proper octane, the total capacity, and the portion of that capacity that is usable/unusable; the average fuel consumption in gph; and the total endurance time. You should also know the capacity and endurance of each individual fuel tank. Running out of gas in an airplane is totally inexcusable.

Disconnect the tie-down ropes as you pass them and visually check the level in all fuel tanks and secure the caps. A lost fuel cap will allow the tank to be siphoned dry in flight; this is expensive and cuts down your range.

If the brakes aren't hidden by wheel pants, check the brake pads and look for leaking hydraulic fluid. There will be one (or two) static openings on the side (sides) of the plane. These should be clear, but never blow in them or into the pitot tube because you might damage delicate instruments.

When you inspect inside the oil compartment door, you should question any petroleum leaks, gummy places, or loose-hanging wires. This sounds ominous, but you very seldom find any—and it never hurts to look. Before checking the oil, always wipe the dipstick; cooling oil may climb the stick and give you a false indication. Be very sure the oil cap is secure: A loose oil cap causes a mess on the windscreen and an unplanned landing. You should know the weight and grade of oil used and minimum and maximum capacity.

Notice that properly secured cowl fasteners and fuel caps are always streamlined so that they can't be unscrewed by the force of the wind. If you really want to check the stall-warning horn, turn on the master switch; if it is electric, lift the metal tab on the wing. If it is a reed, you would have to suck on it. (Most pilots probably skip this task, especially if the temperature is below freezing.)

Check the prop for security and the blade for nicks; most props have some.

A sharp nick on the prop blade, if left untended, can cause an invisible crack down deep inside the blade. The high vibrations they must endure can cause a portion of the blade to fly off. The blade can be dressed with a file by a qualified mechanic, so report any serious rough spots. You can help prevent this problem by avoiding starts, run ups, etc., over gravel surfaces.

See that the air filter is clear of obstructions; the nose strut (and mains in some airplanes) should be properly inflated. While you are standing in front, push the airplane back far enough to check all the way around the tires. If a tire is low, or bald enough that the threads show, call the mechanic. When you have drained, checked, unchocked, and untied your way to the cockpit door again, you can assume it will fly.

If you don't like the looks of something, yell for someone else's opinion: The only stupid question about an airplane is the one you fail to ask.

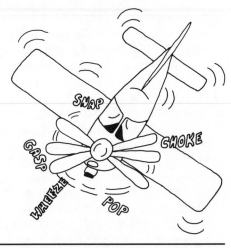

Checklists and Engine Start

Checklist firmly in hand, you proceed. Bear in mind that this is an all-purpose training manual and that your airplane may be different from mine. You may have fuel-tank selectors and boost pumps to deal with—or not. The high-wing Cessna 150 has simultaneous gravity feed; the Cessna 172 has individual tank selectors, but it is still gravity fed and requires no boost pump. Low-wing airplanes, such as Pipers, require both tank selectors and fuel-boost pumps since the fuel tanks are lower than the carburetor. There is no point in arguing the merits of either here. There are advantages and disadvantages to both types, or the manufacturers wouldn't sell so many airplanes.

The checklist provided in the owner's manual is the final authority, but there are a few unintentional problems inherent in following the factory checklist. It is bulky and awkward and it contains a number of items that you are not going to need to refer to every time you start the airplane. For example, you will soon know by heart the recommended power setting for run up and the maximum allowable magneto drop. Having to sit there and reread these items time after time contributes through sheer boredom to carelessness in the use of the checklist. The purpose of a checklist is not to provide you with directions on how to start the airplane. A checklist is used to make certain that you don't skip any safety items, which makes it a very important piece of paper.

Sit in the cockpit with the owner's manual in your lap and construct your own checklist. Cockpit time such as this is very valuable self-training; it is also free. Moreover, a properly organized checklist procedure will save you some "big bucks." Most student pilots can make an engine start and run up last twice as long as necessary, and the Hobbs meter can't tell ground time from flight time.

Organize your checklist into logical groupings of items and memorize each group. For example, in the engine-starting procedure, check the oil pressure and turn on radios and rotating beacon. Review this group prior to starting the engine, and then accomplish the entire sequence from memory. While the engine and the radios are warming up, refer to the checklist to see that you didn't skip anything and review the next group of items to be checked.

This is especially valuable in the run-up sequence. The extended time spent at a high power setting while you search for your place on the checklist can allow the engine to overheat. Review the checklist prior to advancing the throttle, and double-check after the power is reduced.

Establish some additional procedures for use during the times when it is impractical, or even unsafe, to refer to a printed checklist. For example, form the habit of turning on the strobes and the transponder and double-checking the boost pump as you taxi across the hold line into position for takeoff. Turn them off as you taxi clear of the runway after landing. At a busy airport you may be forced to hold short of the runway for some time after you have called for takeoff clearance. Reinforce such last-minute items by repeating to yourself, "strobes to go, transponder to go, boost pump to go." It is at such times that a well-established procedure will keep you from forgetting something important.

A prelanding checklist should also be a simple and concise procedure, followed consistently. During an approach to a busy airport, you will be far too busy spotting traffic and handling communication to have your head buried in a printed checklist. Many airplanes have an excellent pretakeoff and prelanding checklist placarded in a handy place on the panel for a quick review.

Shutdown is a simple and logical sequence. Turn off all radio equipment first to prevent voltage surges that can cause damage. The electrical switches are located in a group, so turn them all off next. Close the mixture, and after the propeller stops, turn off the magnetos and master switch. Review the printed shutdown checklist.

Do not interpret this to mean that you are free to memorize the checklist and then discard it—that would be dangerous. This method of checklist procedure will increase efficiency and contribute to proper and therefore safer habit patterns.

There are too many special procedures involved in detailing an engine start to be very specific here. There are normal starts, cold-weather starts, hot-engine starts, flooded starts, and engines of different makes and different horsepowers respond better to their own factory-recommended procedures. Occasionally you may feel the need to grow a third hand to keep the engine going after it fires. About the only common factor is—check the oil pressure. If you don't have pressure within 30 seconds on a warm day, or within 1 minute when it is cold, shut down and report the problem to the mechanic.

Fuel-injected and/or turbocharged engines are not normally found in primary flight trainers. Therefore we will confine ourselves to normally aspirated engines with carburetors, which may still be of the float type or the pressure type. Nothing worthwhile is ever simple, is it?

Any engine needs some amount of priming in order to fire. Some may be primed by placing the mixture in the full rich position and pumping the throttle: Do not do this unless you are ready to start the engine *immediately.* Excess fuel will begin to leak out of the carburetor and pool in the engine compartment, creating a fire hazard. The best method (and only method in many airplanes) is to use the primer located on the panel. This will squirt fuel directly into the in-take manifold. Some engines are primed by switching on the electric boost pump momentarily, but these are usually fuel-injected engines. If your checklist calls for switching on the boost pump momentarily, the purpose is to check that the electric boost pump is functioning; it will not prime the engine. Some engines like a lot of prime, and some are easily flooded. Refer to your owner's manual for the proper procedure.

Engine fire during start is not pleasant to consider, and fortunately it is relatively rare if the proper starting procedures are observed. Should an engine fire occur after you have succeeded in starting the engine, keep it running. The flames will be sucked into the cylinders where they belong, and the fire will soon be extinguished. Should the engine catch fire and you are still unable to get it started, close the mixture, shut off the tank selector at the fire wall, and get clear of the airplane. The fire will probably contain itself in the engine compartment and soon burn itself out; but there is no reason to sit around and wait to see if it does. Most airplanes are equipped with a fire extinguisher—get out and use it. With all the airplanes I've started, I've only caught one engine on fire. That was stupidity on my part. I know how foolish I must have looked flinging snow all over that smoking Aeronca. At least there was no permanent damage done.

The Golden Rule of engine care is: Do unto your engine as you would have it do unto you. Monitor the engine gauges during ground operation and throughout the flight. Make a note to discuss the use of the mixture control with your flight instructor.

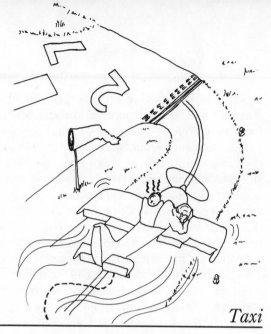

Taxi

Assuming you are taxiing a fixed-tricycle-gear aircraft with steerable nosewheel, you don't really have problems; you only think so at the moment. You push on the throttle when you should be pulling, and vice versa. You twist the yoke when you want to turn and nothing happens. Do not despair—you are not alone. This is the biggest put-down of the entire first flight. "How," you ask yourself, "can I possible *fly* it, when I can't even *drive* it?" Forget everything you know about driving; airplanes do not handle or react in any way, shape, or form like any automobile.

You are seated a comfortable distance from the yoke, heels on the floor, with the balls of your feet resting comfortably on the rudder pedals. The nosewheel is linked to the rudder pedals and will turn 30° (or so) either side of center. Pressure on the left pedal will turn you left, and vice versa.

Holding the aileron while taxiing in a brisk wind is important. Study the taxi diagram in the owner's manual concerning the proper aileron positions for taxiing in a quartering wind. Your airplane is very light and flies at a very low speed. Add taxi speed to wind velocity, and the wing has gained enough airspeed for the control surfaces to be effective. If gusty wind conditions prevail, it may slam the control surfaces around so that the yoke smacks you on the knee. Practice positioning the aileron and elevator properly according to the prevailing wind, even when the wind isn't strong enough to matter. One day it will be blowing hard, and you won't want to get this backwards. In light trainers, surface winds of more than 25 knots are grounds for a no-go decision, even in the hands of an experienced pilot.

The brakes are engaged by applying toe pressure to the extensions on top of the rudder pedals. Bear in mind that each brake is independent; if you wish to stop pointed in the direction you were moving, simultaneous and equal pressure on both brakes is required. A sharper than 30° turn may be accomplished by holding the brake on the side you want to turn toward. Test the brakes very early in the taxi, before you really need them. If you have a hand brake, test that also, and note if it pulls to one side.

For a machine so graceful and free in flight, an airplane is a clumsy and awkward beast on the ground. Never taxi faster than a brisk walk. Slow nearly to a stop before starting a turn, especially when turning from a downwind taxi. The turn will become more enthusiastic when the wind strikes the vertical tail fin; this is called "weather vaning." Use extra caution when taxiing near parked airplanes—damaging one airplane at a time is expensive enough. If clearance is difficult to judge and you have no wingman, look to see if the shadows will clear each other.

Pay attention—this is important: Riding the brakes during taxi causes excessive wear and tear. It may also cause serious overheating of the brakes so that they may fail when you need them the most. Control taxi speed with throttle. PLAN AHEAD to avoid excessive use of brakes. Brakes should be used only for making sharp turns, full stops, or holding still. Anything more is evidence of poor planning and bad technique.

This is a good time to mention torque and spiraling (or corkscrewing) slipstream, because they account for the tendency of the airplane to turn left as you taxi. Some amount of right rudder is normally needed to keep the nosewheel on the centerline. These and other left-turning tendencies will be explained in detail in Chapter 2.

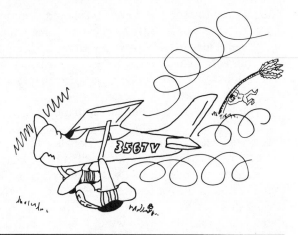

Run Up

Aim the airplane into the wind, and straighten the nosewheel. You are about to increase the power, and you don't need a side load on the nose gear if the brakes slip. Exercise consideration for pedestrians and parked aircraft that have to endure the mighty blast of dirt and rocks from your propeller. Again you must adjust your actions to your airplane and follow your own checklist.

Check that doors and windows are latched and that seatbelts and shoulder harnesses are fastened. Be certain that the fuel selector is on the proper tank and that the boost pump is set as required. Make it a point to taxi and run up on the fuel tank you plan to fly on first; takeoff is a poor time to discover a clogged fuel line.

"Flight controls free and correct" means that you push full forward and twist both ways; then pull full back and twist both ways. By this action you will know if anything is binding or blocking the full use of your control surfaces. At the same time you should look to see if they move the right way.

Idle at the manufacturer's recommended power setting—normally 1,000 rpm. At lower power settings there may not be enough heat to prevent spark plug fouling. Firmly holding the brakes, advance the throttle to the recommended power setting for checking the engine gauges, ammeter, suction, magnetos, and carburetor heat; then reduce the power to idle.

Airplanes have a dual magneto ignition system, that is, two sets of spark plugs are firing all the cylinders. If one magneto fails, you haven't lost all or even half your cylinders; the remaining set of plugs can do the job with only a small loss of power. The owner's manual tells you how much rpm drop is acceptable when only one magneto is operating. Check the right mag first; this means two clicks left and two back (to "both"); then one click left and one back. That sounds "picky," but reversing this sequence has resulted in pilots coming back to the left magneto position instead of all the way to "both" for the takeoff, thus eliminating the dual safety feature. If you are going to form a habit, it may as well be the safest one. Keep one hand on the throttle during the magneto check. If you inadvertently turn the switch all the way to "OFF," reduce the throttle to idle before turning the key back on. Otherwise, you are likely to get the biggest backfire you've ever heard and blow the exhaust stacks right off the engine.

Pulling the carburetor heat on caused an rpm drop. This happened because the fuel/air ratio in the carburetor was at its best and produced optimum results. You opened a butterfly valve that allowed hot air from around the exhaust manifold to flow directly into the carburetor. This hot air was expanded and caused the mixture to become too rich, unbalanced the fuel/air ratio, and caused a drop in rpm. This is a very important safety feature; be sure it is working properly.

The vaporization of fuel in the carburetor causes a dramatic temperature loss—as great as 30°–40° due to reduced molecular friction. The fuel is mixing with air, and if the air is humid the moisture may freeze. Should ice build up and block the carburetor throat, the engine will quit due to fuel starvation. Use of carburetor heat is a prevention, not a cure. If the engine has already been allowed to quit, it won't develop any more heat. Be alert for symptoms of carburetor icing before it gets out of hand.

Carburetor ice occurs most often at low power settings when the engine is developing less heat of its own. Pull the carb heat on prior to reducing the power, and push it off once the throttle has been restored to cruise power. Carb ice may occur at outside air temperatures as high as 70°, and ice has been known to occur at cruise power settings, as well as in descents. If you are conscientious about maintaining your altitude, a decrease in airspeed should first alert you to check your power setting. If you knew what power setting you were using, a drop in rpm is a pretty conclusive signal of carburetor ice. By the time the engine begins running rough, the icing condition has gone pretty far— get the heat on fast. This will cause a further drop in rpm and possibly some serious sputtering as the resulting water runs on through the carburetor. If this hasn't brought on a major heart attack, everything will now be back to normal. Now that you know that carburetor icing conditions prevail, you won't let it go that far again.

Engines with float-type carburetors are more susceptible to icing than those with the pressure-type carburetor. Learn what your manufacturer recommends about the use of carburetor heat. One more word of caution: When the carb heat is on, the air filter is by-passed. During ground operation, dust and dirt can be sucked into the carburetor. Take care that carb heat is off during taxi.

Set trim and flaps for takeoff, set the current barometric pressure in the Kollsman window of your altimeter, and note if there is a difference between the altimeter reading and the field elevation. Set the heading indicator to agree with the magnetic compass. You will cover the flight instruments in Chapter 2. Right now we don't want to trip your overvoltage relay.

To summarize, you have just checked your airplane and its systems and found everything functioning perfectly. Someday this may not be the case. If you determine that some item is not up to its usual standard, you must decide whether or not that item is necessary to the successful completion of the flight. Otherwise, taxi back and discuss it with the mechanic. There are three problems with which you would never attempt a takeoff:

1. The engine is not operating normally.

2. The flight controls are not functioning normally.

3. The fuel is not sufficient to complete the trip (with reserve).

We have now covered most of what you will encounter from the parking ramp to the runway, with the exception of radio communication.

Communications

Close attention to communications, and time spent with it in the kitchen simulator, is doubly important to those students who are training from a non-tower airport. The proper procedures should not come as news to you the first time you encounter the situation. I have known otherwise proficient pilots who refuse to fly into a tower-controlled airport just because they are afraid of the radio. This attitude results in a pitiful waste of the versatility afforded by light aircraft. Right now, the radio is a big distraction for you. If your instructor hands you the mike, you probably have trouble remembering your own name, much less the aircraft number.

Radio communication is another brand new area to most student pilots. Many words, and especially letters and numbers, are harder to understand over the radio; thus some basic phrases have come to be accepted. When you have heard them a few times, understanding becomes easier because you already know what you expect to hear, and you are listening for it. If you are a CB radio nut, please confine your CB terminology to that area and aim for professionalism in your pilot talk. The chapter on "Radio Communications Phraseology and Techniques" in AIM would be of great value to you now. Read it and practice in the kitchen simulator.

You have a noise-canceling carbon microphone; it has holes in front where you speak and another hole on top. Sounds that are directed into both sets of holes cancel each other out so that you don't broadcast your own engine noise. Get your lips close enough to talk into the proper set of holes, or you won't be heard. Brush the mike with your mustache, or get lipstick on it—whichever applies. Pause and listen before transmitting to verify that the channel is clear; when you press your mike button, you cut everyone else out. Hold the button down to transmit, and release it to receive. Speak slowly and distinctly, and be as brief as possible. Say three things: Who you are, where you are, and what you want.

DEPARTING, CONTROLLED AIRPORT

If your airport has a tower, don't move without clearance. If the airport has ATIS (Automatic Terminal Information Service), listen to that first. It is a recorded message giving wind direction and velocity, current barometric pressure, active runway, and anything else you should know before leaving or arriving. The recording is coded "Information Alpha, or Bravo, or Charlie"— moving on through the phonetic alphabet as conditions change. Use that letter when you call for taxi, and ground control knows you have the latest data. This cuts down on radio clutter, and you can listen to ATIS until you get it right.

Tune the published ground control frequency on the communications (Comm) side of the radio, adjust the squelch, and verify that the channel is clear of conversation. Address the controlling agency first, so you have his attention: "Homefield ground, Cessna 3567 Victor (who), Mile High Flying Club (where), taxi with Charlie (what)." Omit extraneous and unnecessary words such as this is, to, and, er, at, uh—.

After you are cleared you should acknowledge, or the controller may keep repeating himself. He already has your full tail number, so give him your last three digits, "67 Victor." This is permitted after he has addressed you in this shortened manner, but use caution if another airplane with a similar call sign is on the same frequency.

In the verbal shorthand of radio communicationese, you only said "67 Victor"; but he understood you to mean, "Cessna three five six seven Victor understands and acknowledges your transmission and will comply with your instructions." If you didn't get it all, ask him to "say again for 67 Victor." This sounds professional and cuts down on verbiage. Keep on asking until you are certain you understand.

Realize that the controller is doing his job, and that job is to serve you. True, he is a professional and you are a novice—and that feels a little intimidating at first. Remember that his profession is to serve the flying public in the interests of safety. He is a dedicated professional who may get a bit testy when he is busy because he sometimes has to get things sorted out in a hurry. If *you* ever need his help, tell him so, fast! You'll get it.

If you were cleared to the active runway, it is legal for you to continue across other inactive runways. However, it is still good practice to look up and check before crossing any runway. Even ground control is not infallible, and the final responsibility for the aircraft and its occupants rests solely with the pilot in command. After you have completed your run up, taxi to the hold line. Change to the tower frequency and call, "Homefield Tower, Cessna 3567 Victor ready for takeoff." Please don't make this call until you really are completely ready to go. You should receive one of the following replies:

1. "67 Victor cleared for takeoff." (You may taxi out, line up, and get on with it.)

2. "67 Victor taxi into position and hold." (You may taxi out, line up, and await further clearance.)

3. "67 Victor hold short." (Don't you dare cross that line until I say so.)

Under these circumstances, you are in a position to promote good pilot/controller relationships by briefly repeating his clearance: (1) "67 Victor cleared," (2) "67 Victor position and hold," and (3) "67 Victor holding short." This is quickly done, the controller will feel better about it, and it gives him a chance to clear up any serious misunderstandings. There is a fourth possible clearance given at busy airports in which the tower says, "cleared for immediate takeoff or hold short." Exercise your option and your judgment. Don't let anybody rush you into anything.

ARRIVING, CONTROLLED AIRPORT

At tower-controlled airports, you must establish two-way radio communication *more than* 5 statute miles from the airport. As you did on your departure, listen to ATIS first. This should be a clue that you must plan ahead, because you can't hover. Listen to ATIS before you depart the practice area, and you can have your approach planned. Take this opportunity to rehearse your call to the tower. When you tune in the tower and they are so busy you can't get a word in edgewise, you've got another clue. If the radio is saturated, so is the traffic pattern. Take the opportunity to practice 360° turns until things quiet down. "Homefield Tower, Cessna 3567 Victor, 8 South, landing with Delta" should get you permission to enter the airport traffic area with instructions to report downwind, base, or whatever is most efficient for the circumstances. Possible communications between this point and "67 Victor cleared to land" should be discussed with your flight instructor as specific situations arise.

After touchdown and while still rolling, the tower will probably say something like, "turn left next taxiway, contact ground point niner." Turn completely clear of the runway and stop before you tune. The aircraft comes first, and as long as you are on the active runway, you should be listening to the tower. "Point niner," or "point 7," etc., in conjunction with ground control, always assumes 121 point—so memorize it.

Ask your instructor about how to visit the tower. The controllers always welcome student visits, and you can listen and watch as long as you like if you don't get in the way. When controllers aren't busy, they are really nice people. If you have a radio that will pick up aircraft frequencies, listening for a while is a great way to become familiar with the phraseology. You will probably hear a lot of "goofs" to guard against. It isn't necessary to actually experience a situation to learn from it.

UNCONTROLLED AIRPORTS

Flying in and out of a nontower airport requires no clearances; it does call for a sharp eye and a keen sense of self-preservation. Communication at an uncontrolled airport is a matter of reporting your position and intentions to other interested parties who may or may not be listening. For traffic separation, depend only on the primary rule for visual flight—see and avoid.

If there is a Unicom (aeronautical advisory) on the field, the frequency will be printed on the sectional chart along with other airport information. It will also be published in the *Airport/Facility Directory* of AIM. The standard Unicom frequencies at nontower airports are: 122.7, 122.8, and 123.0. Private airports may use 122.725 or 122.75. You can obtain traffic pattern advisories from the Unicom operator. Many Unicoms offer excellent advisory services, but be advised that these reports are just that—advisories—not clearances. It is possible that the person you are talking to is a nonpilot who can't even read the wind sock. Spend some time in the kitchen simulator with AIM on the sections entitled "Airport Operations" and "Services Available to Pilots." Memorize the frequency for Multicom, 122.9. In the traffic pattern at a nontower, non-Unicom airstrip, broadcast your intentions just as you would on Unicom for the edification and enlightenment of other possible traffic. Do not abuse the Unicom and Multicom frequencies. Many inconsiderate and unprofessional pilots tend to use 122.9 as if it were a private telephone and chat back and forth throughout the entire flight. It is a very useful frequency if you need to keep track of a friend in another airplane, but nobody else in the area cares to hear that you are watching a beautiful sunset. Parachute jumping and glider towing activities are usually coordinated over Multicom. If you have to listen to it all day while trying to make a living, the chatter wears a little thin. Try to be as professional as possible during *all* radio communications; it would be fun to be mistaken for an airline captain.

Tower airports also have Unicoms, but these are strictly for services such as calling for fuel, transportation, etc. The standard Unicom frequency for use at tower airports is 122.95. Later you may impress your passengers by calling ahead so that the limosine is waiting when you arrive.

If your home airport is located in a Terminal Control Area (TCA) or a Terminal Radar Service Area (TRSA), you may be dealing with another radio call prior to departure that is known as "clearance delivery." If you are, turn to

Chapter 4. If your trainer is transponder equipped, check on transponders in Chapter 4. These are some of the subjects in flight training that can be absorbed far more easily on the ground. If you don't understand them, you probably don't realize how much they add to your load of confusion in flight and distract your attention from the basics of operating the aircraft.

In the kitchen simulator, think through the sequence of events occurring during a normal departure and arrival at "Homefield." Write down your most frequently used radio frequencies on your checklist, in case your memory fails. Aviate, navigate, and communicate, in order of importance. Radio proficiency will take care of itself. Every pilot has experienced mike fright. Console yourself—your favorite disc jockey probably can't fly an airplane.

Takeoff

To the layman, the most spectacular and critical part of flying is the landing; to the pilot, it is the takeoff. It is unfortunate that in the process of flight training, takeoffs must preceed landings.

Consider the differences from the standpoint of safety. On a landing, you are physically and mentally prepared to land; the engine has been running fine for hours; you have a concrete surface within reach ahead, airspeed is plentiful, landing checklist is complete; pilot psychology is all set for the task at hand. On takeoff, most of the opposite is true.

Conscientious pilots approach initial takeoff mentally prepared for the worst. They have calculated their weight and balance and know they are within limits. They know their fuel consumption in gph and that their supply includes an adequate reserve. They know the wind direction and velocity and its angular difference from the runway heading. They have computed density altitude and know that they have enough distance available to lift off and climb clear of obstacles. They are mentally prepared to abort the takeoff any time things don't look, feel, or sound right—even if this means gliding to the field beyond the departure end. They are disciplined enough to avoid a low altitude, low airspeed attempt to turn back to the runway. Pushing the nose down (when you desperately want altitude) is one of those contrary habits that comes only from knowledge, practice, and self-discipline. These habits are what flight training is all about.

The mechanics of the takeoff are simple and natural when you understand the basic principles of aerodynamics. Line up on the centerline and add takeoff power, keeping the airplane on the centerline with rudder pressure. Hold a small amount of back pressure on the yoke, and the airplane will fly when it is ready.

It is time to examine how and why the airplane flies. Chapter 1 was intended to reduce the somewhat awesome load of clutter encountered between the parking ramp and getting airborne and to free your mind for more important concepts. Combine Chapter 2 with a thorough reading of other home-study materials you may have on aerodynamics (principles of flight) and engine operation. Your next flight will be far more meaningful to you if you understand these principles. Otherwise that flight will deteriorate into a "monkey see, monkey do" proposition.

Basic Air Work

2

Basic Aerodynamics

THINK of the wing—that is all an airplane is, really. They hung a motor on the front to get it airborne, stuck a tail on the back for balance, and fixed a place under it (or on top of it) for you to sit. When you understand what is happening with the flow of air over, under, and behind the wing and what effect it has, everything you need to do comes naturally. The wing is flying because air is flowing smoothly over the upper surface, developing low pressure on top and high pressure underneath. This pressure differential is the basis of lift. Bernoulli's theory proves that the wing will fly as long as adequate airflow is allowed to continue.

Two very important terms you must understand are "relative wind" and "angle of attack" (Fig. 2.1). The direction of flight of the wing is directly opposite to the relative wind. The chord line of the wing is drawn from the leading edge to the trailing edge. The angle between this line and the relative wind is the angle of attack.

FIG. 2.1. *Very basic aerodynamics.*

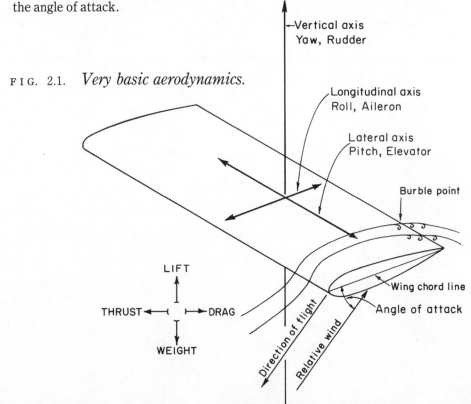

22

There are four forces affecting the wing: lift, weight, thrust, and drag. These four forces are in constant interaction with each other in flight. Reams of mathematical formulas may be produced to prove how any given control input affects these forces. Basically, when the forces are balanced, you are in straight-and-level, unaccelerated flight. Develop more lift than weight, and you go up; decrease lift so that weight is the greater, and you come down. Increase thrust to be greater than drag, and you go faster; allow drag to exceed thrust, and you slow down. Any combination you desire (within the physical capabilities of the aircraft) may also be achieved, such as accelerating or decelerating in level flight or while climbing or descending.

The airplane has three axes of rotation: (1) longitudinal (nose to tail) in which the aileron rolls the airplane around the longitudinal axis; (2) lateral (wingtip to wingtip) in which the elevator pitches the airplane around the lateral axis; (3) vertical (located approximately between the two pilot's seats) in which the rudder yaws the airplane around the vertical axis.

Since we complicated our wing by the addition of an engine and movable control surfaces, we caused it to have a tendency to yaw to the left under conditions involving high power settings and/or low forward speeds, making it necessary to correct with right rudder to maintain coordinated flight.

Oversimplified, "being coordinated" means pointing the nose in the same direction that the wing is going. If you are coordinated (not yawing), the little ball in the curved glass tube on the instrument panel will remain in the center of the tube. If you are yawing (uncoordinated), centrifugal force will pull the ball out to the side of the tube. Just remember to step on the ball; the rudder pressure will yaw the nose back where it belongs.

The following four factors are responsible for the airplane's tendency to turn left (Fig. 2.2):

1. Torque. For every action, there is an equal and opposite reaction. Viewed from the pilot's seat, the propeller spins clockwise; visualize a toy airplane with a rubber-band-powered propeller, wound up tight. What happens if you hold the prop and release the fuselage?

The slide-rule boys fixed this for us to some extent. The left wing is attached (angle of incidence) at a slightly higher angle of attack than the right wing; this causes more lift and compensates for torque at normal cruise power settings. Otherwise, you would have to hold right rudder all the time that the engine is running. This added lift on the left wing would drag the nose to the left, so the same design geniuses offset the vertical fin on the tail. At power settings above normal cruise (in a climb) this design factor isn't enough, and you must help it with right rudder. Climbs also add P-factor (discussed next) that further increases the need for rudder compensation. In a power-off glide, you have the design factor and no torque; therefore you compensate with left rudder.

2. Asymmetric loading of the propeller, or "P-factor." This factor is tougher to understand. Propeller blades are airfoils just like the wing is, and as such they are subject to angle of attack. In the level-flight attitude, the down-flying blade has an angle of attack that is equal to that of the up-flying blade. If you increase the angle of attack of the wing, what happens to the propeller?

The angle of attack of the down blade increases (more lift), and the angle of attack of the up blade decreases (less lift). This action causes your heading to wander when you try slow flight. Your power setting isn't that high, so it isn't all torque. Blame P-factor and add right rudder. This will always be true in high angle of attack, high power situations.

·**3.** Corkscrewing (or spiraling) slipstream. In Figure 2.2 observe how the flow of air from the propeller twists around the airframe and strikes the vertical tail surface on the left side. If we could add an equal surface below, we could eliminate this problem. Obviously that modification would cause other difficulties, so we'll just live with this. Notice that at high propeller speeds and low forward speeds, the corkscrew is tight. At higher forward speeds the corkscrew is elongated and less effective. Corkscrewing slipstream pushes your nose to the left on takeoff and has the same impact upon your slow flight maneuver; its effect will increase as forward speed decreases. This will also contribute to a rolling moment to the right. Try to detect its effect the next time you practice flight at minimum controllable airspeed.

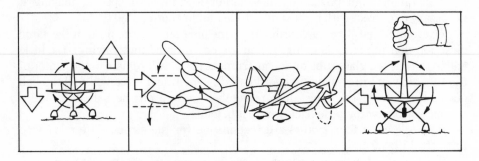

F I G. 2.2.   *Left-turning tendencies.*

4. Gyroscopic effect. Unless you fly tail draggers, gyroscopic effect won't affect you very much. If you do, its action will explain why your airplane tries to jump in the bushes on takeoff when the tail comes up. Your spinning prop is a gyro; when the tail goes up, the gyro goes down and reacts like all gyros do—90° in the direction of rotation.

A thorough understanding of these left-turning tendencies is vital to coordination. With the possible exception of straight-and-level flight, one or more of these left-turning tendencies will have an effect on every flight maneuver you will perform. Keeping the ball centered assures you of more efficient performance from the airplane and may save you from some verbal abuse from your flight instructor.

Trim and Throttle

Before getting serious about flight maneuvers, examine your progress in the use of trim and throttle (Fig. 2.3). The trim tab is a very handy gadget.

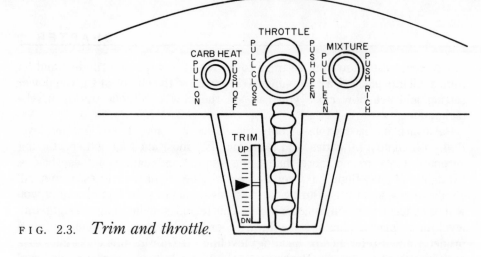

F I G. 2.3. *Trim and throttle.*

When properly set, it will allow the airplane to fly "hands-off" throughout its entire airspeed range. If you aren't using trim you are working too hard. Possibly you are making yourself airsick; the airplane usually flies much smoother when you leave the controls alone.

You have now discovered that you can move the nose up and down with the trim tab alone. You can move it, but you will never get it properly set doing it that way. The correct technique begins with placing the nose of the aircraft where you want it (relative to the horizon) and holding whatever elevator pressure is necessary to keep it there. We know you have a terrific handgrip, but don't use it on your airplane. Try holding the elevator in position with the flat palm of your hand or with your fingertips.

The trim tab will move without being stared at and so will your pitch attitude—figure out which one you should be watching. Gently roll the tab until the pressure you are holding is gone. You will probably be moving the tab backwards at first, just as you did with the throttle when you first tried to taxi. It takes a light touch to feel the pressure changes—they will be delicate, like milking a mouse.

Any power change or any flap change will necessitate a trim change; you are rearranging the four forces acting on the wing. Trim may be used to reduce strong control pressures while airspeed is stabilizing in the new configuration. However, the final trim setting will not be found until after the airspeed stabilizes.

When moving the throttle, you should be firm and positive, smooth but not abrupt. Most new students hesitate to shove the throttle all the way to the firewall. An aircraft engine is designed to do its very best work at two power levels—cruise range, and full bore—so don't be afraid to use full throttle when you need it. You can abuse the engine by yanking the power off abruptly. The engine develops a lot of heat while running at high power settings and cools off quickly at low power settings. Picture those moving parts expanding and contracting like a balloon—something might crack. Conversely, sudden jamming of the throttle all the way forward may flood the engine; it will hesitate and possibly quit. You will never go wrong with a smooth, steady power increase or decrease all the way to your desired power setting, be it high or low.

Learn to use the numbers on the tachometer. Given the same percent of power and the same pitch attitude, the airplane performs the same way every time. Memorize a few rpm settings to go with a few pitch attitudes, and let things fall into place. Start listening to the sound of the engine at a given power setting and see how close you can set the power without staring at the tachometer.

An airplane is capable of only four basic actions: (1) straight-and-level flight, (2) climbs, (3) glides, and (4) turns. The most exciting and spectacular aerobatic feats are no more than some exotic combination of these basics. Straight-and-level flight has been defined as a series of recoveries from small climbs, dives, and turns. During the next few hours of your flight training, you will be concentrating on basic air work. This includes maintaining straight-and-level flight; maintaining altitude during coordinated turns and rolling out on a predetermined reference or heading; leveling off from climbs and glides at a predetermined altitude, both wings level and while turning; recognizing and recovering from stalls with and without power; flight at minimum controllable airspeed; steep turns; and ground reference maneuvers.

Some amount of proficiency in these areas is necessary prior to traffic pattern work—takeoffs and landings. Once again, the kitchen simulator will save you a lot of flight time and help establish more solid habit patterns.

To hold a heading and altitude precisely, you need to be able to interpret the altimeter and the heading indicator. Thus a discussion of the primary flight instruments and the systems which make them work is in order.

Primary Flight Instruments

As far as the instrument systems go, the explanations given here are *very* basic. They may be oversimplified to the point of being downright insulting to anyone with a technical background. When I started taking flying lessons, I didn't have any technical training at all. If you don't either, perhaps this section will help. You will need more information than is provided here before you go for your instrument rating.

GYROSCOPIC INSTRUMENTS

The engine drives a small vacuum pump. This pump sucks a stream of air through the cases of two of your gyroscopic instruments. The stream of air strikes little rotor vanes and spins the gyros, similar to the principle operating a waterwheel. There is a vacuum gauge on the instrument panel; if the vacuum pump fails, the low pressure reading on the vacuum gauge would tell you that those gyros are no longer reliable. The vacuum-driven gyro instruments are the Heading Indicator and the Attitude Indicator. The third gyro is the turn and bank and that one is usually electrically driven. Thus you are assured that you always have a gyroscopic attitude instrument, should either system (electrical or vacuum) fail.

Attitude Indicator. The little airplane in the Attitude Indicator (AI) remains fixed inside the case (Fig. 2.4), although it is adjustable up or down for taller pilots. The horizon bar is kept rigidly parallel to the surface of the earth by the spinning gyro. Between the two of them (the airplane and the horizon) you get the same attitude picture as you would by looking outside. However, any pitch attitude change you make on the instrument will correspond to a proportionately larger change on the outside horizon. Flying by reference to instruments is a very delicate operation.

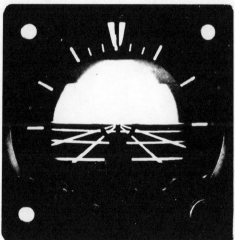

F I G. 2.4. *Attitude indicator.*

Degrees of bank may be determined by the "bug" at the top of the case (which goes the wrong way.) The bug is also "fixed" with the horizon bar, and will remain perpendicular to the earth. The hash marks at the top of the case indicate 10°, 20°, and 30° of bank. The next mark indicates 60°, so you can estimate 45° halfway in between. If the AI has painted lines on the bottom half of the case (resembling section lines in Kansas), placing the lower wing on the proper line will depict the amount of bank in a less confusing manner.

Following the discussion of each instrument in this section, there will be a short description of the operation of the instrument "Under the Hood." In case you have not yet been subjected to this experience, a "hood" is a plastic device that restricts your visual range to the instrument panel of the aircraft and may otherwise be known as a "portable cloud." This topic will be considered in greater depth in Chapter 4.

> UNDER THE HOOD: The AI will be your most valuable reference when flying under the hood because it gives both pitch and bank information simultaneously; your scan of the instruments will include it most often. The AI will be primary during any change in pitch or bank.

Heading Indicator. Figure 2.5, the Heading Indicator (HI), depicts a compass rose. Properly set to correspond with the magnetic compass, the HI will not be subject to the usual errors inherent in the magnetic compass. The HI is much easier to read accurately than is the mag compass. However, the HI is just a gyro—it is not North seeking. You must take an accurate reading from the magnetic compass and set the HI. Always pull the setting knob out and give it a twist to make sure it doesn't remain locked in place.

F I G. 2.5. *Heading indicator.*

Gyroscopes will precess due to friction generated by their spinning, so you need to check the HI periodically and reset it as required. If your HI is precessing more than 3° every 15 minutes, write it up in the aircraft squawk book.

An astounding number of people do not have the faintest idea of the purpose and function of the compass rose. Many who do think they understand it don't seem to apply the information when in flight. Basically, there are 360° in a circle; therefore there are 180° in a half circle, and 180° would be the reciprocal (the opposite direction) from 360°.

A heading of North would be referred to as 360° or 0°, either one. A heading of East is 090°, South is 180°, and West is 270°. These are called cardinal headings. Where students often fail to apply cardinal heading information is when the heading flown is somewhere in between. If you are flying a heading of 030°, don't think of it as just a number; think of it as "going Northeast." If your course calls for a heading change to 050°, is that a left turn, or a right turn? The rule to memorize is: Turn left to a lesser heading, right to a greater heading. I'm trying to emphasize—study the compass rose and relate the numbers to real directions. You have to know where you are at all times in an airplane; "temporarily disoriented" is a fancy way of saying "lost."

Situations will arise in which you will need to figure out the reciprocal of your heading. In the traffic pattern, the downwind is the reciprocal of the direction of landing. If an unfamiliar field has three or more runways, it is embarrassing to line up on the wrong one. Very High Frequency Omnirange (VOR) navigation is another area that will demand a certain facility with the compass rose. Your instructor will show you his way of figuring out reciprocals. I can't add and subtract 180 in my head, but I *can* do it this way: $-2+2$, $+2-2$. Here is how it works: Headings always have three digits, even if the first one (or two) is zero. For example:

$$(1)\,045 \quad (2)\,340 \quad (3)\,248 \quad (4)\,134$$

If you can add 2 to the first number, then subtract 2 from the second number; vice-versa, if you can subtract from the first number, add to the second. The third number never changes. For example:

$$
\begin{array}{llll}
(1)\ \ 0\ \ 4\ \ 5 & (2)\ \ 3\ \ 4\ \ 0 & (3)\ \ 2\ \ 4\ \ 8 & (4)\ \ 1\ \ 3\ \ 4 \\
\ \ \ +2-2 & \ \ \ -2+2 & \ \ \ -2+2 & \ \ \ +2-2 \\
\hline
\ \ \ 2\ \ 2\ \ 5 & \ \ \ 1\ \ 6\ \ 0 & \ \ \ 0\ \ 6\ \ 8 & \ \ \ 3\ \ 1\ \ 4
\end{array}
$$

With a minimum of practice, you can figure reciprocals quickly and accurately in your head.

> UNDER THE HOOD: the HI will be the primary instrument for bank information, provided you are not supposed to be turning. It is supported by the AI and the turn and bank.

Turn and Bank. The turn and bank (Fig. 2.6) also may be called the "turn and slip", "turn coordinator," "rate-of-turn," "needle and ball," or "slip and skid." Whatever it is called, it might look like either of the pictures, and it is the source of the noise you hear when you turn on the master switch. It is the electrically driven gyro.

F I G. 2.6. *Turn and bank.*

The turn and bank is really two separate instruments in one case. You are already well acquainted with the ball that lies in a curved tube full of white kerosene (to dampen motion). The ball is not connected in any way with the turn needle.

The turn portion of the instrument is calibrated so that when the needle is in the doghouse (or when the little airplane's wings are on the hash marks) you will make a 360° turn in 2 minutes. This is called a standard rate turn.

Instrument rating applicants, whose instructors take their other gyros away from them, are expected to make accurate heading changes by reference to the turn needle and the clock; 3° per second, 30° in 10 seconds, etc. This is fun, but you don't have to do it (yet). Just remember that when you are flying by reference to instruments, NEVER bank more steeply than the amount required to maintain standard rate. In steeper banks it is far too easy to lose control. Whenever you are operating under Visual Flight Rules (VFR) under positive radar control, the controller expects all turns to be made at a standard rate, and he bases his instructions to you on that assumption.

UNDER THE HOOD: The turn needle gives primary bank information in turns and supports the HI in straight flight.

MAGNETIC COMPASS

The magnetic compass or "wet compass" or "whiskey compass" is an instrument system by itself, dependent on no outside power source (Fig. 2.7). If this makes it the most reliable instrument in the airplane, it doesn't save it from being the most frustrating to read because it can only be read accurately when the airplane is in straight-and-level, unaccelerated flight. There are six built-in errors you must understand to use the compass effectively. And that isn't really whiskey in the case; it is acid-free white kerosene. Built-in errors in the use of the magnetic compass are: (1) variation, (2) deviation, (3) magnetic dip, (4) northerly turn error, (5) acceleration error, and (6) oscillation.

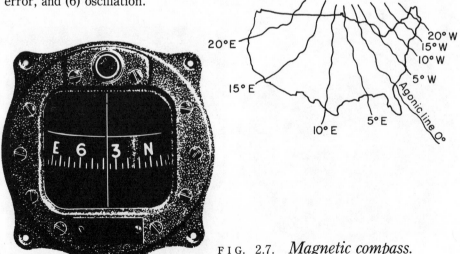

FIG. 2.7. *Magnetic compass.*

1. Variation is the angular difference between True North and Magnetic North. In Figure 2.7 the line of zero variation is called the agonic line. Radiating from that are isogonic lines, depicting the degrees of variation, East and West. On the sectional chart the isogonic lines are depicted by dashed red lines; the degrees of variation (East or West) are printed along the line. In flight we can deal only with magnetic headings, having no equipment that will point to True North. However, in your preflight planning you will have to measure your course relative to True North and then correct it to Magnetic North: "East is Least, and West is Best." Subtract an easterly variation, and add a westerly variation.

2. Deviation. Large hunks of metal (such as aircraft engines) and operating electrical equipment can generate enough of a magnetic field of their own to interfere with your compass needle. The compass is adjusted (swung) after it is installed in the airplane. This is done while the engine is running, the lights are flashing, and all other other equipment is turned on. Even at that it may not be possible to match everything up all the way around the compass card. The mechanic will compromise and adjust the compass perhaps 2° off on North and 2° off on South, rather than making it perfect on a North heading, while leaving a 4° error on South. He will place a compass correction card on the instrument case so that you can adjust your magnetic heading accordingly. Avoid carrying objects in the airplane that could interfere with the compass, such as that new flashlight with the nice magnet on it.

3. Magnetic dip is the mischievous tendency of the compass needle not only to point to Magnetic North, but to point *down* as well. This doesn't happen if you are flying along the equator, but the farther from the equator you go, the more the compass needle points down. The next two errors on the list are a direct result of this magnetic dip error.

4. Northerly turning error is the most pronounced of the dip errors, and it is most apparent on headings of North and South. Making a 180° turn from a heading of North, the compass will momentarily indicate a turn in the opposite direction. It will catch up and be pretty accurate as you pass through East (or West) and then speed up and beat you to your South heading. You will have to lead the indicated heading by about 30° if you want to roll out on a 180° heading. Conversely, in turning from South to North, as you turn from the South heading the compass will indicate a turn in the correct direction, but at a much faster rate than you are really going. Again it will be accurate as you pass through East or West, but as you approach North it will begin to slow down. You will have to overshoot your heading by 30° and wait for it to come around. The 30° correction works fairly well in the continental United States because it lies approximately 30° North Latitude. If you move to Mexico, to 20° North Latitude, you can reduce the corrections to 20°.

5. Acceleration error occurs due to the pendulous-type mounting of the compass card, combined with dip error. The whole card tilts upward when the airplane is accelerating and downward when decelerating. This is more pronounced on headings of East and West. When the airplane is accelerating the card will indicate a turn to the North, and when it is decelerating the card swings South. Remember ANDS: Accelerate North, Decelerate South.

I hope someday you may make such a wonderful flight, but if you ever go south of the equator, everything you have just learned about the magnetic compass will work exactly backwards.

6. Oscillation error is the annoyingly erratic movement of the compass card sloshing around in turbulent air. The best you can do under these circumstances is to take an average. Take your best guess, locate a point on the distant horizon, and go for it. When you get there, take another average and try again.

PITOT-STATIC SYSTEM

The pitot-static system depends on two (or more) outside air sources. Impact pressure, or "ram pressure," is taken from the pitot tube, which is mounted outside so as to encounter a minimum amount of airflow disturbance. The pitot tube may be protected by electric heat for use during icing conditions or heavy rain. The pitot heat switch is located on the panel and draws a heavy load of battery juice, so monitor your ammeter whenever the heat is in use. The pitot-static system itself doesn't depend on electricity—the heat is only for protection. If the pitot tube becomes clogged, your airspeed indicator will be inaccurate.

The static pressure source provides atmospheric pressure and is necessary to the functions of all three pitot-static instruments (airspeed, altimeter, and vertical speed). Lose all of those while in the clouds, and you are in trouble. Instrument airplanes are equipped with an alternate source of static pressure in case the primary source ices over. This is usually vented somewhere inside the airplane, and its use causes a few small instrument indication errors. It is still better than losing the works.

Altimeter. The altimeter (Fig. 2.8) is one of the most important instruments in the airplane—if not THE most important—and remains an area of mass confusion; the most-missed questions on the written exam are the ones on altimetry.

The altimeter is basically a barometer. Inside the case it contains a stack of hollow, elastic, metal wafers (aneroid wafers) that expand and contract as atmospheric pressure changes. The mechanism that moves the needle is geared like a clock and is based on a fixed set of standard atmosphere values; for every 1,000 feet you climb, the pressure will decrease "so much" and the temperature will decrease "so much." The trouble is that actual conditions are seldom standard, and the altimeter is going to present you with standard information anyhow. Setting the actual current barometric pressure in the Kollsman window gets the mechanism joined up with the standard atmosphere value scale again.

On the ground with the current pressure properly set, the altimeter should read close to the correct field elevation Mean Sea Level (MSL). If you increase the barometric pressure setting, the altitude reading will also increase, and vice versa. The gearing mechanism will change the altimeter reading according to this easy table: One inch (of barometric pressure) = 1,000 feet; one-tenth of an inch (0.1) = 100 feet; one-hundredth of an inch (0.01) = 10 feet.

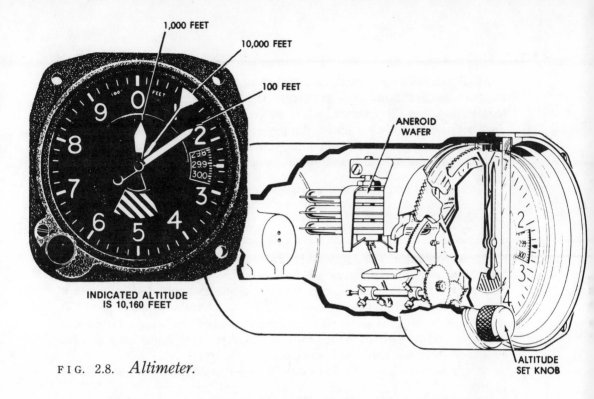

1,000 FEET

10,000 FEET

100 FEET

ANEROID
WAFER

INDICATED ALTITUDE
IS 10,160 FEET

ALTITUDE
SET KNOB

FIG. 2.8. *Altimeter.*

I'm sure that by now you know how to read your altimeter. "The big hand points to—." Let's get on with the types of altitudes—all five of them: indicated, pressure, true, absolute, and density.

1. Indicated altitude is what you read on the instrument, assuming the current barometric pressure is properly set.

2. Pressure altitude is indicated altitude with standard barometric pressure (29.92) set in the Kollsman window. This is the altitude you will use to make density altitude and true airspeed computations. You will also fly with 29.92 set if you can ever hustle your airplane up above 18,000 feet (see Chapter 3 on airspace).

3. True altitude is true height above sea level. This is a mathematical value of interest only to a computer and of no value whatsoever to a pilot.

4. Absolute altitude is how high you are above the surface. If you need to know, subtract the known surface elevation from your indicated altitude.

5. Density altitude is even more important to you than indicated altitude, because it is the only altitude your *airplane* understands.

Density altitude is pressure altitude corrected for nonstandard temperature. That seems straightforward enough, but consider the ramifications relative to your airplane's performance. For example: Your airport's field elevation is 6,000 feet MSL; standard temperature at 6,000 feet is approximately +5°C. If the Outside Air Temperature (OAT) is +30°C, then the density altitude corrects to 9,000 feet, even though your altimeter still reads 6,000 feet.

You know you are at 6,000 feet, and your *altimeter* knows it; but the *airplane* reacts as if it is at 9,000 feet and that is how it will perform. It will not climb as well. Vacationing flatlanders wreck airplanes around high altitude airports all summer long. COMPUTE DENSITY ALTITUDE EFFECTS ON AIRCRAFT PERFORMANCE BEFORE YOU ATTEMPT TO TAKE OFF. The airport is already high enough, but I'll bet they built it on the lowest, flattest spot in the area. Just because you made it up off the pavement, your troubles are not necessarily over. Don't stop with computing runway length required; include finding out what your rate-of-climb performance will be at that density altitude.

> UNDER THE HOOD: The altimeter gives primary pitch information in level flight and in level turns. Any time the objective includes a constant altitude, the altimeter is primary, supported by airspeed, attitude, and vertical speed.

Airspeed Indicator. The Airspeed Indicator (ASI) works by measuring the difference between ram air pressure and static pressure. The greater the difference, the faster you are going. Just like altitudes, there are five types of airspeeds, and we could almost add a sixth if we consider ground speed. We will ignore "equivalent airspeed" and "mach number" as being a little out of our class, and save ground speed for cross-country. That leaves us with three airspeeds: indicated, calibrated, and true.

1. Indicated Airspeed (IAS) speaks for itself; read the numbers off the instrument.

2. Calibrated Airspeed (CAS) is IAS corrected for installation error, namely, position and instrument errors. If the pitot tube adjusted automatically so that it remained parallel to the relative wind, and you always flew with the ball dead center, there should be no difference between IAS and CAS.

You have seen the needle pegged at the top of the case during minimum controllable airspeed practice. You can't be going zero knots, because the owner's manual plainly states the airplane stalls at 50 knots. The published speed and the colored marking on the ASI are both CAS. The difference occurred because ram air can't blow directly into the pitot tube due to the excessively high angle of attack. Slips and skids will foul up airspeed indication by allowing some ram air to blow into the static source; thus in a slip the ASI lies. Depend on pitch attitude in order to ensure a safe airspeed.

The difference between IAS and CAS will be greater if airflow into the pitot source is not direct, or if it is blowing directly into a static source. The number the needle points to on the ASI is the IAS; but the colored markings reflect CAS. The aircraft owner's manual supplies a correction table.

Pay attention to the "V speeds" denoted by the colored markings on the ASI. There are more V speeds that are not so marked. You will encounter more as you progress to complex and multiengine airplanes. Definitions of V speeds may not seem vital to you now, but they are a part of the vocabulary of pilots. No one wishes to appear ignorant around the hangar.

3. True Airspeed (TAS) is important to know for flight planning computations (Fig. 2.9). It is the true speed at which the airplane is moving through undisturbed air. TAS will *increase* with altitude (the air becomes thinner and offers less resistance), while IAS *remains the same.* This concept will keep you out of trouble during high altitude airport operations. Fly the same indicated approach speeds you are accustomed to, and don't be deceived by the faster ground speed as the bushes flash past.

FIG. 2.9. *Airspeed indicator.*

In flight, you need to know your TAS so that (based on the forecast winds aloft) you have the information necessary to compute your ground speed. The example shown in Figure 2.9 is a true ASI, and it is very simple to use. The numbers in the white windows will rotate when you twist the knob on the lower right. Set 29.92 in the Kollsman window of the altimeter to get the pressure altitude and reset the altimeter correctly. On the top scale of the ASI, line up the pressure altitude with the OAT in degrees Celsius. (The OAT indicator is located somewhere around the windscreen.) Now you can read your true airspeed under the needle on the white portion of the scale. If your ASI is not equipped with this handy gizmo (it was probably an expensive option), you can do the same thing on your flight computer.

I'll let you in on a deep, dark secret. Most pilots don't fool with changing the altimeter to pressure altitude; they go ahead and use indicated altitude. This is close enough for practical purposes; but in this case it is *not* close enough for government work. You will miss the TAS question (and the density altitude question) on the written exam if you fail to convert to pressure altitude.

> UNDER THE HOOD: When in level flight, the ASI will supply supporting pitch information and will be the primary power instrument. Airspeed is primary for pitch when the objective is a constant airspeed climb or descent.

Vertical Speed Indicator. The Vertical Speed Indicator (VSI) may also be referred to as the Vertical Velocity Indicator (VVI) or the rate of climb; the latter is not strictly accurate since the instrument can also indicate rate of descent (Fig. 2.10).

FIG. 2.10. *Vertical speed indicator.*

The instrument is in a sealed, airtight case that is connected to the static pressure line through a calibrated leak. We mention this because it accounts for the lag in the VSI indication if altitude changes are abrupt. Differential pressures between the static line and the pressure trapped in the case will need about 6–9 seconds to stabilize. Rough control technique or turbulent air will cause unreliable indications on the VSI. Handle matters smoothly, and the VSI will indicate your rate of climb or descent in hundreds of feet per minute (fpm). At a constant altitude, the needle should stay pegged at zero.

> UNDER THE HOOD: Use the VSI to warn yourself that a trend is developing; this is good information supporting pitch. The VSI would be primary for pitch if the objective were a constant rate climb (or descent).

Primary Flight Maneuvers

This section was carefully designed for use in the kitchen simulator. You are now in an area in which memorizing procedures and practicing in your mind will save you flight hours and money and will make you a safer pilot.

CLIMBS

We will assume you are training in an airplane that is in the 100–150 horsepower range, with a fixed-pitch prop and fixed gear. Any climb to gain more than 100 feet of altitude is going to require full power. You might sneak up there without it, but it will cost you some airspeed.

MEMORIZE THIS PROCEDURE: To enter a climb, place the nose in the climb attitude as you smoothly apply full power; add right rudder as necessary.

Remember to continue holding right rudder to correct for torque as long as you maintain full power, even in turns. During the left turn torque is helping, so it will take a little less right rudder. Conversely, torque is against you in the right turn, so lean a little heavier on the rudder. You will be reminded of this procedure when you are introduced to full power stalls.

Climb rate and climb airspeed are limited by available power. MEMORIZE THE THREE CLIMB AIRSPEEDS recommended by your airplane's manufacturer:

1. V_x (best angle of climb). This is the speed at which you will gain the most altitude in the least forward distance, and it must be maintained so long as obstacle clearance is in question.

2. V_y (best rate of climb). This will gain the most altitude in the least amount of time.

3. Cruise climb speed. This may not get you to altitude as quickly, but it will get you down the road faster, provide better engine cooling, and better forward visibility to look for oncoming traffic.

It is good practice to make a shallow turn occasionally during a prolonged climb. Forward visibility is somewhat restricted, even in the cruise climb attitude. The silhouette of another airplane coming straight at you is difficult to see. The turn will alter your silhouette for his benefit and also provide you with a broader scan while you look for oncoming traffic.

When you are ready to go somewhere besides the local practice area, you will want to know more about planning the climb to the level off. You might need to compute the distance you traveled to the Top Of Climb (TOC) to figure out if you are going to have to circle or alter course to clear a mountain. The owner's manual provides data for computing your average rate of climb. For example: You are climbing from sea level to 7,000 feet at an airspeed of 90 knots and an average rate of 500 fpm. The airplane is traveling 1½ mi/min and will level off in 14 minutes. The level-off will take place 21 miles down the road. If the mountain is farther away, you can go direct.

To level off from a climb at a predetermined altitude, you must plan ahead; lead the altitude slightly. Push the nose down to the level-flight attitude, and hold the forward pressure as airspeed builds up. Rpm will increase as well, so reduce power to the desired rpm and retrim as soon as airspeed is stabilized. Correct any altitude errors of less than 100 feet with elevator pressure; remember that climbs and dives will affect your airspeed, which will affect trim. Hold the attitude and don't bother retrimming until airspeed has stabilized.

MEMORIZE THIS PROCEDURE: To level off from a climb, lower the nose to level flight attitude, reduce power to cruise, retrim after airspeed has stabilized.

GLIDES AND OTHER DESCENTS

MEMORIZE THIS PROCEDURE: To enter a glide (pull carb heat on), reduce power, lower the nose to the glide attitude, and retrim after airspeed stabilizes.

"Glide" implies a lower power setting or no power at all. "Descent" implies a higher power setting and probably a higher airspeed. First let's examine the power-off glide.

The manufacturer recommends a best glide speed for your airplane. This is the speed that will allow you to glide the greatest distance; in the event of engine failure it is worthwhile to know. They figure the best glide speed to be 1.3 times the lowest power-off stall speed (V_{so}). It usually works out pretty close to V_y. In a power-off glide, the airplane feels and sounds a little different. It is obviously quieter, and the controls feel a little less responsive without the airflow from the propeller. The rate of descent in the power-off glide may vary according to weight, but it will probably be close to 500 fpm. In Chapter 4 (under off-airport landing) stopping the prop from windmilling is discussed. The consensus is—don't do it. Emergency descents will be covered in the section describing forward slips.

Descents at landing approach speed merit some practice prior to traffic pattern work. Your instructor will tell you what power setting to use; this is usually 1,500 rpm in most trainers. Pay close attention to the pitch attitude required to maintain approach speed, especially during turns. In the traffic pattern at low altitude, with other airplanes to watch out for and the radio to handle, is no time to be staring at the airspeed indicator. FLY ATTITUDE when making gliding turns. Control the *rate of descent* with the *throttle*.

The *throttle* is your airspeed control in a *cruise* descent. You can descend at any airspeed your airplane can handle and at any rate (controlled by pitch attitude) that your eardrums can handle. The most comfortable rate for your eardrums is around 500 fpm; so PLAN descents far enough AHEAD. En route (or cruise) descents is another area that merits discussion and planning.

Suppose you had to climb en route to 7,000 feet to clear a mountain range, and that you would be descending to sea level again for the landing. It took a fair amount of expensive time to climb that high; you can make up for some of that time by descending at an increased airspeed. You can go faster downhill than you can at cruise. Just be sure that the air is smooth enough, and that you don't redline the engine rpm. Pitch to the rate, power to the airspeed (just the opposite from controlling your descent in the traffic pattern). Push the nose down until you establish the desired rate of descent; adjust the throttle to establish the desired airspeed. Trim to maintain attitude.

The next step is to plan WHEN to begin the descent. Suppose you choose to descend at 500 fpm at a speed of 120 knots. You are traveling 2 miles per minute and you are going to lose 7,000 feet—that will take 14 minutes. Therefore, you will begin your descent 28 miles from the airport. It is extremely uneconomical to arrive over the airport 7,000 feet too high and have to spiral down. Students do this all the time when returning from the practice area. There goes more of their valuable practice time, ticking away.

To level off from the descent, lead your altitude by approximately one-tenth of the rate of descent. For example: If you are descending at 500 fpm, begin the level-off procedure from 50 feet above your desired altitude; if you are descending at 1,000 fpm, lead the desired altitude by 100 feet.

MEMORIZE THIS PROCEDURE: To level off from a descent, add power to the cruise power setting (carb heat off), raise the nose to the level-flight attitude, stabilize airspeed, and retrim.

Entering and leveling off from climbs and glides while turning is no different than doing so when the wings are level; pitch control and bank control just take a little practice. It would be much easier if the hand gripping the yoke didn't have white knuckles. Two fingers of one hand is enough to hold all the pressure your airplane requires. Catch yourself if you are tensing up and make some conscious effort to relax and quit fighting it—make love, not war.

TURNS

Now that you are using the rudder properly to compensate for all torque-related maneuvers, let's see if we can sort out why you abuse it while making turns. Start with an airplane perfectly trimmed to fly level with hands off.

We have to go back to aerodynamics and control functions to figure out what makes the airplane turn. In straight and level flight, the lifting force, which always remains perpendicular to the wing, is directly opposing gravity, or weight. When you move the aileron control to the left, you cause the left aileron to be raised and the right aileron to be lowered; thus changing camber and increasing lift on the right wing while decreasing lift on the left. The airplane will rotate around its longitudinal axis; the wing's lift is now pulling you around in a left turn.

Observe that we haven't mentioned rudder or the elevator and still we are turning. The rudder does not turn the airplane—it merely yaws it. Of course your turn *entry* without rudder was uncoordinated—actually downright sloppy—and without up-elevator you are losing altitude.

If the rudder doesn't turn the airplane, why use it at all? If you had your eyes on the ball when you made this turn without rudder, you saw it slide out to the left on the entry and sneak back to the center. When you rolled level again, it took off to the right and came back. *Observation*: Even without holding rudder, the ball was centered during the turn itself; it left home only during the entry and the rollout. *Conclusion*: You need to use rudder only during the entry and the recovery, not during the established turn. You can see the same thing by watching the nose skate around on the horizon instead of pivoting around its axis.

The culprit in this instance (left-turn entry) is the right aileron. Remember that increasing lift causes an equal amount of increased drag. This drag causes yaw around the vertical axis, known as "adverse aileron yaw." The nose will yaw toward the lifting wing and will stop yawing as soon as you stop increasing the drag. *Conclusion*: Use a little rudder in the direction of roll, and get off it when the roll stops.

Now let's discuss use of the elevator in the turn. Centrifugal force is going to make your airplane heavier, and you are also losing a portion of your vertical lifting component because the lifting surface (the wing) is no longer perpendicular to the ground (gravity). The steeper you bank, the heavier you become and the more vertical lift you lose. To compensate, you must increase back pressure on the elevator (rotate around the lateral axis), thus increasing the wing's angle of attack and gaining enough extra lift to maintain altitude (Fig. 2.11).

The difference in the amount of up-elevator needed between a 10° bank and a 60° bank is impressive. The need for up-elevator will increase steadily as the bank steepens and will decrease steadily as it shallows. The common error

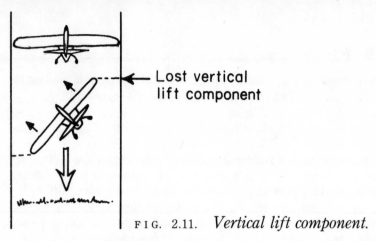

Lost vertical
lift component

F I G. 2.11. *Vertical lift component.*

is to hang on to all of the back pressure throughout recovery and roll out nose high and climbing. The back pressure must steadily increase on entry and steadily relax on rollout. A word about good posture—you won't fall out, so don't lean away from the turn.

Unless your airplane has tandem seating, the horizon reference will be different during left and right turns because you are sitting off center. Most students tend to dive to the left and climb to the right.

Turns to Headings. To roll out of a turn on a predetermined heading, lead the heading by some amount or you will turn past it. The rule of thumb for turns to headings is to lead the desired heading by one-half the amount of bank.

Example: If the amount of bank is 30°, begin the rollout 15° ahead of the desired heading. Roll out smoothly and consistently, with your eyes on the horizon to eliminate any tendency to yaw or pitch. The heading will take care of itself. Never enter a turn without looking carefully for other traffic. Airplanes in flight seldom get by with having fender benders.

Steep Turns. This maneuver is no longer listed in the private pilot flight-test guide, and I don't understand why. They are certainly done, even at very low altitudes while practicing ground reference maneuvers. The accelerated stall should certainly point out the necessity for doing them correctly. Even though you will not be flight checked specifically on steep turns, put in a little time on "steep 720s."

Line up with a point on the horizon and note your heading; enter a 45° bank and hold your altitude constant throughout two complete 360° turns. Roll out on your starting point and see if your heading is ±10° of your entry heading. Your altitude should never vary more than 100 feet throughout, and you really shouldn't settle for *any* altitude (or heading) deviation. You will climb during the rollout if you do not make a positive correction with the elevator. In your trainer it may be necessary to add full power to help maintain altitude in a steep turn. If so, add the power gradually as the bank steepens, and reduce it again to cruise as you recover, just as you alter the amount of back pressure you hold. Once established in a steep turn, use the elevator to maintain altitude, keeping the bank constant. Aim for precision in steep 720s, both left and right.

Warning: If the attitude really gets away from you and airspeed begins to build rapidly, abort the maneuver and start over. Level the wings in a high airspeed descent (dive) before applying up-elevator. Further increasing back pressure in a steep turn only tightens the turn, thus further increasing wing loading and further increasing weight. This is the beginning of the old "graveyard spiral" (Fig. 2.12). Airspeed has decreased in the steep turn, and due to wing loading, stall speed has increased. If the two should meet, you may be in for some excitement. Accelerated (high airspeed) stalls are generally snappier than the regular kind and will be discussed in Chapter 4.

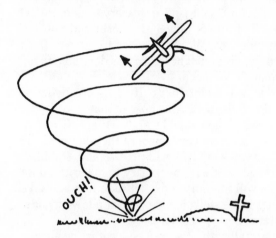

F I G. 2.12. *Graveyard spiral.*

"G forces" (gravity forces) increase as centrifugal force is added to gravity. At 2 Gs the airplane and everything in it doubles its weight. This 2 G point is reached mathematically, coinciding with a constant altitude, 60°-banked turn. At 2 Gs, your cheeks begin to sag, and your lower lip wants to droop. If you reach up and touch the overhead, you may bruise your elbow when you let your arm back down. At 4 Gs, (approximately 80° of bank) you may have difficulty touching the roof at all, and you are very near the structural limitations for a utility category airplane; you have already torn the wings off a normal category machine. Positive G limitations for normal category is 3.8, utility is 4.4, and aerobatic is 6.0. By 6.0 Gs, untrained people have already blacked out. Sensible practice dictates that when your cheeks begin to sag, level the wings before increasing back pressure.

STALLS

Not too many pilots actively enjoy stall practice, but practice you must. You will demonstrate a number of stalls for the examiner on your flight check, but that is not the reason for practicing them. The actions necessary for stall recovery are contrary to your basic survival instincts. When the airplane is descending rapidly toward the trees, a beginner wants to pull back on the stick and get *up* there again. If he has programmed himself to think of the wing and the airflow over it, he would instinctively push the nose *down* toward those trees to recover the flow of air that gives the wing lift. A habit pattern this basic takes plenty of practice.

A stall is a function of angle of attack; it can occur at any pitch attitude or any airspeed when the angle of attack becomes too great. Picture the air flowing smoothly over the upper wing surface and breaking away in turbulence near the trailing edge. As the angle of attack increases, this break-away (or "burble") point moves forward. The stall occurs when the burble point moves so far forward on the lifting surface that there is no longer enough lift to support the weight.

Suppose this point was reached at 50 knots (remember that the wing was still flying at 51 knots and will do so again), so it isn't necessary to dive to 100 knots to recover. Decrease the angle of attack (lower the nose) and you are back in business with minimum altitude loss. We do not wish to recover from the stall only to fly the airplane into the ground. Therefore it is desirable to accelerate *to* but not *through* your airplane's V_x speed.

You know the pitch attitude that will maintain V_x. If you were flying at cruise speed and you added full power while raising the nose to that V_x attitude, airspeed would decrease until it reached V_x and would stabilize there. If you increased angle of attack until the airspeed was very low and then lowered the nose to that same V_x attitude, airspeed would *increase* to V_x and stabilize. Therefore, when recovering from the stall, it isn't necessary to lower the nose THROUGH that ATTITUDE. This will minimize your altitude loss and give you the best chance to clear obstacles if the stall should occur at a low altitude. We are hammering home habit patterns here: *pay attention*.

The wing would recover from the stall with power off, since it is the airflow over the upper surface that counts. Because more power makes more air, include the addition of full throttle in your habit pattern. Leveling the wings will aid recovery because stall speed is lower with wings level than it is in a bank, and stall speed is lower with power than without. You must practice stall recognition and recovery until the proper actions are automatic.

In low airspeed stalls such as you are practicing, you have plenty of clues that the stall is approaching. The nose is high and airspeed is deteriorating, the controls feel mushy and unresponsive due to reduced airflow, the control movement necessary to accomplish the desired result becomes exaggerated, the airplane becomes increasingly nose heavy, and the stall-warning horn is blasting in your ear.

You still persist in increasing back pressure until you feel some amount of buffeting (imminent stall). When the stall fully occurs, you feel a slight bump followed by an uncontrollable pitch down by the nose (full stall). This is fine because that is where you would put the nose yourself, if you had any choice in the matter. The wing is no longer developing lift, so the heaviest end heads for gravity the fastest. The nose goes down and airflow over the wing recovers quickly. You won't lose much altitude, so there is nothing to fear from stall practice with 3,000 feet or so of clear airspace below.

You started with straight-ahead (wings level), power-off stalls and progressed to straight-ahead stalls with full throttle. By now you probably believe in torque and the need for right rudder in a full power climb. If you are still rolling to the left, you had better review the four left-turning tendencies.

When the rudder is coordinated (ball centered), the wings stall simultaneously and the nose pitches down with the wings level. When uncoordinated (ball off-center), the flow of air over one wing is partially blocked or disturbed by the nose, allowing that wing to stall slightly ahead of the other one. With one wing stalled and the other one lifting, the airplane will roll toward the stalled wing as the nose pitches down. Rolling to the left is most common due to torque. The nose yaws to the left and blocks airflow to the left wing. The ball is out to the right, so step on the ball. The airplane is aerodynamically capable of recovering itself from the stall, provided it has enough altitude. However, it was carefully streamlined for maximum performance, so airspeed will build rapidly in an exaggerated dive. Practice recovering immediately to the ATTITUDE that will provide V_x and maintain that airspeed until you have a positive rate of climb established. Make all control movements—including addition of throttle—smooth and positive but not abrupt. Stay loose, and make another clearing turn before you try it again.

MEMORIZE the stall recovery procedures: *simultaneously* add full power (carb heat off), level the wings, and place the nose in the V_x attitude; recover flaps; maintain V_x until a positive rate of climb is established.

SPINS

Spins are discussed at this time merely to lay another demon to rest. You have probably heard many hairy hangar stories concerning spins. Pilots love to talk about flying, and many of them excel at making a good story even better. *Did I ever tell you about the time . . . ?*

Flight instructor applicants are required to show a logbook entry attesting that they have entered and recovered from spins in both directions. At this time, spins are not a requirement for any other certificate or rating. You can start a lively discussion in your next hangar session by raising the question of spin training for private pilots. Do what you want about it; spin training is optional, but it certainly won't hurt you.

If you fly a 40-year-old airplane, you had better practice spins. In the olden days, airplanes were much easier to spin unintentionally than modern models are. Nowadays you must encourage your airplane to enter a spin and then hold it there; if you let go, it recovers itself.

A spin may be defined as an aggravated stall that results in autorotation.

Observe that it is a stall; the airplane cannot spin if it is not stalled. Recover by stopping the rotation with rudder and breaking the stall with forward elevator pressure. You really aren't pointed straight down, no matter how things look.

Airspeed in a spin is very low, probably not exceeding 80 knots (indicated) in your trainer. There are no undue positive or negative G forces. Thus the only things in line for possible damage are your delicate (and expensive) gyroscopic instruments. Most trainers that are certificated for intentional spins will lose approximately 500 feet of altitude per turn. Check your owner's manual for information about your airplane's Center of Gravity (CG) loading, spin characteristics, and recovery technique; some vary slightly, and many airplanes are not certificated for intentional spins. In any case, don't try it alone the first time—it makes you dizzy. Most beginners sit there goggle-eyed during their first spin. With practice, you can sort it out and recover within 10° of a predetermined heading.

Even if you practice spins until you can recover accurately, it won't help you one bit if you enter a spin at traffic pattern altitude; the airplane simply doesn't have enough room to recover. Spin training is a confidence maneuver. Stall recognition and recovery is your real ace in the hole—no stall, no yawing moment, no spin.

MINIMUM CONTROLLABLE AIRSPEED

Flight at minimum controllable airspeed means maintaining the airplane in a condition whereby any pitch increase or power reduction would result in an immediate stall. This maneuver will hereafter be referred to as "MCA" or "slow flight." The student's first question after being introduced to this maneuver is usually, Why learn this, and what good is it?

MCA is basic; it teaches you more about your airplane than any other maneuver you can perform. Practice it once in a while after you are certificated and no longer flying regularly with an instructor. Never fail to include slow flight practice when you are checking out in any new type of airplane.

MCA familiarizes you with the feel of your airplane in a critical speed range. You know how the controls feel, how the pitch attitude looks, and how much rudder is required to maintain coordination. You can see how much the nose pitches when flaps are added, and you can learn the pitch attitudes and power settings the airplane requires to maintain altitude. You will understand what the phrase "behind the power curve" means when the airplane refuses to climb, even with full power. You are operating in an area of reverse command in which more power is required to maintain altitude at a lower airspeed.

You can see how airspeed affects turn radius, and you will get the elevator and the throttle working together to maintain altitude and airspeed in turns. You will see how much the addition or retraction of flaps (and gear) affects pitch and sink and/or climb rate. You will learn to anticipate the reactions of the airplane to all control surface, attitude, and power changes. Finally, you will get ahead of your airplane mentally, instead of letting it pull you around the sky.

Flight at MCA will also show you if you have allowed your technique to become sloppy. If you can't perform slow flight to acceptable standards, some practice (or dual instruction) is in order in the interests of safety (Fig. 2.13). You should be able to enter and recover from MCA on a predetermined heading and altitude. You should also be able to maintain altitude during turns of any degree of bank and with any amount of flaps. Don't be satisfied with less, no matter what the minimum standards in the flight-test guide are. Your airplane can do it perfectly; anything less is pilot error.

F I G. 2.13. *Minimum controllable airspeed.*

Begin by clearing the area and noting your heading and altitude so that you can score your results. Pull carb heat on and reduce power to 1,500 rpm. Anticipate the immediate nose heaviness and be ready with back pressure to maintain altitude. You have already begun slowing down.

Begin a slow, steady pitch increase to your predetermined attitude and maintain wings level. A quick glance at the altimeter will verify whether the rate of pitch increase was correct.

Very soon you will be treated to the sound of your stall-warning horn. This is a great angle-of-attack indicator; as soon as it comes on, begin a steady power increase. The nose will yaw to the left, so be ready to add some right rudder. Keep your eyes fastened on the nose; if your nose doesn't wander around, neither will your heading. When you find the pitch attitude and power setting that will maintain the desired airspeed and altitude, remember what they are. They will work next time and avoid all that searching around. Add and retract flaps (and gear) and learn to anticipate the elevator pressure changes necessary to maintain altitude and airspeed.

On the recovery, add power to cruise (carb heat off) and slowly lower the nose to the level-flight attitude. Glance at the altimeter once in a while to verify that the rate of decreasing pitch is correct. As airspeed builds, gradually retract the flaps to minimize sink. Keep your eyes on the horizon reference, and prevent the nose from wandering.

Practice turns to headings in the slow flight configuration, and use varying degrees of bank. Remember the loss of altitude in a bank, and if you are truly at minimum controllable airspeed, you have no further up-elevator available without bringing on a stall. Adding power in the bank will prevent sinking; reduce it again on rollout, or you will climb.

Observe that one idea keeps appearing over and over—anticipate. You are trying to maintain heading, airspeed, and altitude; but the real objective is knowing your airplane well enough and gaining the skill to perform any specific task. You are moving along at a good clip, and you can't hover. You must be somewhere ahead of your airplane mentally, and the faster your airplane is, the farther ahead of it you had better be. The airplane performs exactly the same way every time, so learn what it does and be ready for it. That is the key to smooth, safe, precision flying.

MEMORIZE THESE PROCEDURES for entering and recovering MCA: (carb heat on) reduce power to 1,500; increase pitch to the slow flight attitude; when the stall horn comes on add power to the predetermined power setting (carb heat off). Add flaps as desired.

Recovery: add power to cruise, lower the nose to level-flight attitude, and slowly retract flaps. While in the slow flight configuration, CONTROL AIRSPEED WITH ELEVATOR; CONTROL ALTITUDE WITH THROTTLE.

GROUND REFERENCE MANEUVERS

Ground reference maneuvers include S-turns across a road, rectangular courses, turns about a point, 8s around pylons, 8s along a road, and 8s across a road. When you can do one, you can do them all.

Your instructor will probably start with S-turns across a road. The first objective is to force you to expand your attention. You have been completely wrapped up in the airplane until now. Sooner or later you will have to maneuver the airplane relative to an outside reference point, and you may as well start now. The main objective, however, is to show you the effects of wind (drift) on your ground track and to teach you how to compensate for it.

FIG. 2.14. *Boats (ground reference).*

Look at boats 1 and 2, trying to row from point A to point B in Fig. 2.14. Boat 1 is going to end up downstream at point C; boat 2 might just make it, because of his "crab" into the current. He does not have the boat tipped over on its side; his rowing is just as level and coordinated as that of boat 1, but his heading is different. This example is not intended to insult your intelligence; just because airplanes can fly sideways without sinking, some people get the idea that is how it is done.

Figure 2.15 depicts a constant 30° banked turn. The path through the air is a perfect circle; the ground track would also be a perfect circle if there was absolutely no wind. The airplanes in the other diagrams are making the same perfect circle through the body of air, but the body of air is moving over the ground. In order to make the ground track be the perfect circle, you must alter your path through the air by steepening or shallowing the bank.

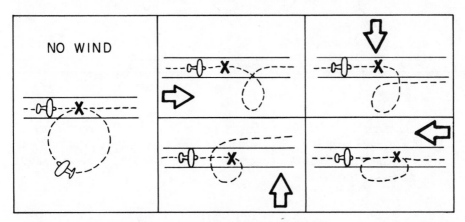

F I G. 2.15. *Wind circles (ground track in turns).*

It is preferable to enter all ground reference maneuvers downwind, so that you can establish immediately what your steepest bank will be. These are done at a very low altitude (600–800 feet AGL) and you should plan your steepest bank not to exceed 45°. Drift is easier to see the closer you are to the ground. Your instructor will have a place picked out where you won't get "canned" for "buzzing." FAR 91.79, minimum safe altitudes, is the regulation that applies.

Establish yourself on altitude, power set at cruise, and trim for hands off. Now leave the power alone; maintain altitude with elevator and bank. If you climb or dive so much that you need a power change to correct your altitude, abort the maneuver until you have everything reestablished, and start over. Avoid this dilemma: Low altitude, steep bank, low power setting, low airspeed. This combination quite frankly scares the daylights out of me. It is easily avoided by leaving the power set at cruise.

Fly the S-turn across a road (Fig. 2.16) in your kitchen simulator. With a constant bank, your ground track would follow the dashed lines, and the S is supposed to be symmetrical. Plan so that the wings are parallel to the road as you cross it, and don't fly straight and level for miles; you roll *through* that turn *as* you cross the road. THE STEEPEST BANKS OCCUR DIRECTLY DOWNWIND, AND THE SHALLOWEST BANKS DIRECTLY UPWIND; CRAB INTO THE CROSS-WIND. Don't forget elevator pressure changes as banks steepen and shallow, or you will end up flying a vertical "S" as well as a horizontal one; the plan includes maintaining a constant altitude.

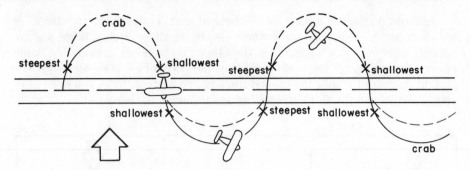

FIG. 2.16. *S-Turns across a road.*

Apply the same principles to the ground reference maneuvers in Figure 2.17. If you have been "logging" simulator time along with your actual dual practice of the basic flight maneuvers, you should be ready to move along to Chapter 3 and a progress check.

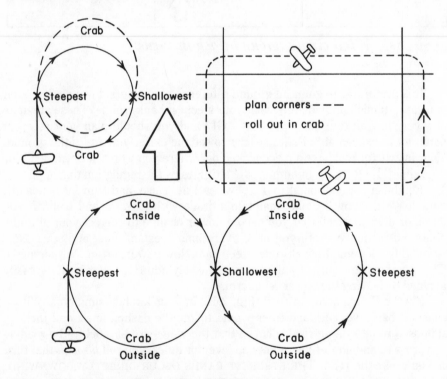

FIG. 2.17. *Ground reference maneuvers.*

3
Getting Ready for Solo

PAUSE a moment for a progress check. Student pilots are in a curious position compared to other learning situations, in that they simply cannot judge their own progress. Consider that your only basis for comparison is your flight instructor, since your instructor is the only one you are allowed to fly with. This may seem unfair since the instructor has presumably had more practice than you have. Students of other skills generally have some opportunity to observe their peers in action. This is not true for the student pilot. You are naturally concerned about the progress you are making, and you must take your flight instructor's word for it.

Five-Hour Check

Generalizations are dangerous in flight instruction because there are so many variables—location, weather conditions, previous knowledge and experience—the list could go on and on. I'll stick my neck out and state what my goals for you would be with five hours of dual instruction behind you. If you feel that you don't meet these standards at this point, perhaps you should be spending more time in your kitchen simulator or revising your estimate of the total flight time you are going to need.

You can handle the preflight, taxi, run up, and takeoff unassisted. Most of the communication duties are yours, but you are still glad your instructor is there to translate occasionally. You can hold an assigned heading and altitude or at least spot the error and make the correction without being told how. The same is true with medium turns to headings and rudders are reasonably coordinated. You can enter and recover unassisted from slow flight and from straight ahead stalls, both power on and power off. You can enter a climb and level off at (or near) an assigned altitude and also enter a glide and level off at an assigned altitude. You can make climbing turns and gliding turns while maintaining a safe airspeed, and you can level off from turning climbs and glides while still maintaining the turn. These maneuvers are not perfect yet, but you have the idea.

You can find your way to the practice area and back. You have been introduced to some ground reference maneuvers, and you have been placed briefly in the portable cloud (instrument hood). You have probably been startled by a simulated engine failure. Your instructor is entertaining thoughts of introducing you to the traffic pattern for takeoffs and landings. You are going to love this part, but prepare to be frustrated from time to time. The traffic pattern is the place where all the basic piloting skills and flight maneuvers thus far practiced begin to come together.

It is beginning to dawn on you that sometime in the not-too-distant future you are going to be expected to fly *all by yourself!*

Takeoffs and Landings

NORMAL TRAFFIC PATTERN

The normal traffic pattern is a rectangle (Fig. 3.1). Turns are planned to keep the corners as square as possible to enable others to better predict what you are going to do next. Enter the pattern already established at traffic pattern altitude, neither climbing nor descending. A low-wing airplane descending into a pattern already occupied by high-wing airplanes is a situation with a large potential for trouble.

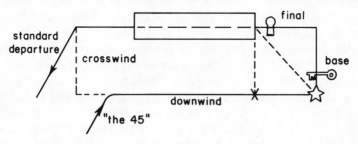

FIG. 3.1. *Normal traffic pattern.*

In a normal traffic pattern, all turns are made to the left (left traffic) unless otherwise indicated by the tower. At an uncontrolled field, the segmented circle depicts the proper direction. Refer to the section entitled "Airport Operations" in AIM. The altitude flown will normally be 1,000 feet AGL, rounded off to the highest 100 feet. Many airports request (or require) that the pattern be flown at some other specified altitude for noise abatement or because of obstructions. Research your destination in AIM's *Airport/Facility Directory* for any nonstandard conditions.

The reasons for the standard departure and the entry at the 45° angle to the downwind leg should be fairly obvious as a collision-prevention procedure. The terms "downwind" and "crosswind" for those sides of the rectangle seem reasonable and self-explanatory. The "base leg" might have been derived from our national pastime in a more diamond-shaped pattern; I have never really cared for the term "final."

The remaining markings on the traffic pattern depicted in Figure 3.1 should be handled as follows (assuming there is no interference from other traffic):

Reduce power (carb heat on) directly abeam the touchdown point (×), slow to descent airspeed, and add flaps as desired.

Establish approach airspeed and descent, and begin a gliding turn to the base leg. Observe that this point (★) occurs approximately 45° from the touchdown point.

At the "key position" begin to judge whether flap and/or power changes are necessary to assure arrival at the touchdown point. Approach airspeed remains constant, appropriate to the selected flap setting. The key position is also the most critical point in the traffic pattern from the standpoint of safety. Most midair collisions and most stall-spin accidents occur right here along the base-to-final. FLY ATTITUDE in gliding turns so that you can keep your head up to watch for unannounced, straight-in traffic. At the same time, look outside to verify the proper attitude to assure a safe and accurate airspeed. When you are ready to make the 90° turn, look around and locate a reference point that is under (or above) the wing; scan for traffic as you turn your head to look. Enter the gliding turn, monitoring pitch attitude relative to the horizon while clearing the area for traffic. Roll out on the wing-tip reference, and you have turned 90°. It works every time. Fly attitude and keep your eyes where potential traffic is, NOT on the airspeed indicator and NOT searching for the runway. A runway has never been known to move; it will still be there when you roll out of the turn (aircraft carriers excepted).

Use a ground reference point on the downwind to maintain a ground track that is parallel to the runway. While you are still abeam the runway, look ahead for a reference point over the nose of the airplane. When you pass the touchdown point and begin to slow and descend, the runway is behind you. This is the point where most students begin to drift inside (or outside) of the desired track. Flying toward an outside reference is preferable to attempting to fly a heading, since it keeps your head outside the cockpit.

The turn from base to final should be made no lower than 500 feet Above Ground Level (AGL), or one-half of the recommended traffic pattern altitude. If you are shooting "touch-and-goes," climb to this altitude before beginning the turn to crosswind.

The "keyhole" in Figure 3.1 is your target, not the touchdown point on the runway. It is also close enough to the touchdown point to allow a glide to the runway with full flaps if the engine quits.

You may be called upon to make many adjustments in the traffic pattern, but plan to arrive in the keyhole with the same power setting and the same airspeed and flap setting every time. If you have added power to make it, reduce the throttle to your normal power setting at this point. If you have had to close the throttle to get down to it, at this point add the power once again. No matter what adjustments you have had to make, the configuration is consistently the same on short final, and the touchdown will be consistent also. A well-planned and well-executed traffic pattern leads to a successful landing. If you have to scramble to keep up with the airplane in the pattern, you are probably going to make a mess of the landing too.

The following is an organized list of procedures for flying a touch-and-go pattern; fly it in the kitchen simulator until it becomes a habit:

1. Descend to traffic pattern altitude, set the power at low cruise, and trim for level flight.

2. Enter the 45, reporting your position on the radio as necessary.

3. Establish on downwind (carb heat on), maintain pattern altitude, and note a reference off the nose; communicate as necessary.

4. Reduce power opposite the touchdown point, add flaps, and maintain pattern altitude while slowing to approach speed. Lower the nose to the glide attitude that will maintain approach airspeed and retrim.

5. Establish descent, note the wingtip reference, and begin the gliding turn to base leg. FLY ATTITUDE and visually clear the final approach path.

6. Roll out on the reference, locate the runway, and add flaps as desired; fly attitude.

7. Plan the gliding turn to final so that you roll out lined up with the runway; fly attitude.

8. Add or reduce power as necessary to arrive in the keyhole position; fly attitude.

9. Reset the power (if necessary) to your normal approach power setting in the keyhole position, add full flaps, and FLY ATTITUDE to the flare. The flare and the touchdown will be discussed later.

Assuming you have chosen an airport with plenty of runway for this operation, don't rush yourself on the rollout. You survived the landing; do not swerve and ground-loop the airplane. Retract the flaps, gently maneuver yourself back to the centerline (you probably missed it on the touchdown), and concentrate for a takeoff.

1. Add power (and right rudder) and accelerate to rotation speed (V_r), maintaining runway heading.

2. Climb at V_x, maintaining runway heading, and further accelerate to V_y once all obstacles are cleared.

3. Note a wingtip reference, and FLY ATTITUDE in a climbing turn to crosswind.

4. Roll out on the reference and look around for traffic, especially in the direction of the normal 45° entry point.

5. Turn to the downwind, leveling off at traffic pattern altitude and low cruise airspeed, and retrim. Report your position on the radio as necessary.

You can plainly see that this "touch-and-go" or "crash-and-dash" or as the British call it, "doing circuits," is a busy operation at first. This is the point in your training where all the basic air work you have been practicing comes down on you at once. Review the procedures until they go smoothly. Let's move on to a discussion of making adjustments for other traffic.

SHARING THE TRAFFIC PATTERN

When you share the traffic pattern with other airplanes, especially if they are slower or faster than yours, you will be obliged to make airspeed adjustments and/or extend your downwind leg to maintain a safe interval. Occasionally, the tower may request that you break out of the pattern, make a 360° turn for spacing, and reenter the pattern. Do not initiate such a maneuver yourself without requesting clearance to do so. The tower doesn't want you to run someone down, but they do need to know what you are up to in case someone else is on the way into the pattern. If you should receive such instructions and they sound urgent, I recommend that you turn first and acknowledge later. Make the turn maintaining traffic pattern altitude, and consider cleaning up flaps, gear, etc., as necessary to maintain a safe airspeed.

A general rule for assuring adequate spacing when following traffic of an approximately equal speed is to begin the turn just after the traffic you are following has passed your wingtip going in the opposite direction. Another good general rule to follow is: On any *extended* downwind, maintain traffic pattern altitude *at least* until you are ready to begin a turn to base. When you are called upon to extend the downwind to make room for other traffic, the task of planning the descent changes. If you reduce power at the usual place (directly abeam the touchdown point), obviously you are going to end up either too low or too slow—or both.

The downwind leg is usually flown approximately ¾ mile from the runway, but to simplify the arithmetic let's call it 1 mile even. Note that the lines between the positions marked are all equidistant (Fig. 3.2). If you fly from A to B to C to touchdown, you have covered 3 miles. Reducing the power to begin the descent at point A works out just fine in a normal traffic pattern. However, if you must extend your base leg 1 mile, turning base at point D instead of point B, then you should maintain pattern altitude to point D and begin your power reduction and descent as you turn base; you are still 3 miles from touchdown. If you have to extend all the way to point E before you turn base, don't begin the descent until you roll out on final.

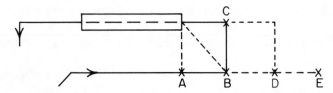

F I G. 3.2. *Extended traffic pattern.*

If the tower gives you a sequence such as, "number three to follow" *never begin* a turn to base leg until you can see all of the airplanes that are ahead of you. If there is any doubt in your mind, call the tower and request that the controller tell you when you are clear to turn base. The controller has binoculars and isn't looking down into ground clutter.

When asked to keep up your speed on final because a faster airplane is behind you, you can handle the situation easily—fly a cruise descent. The tower knows you will have to slow down sometime; plan it far enough ahead so that you arrive at the keyhole position on the proper speed. Practice flying a higher airspeed approach until you can judge when you have to start slowing down. There is more than one way to fly a traffic pattern. Another way involves the following: When the tower says, "Make short approach, cleared to land," the controller wants you to close the throttle, add full flaps, and go for the numbers.

Both of these (high airspeed and short approach) situations are a little too much for you now, but with practice you will handle them smoothly. Fore-warned is forearmed—simulate these situations with your instructor. Any time you are given instructions with which you don't feel prepared to cope, refuse them. Controllers are trained to recognize the capability of your type aircraft, but only you can know your own level of skill.

If an airplane is overtaking you on final, the pilot can always go around. FAR 91.67 is the regulation concerning right-of-way. Look it up—you may be the one overtaking me someday. Now let's discuss go-arounds, landings, and traffic pattern emergencies.

LANDINGS, RECOVERIES AND OTHER EMERGENCIES

Contrary to popular belief, you do not fly an airplane onto a runway. You fly it down close, close the throttle, and prevent the touchdown as long as possible. The perfect landing occurs when the wing stalls at the same moment that the mains touch the pavement. This happens once out of every several hundred landings. In the meantime, we keep trying to get it right.

A tricycle-gear airplane has three wheels; two are for landing, and one is for steering while on the ground. The main landing gear will take an extraordinary amount of punishment, but the nosewheel is a fairly fragile arrangement that has enough to do simply supporting the weight of the engine. Treat the nose gear gently; lift it off first, and set it down last.

The transition from the final descent to the touchdown may be called by a number of terms—roundout, flare, crash. No matter what you call it, all it amounts to is leveling off from a glide. WHEN to do it is a matter of depth perception. However sharp your vision may be, if you fixate on any given point you will be unable to judge when to initiate the flare. Depth perception depends on eye movement. If you stare at a point directly over the nose, you will flare too high and drop it in. If you stare at a point too far away, you will flare too late and pancake. Either way, you bounce. Try to find a happy medium that allows enough eye movement to compensate for the constantly changing focal distance. This is a judgment factor that comes only after some experience.

Start by looking down the runway approximately the same distance you would be looking down a highway if you were driving at a comparable speed. Rotate the elevator to transition from the glide attitude to the level flight attitude and close the throttle. Lift the nose to an attitude slightly steeper than that attitude necessary to maintain level flight, as if you wished to initiate a shallow climb. Then wait for the power-off stall.

As airspeed deteriorates, the nose becomes increasingly heavier, just as it does during stall practice. Maintain a steady increase in back pressure to maintain the touchdown attitude. Remember the nosewheel, and hold it off as long as possible. When the wing is no longer able to support the weight of the airplane, the airplane will settle down to the runway on the main gear.

There is a new factor called "ground effect" that will affect your aircraft's performance between the flare and the touchdown. This phenomenon will be covered in the discussion of soft-field takeoffs and landings in Chapter 4.

If you flare too abruptly or with too much airspeed, the airplane climbs (or "balloons"). You are now very near stall speed, and you still have an increased angle of attack; airspeed will continue to deteriorate. You are also too high above the runway, and the airplane will quickly develop an enthusiastic rate of descent: Add power immediately. That is why you already had your hand on the throttle. Do not lower the nose any further than the normal landing attitude: If you are going to bounce, do it on the main gear.

Most ballooning situations can be recovered easily and turned into an acceptable landing by adding a burst of power to break the rate of descent. However, if the balloon was a really big one, or if there is a crosswind and you have lost your correction and have started to drift, add full power, accelerate in ground effect to V_x, retract flaps, go around and try it again.

The airplane will also go around following a bad bounce. The problems of control following a bad bounce are just the same as with a balloon; add full power and go around before you allow a condition to develop known as "porpoising." This can happen when the nosewheel is allowed to contact the runway before the mains. The airplane begins bouncing back and forth from the mains to the nose, and each bounce gets higher until the nose gear finally gives up and retracts itself. This action is also hard on propellers. If you encounter a porpoising situation, IMMEDIATELY add full power, place the nose in the normal landing attitude, and keep it there. DO NOT ATTEMPT to counter each bounce with opposite control movement. The combined reaction time of a pilot and an airplane is such that the porpoising situation will only be aggravated.

The decision to continue a landing has turned out to be the wrong choice before; a decision to go around has never been proven wrong. Practice the technique of the go-around from the full-flap configuration until you are thoroughly comfortable with it and until directional control and airspeed control are acceptable. Look ahead on final approach, and be alerted if a go-around situation appears to be developing. Don't leave the decision until it turns into a full-grown problem. Being obviously too high or too fast would certainly be grounds for a go-around decision. In this case you would execute the go-around directly overflying the runway. Keep a wary eye on any airplane sitting beside the departure end of the runway—the pilot may not see you coming; be ready to go if the airplane moves. In that case, you would sidestep and keep it in sight to prevent its climbing up underneath you.

For some unknown reason, pilots who make reasonable decisions to abort landings can't seem to properly face the issue of when to abort a takeoff. If the machine isn't behaving right, close the throttle. Whatever the situation is now, you will get in deeper by trying to continue. Most airport runways are long enough to take off and land several times before you run into the fence. Keep this in mind when you opt for an intersection takeoff.

The first 500 or 600 feet after lift-off is the most critical portion of the flight if the engine should fail. Airspeed in the climb is low, and angle of attack is high. As soon as the engine stops, airspeed is going to bleed off very rapidly. You don't have time to think about putting the nose down—just DO it. Attempting a turn back to the airport has gotten a lot of pilots in big trouble. Do the best you can with what you have to work with, keep any turns shallow, maintain best glide speed, and steer for the closest open spot. A long time ago I picked out my spots off the departure end of every runway at Homefield. I hope I never use one, but at least I know where they are.

Play this game with your flight instructor: At altitude and on a cardinal heading, establish a climb at V_x; close the throttle—don't cheat, give yourself a 3-second reaction time before you lower the nose. See how much altitude you lose making a 180° turn. You would never attempt to turn back to a runway. Besides, you would be landing downwind.

One more landing you should be able to demonstrate proficiency in prior to solo is the no-flap landing. Electric flaps can fail, and so can manual ones. I once had the locking mechanism break; the flaps were fine, they just couldn't be set. With no flaps, you will see a flatter, more nose-high approach attitude, and a long, floating flare.

Do not feel too frustrated if you don't see the "landing attitude" picture right away. There is really nothing magic about it. It is great fun to watch a student suddenly get the picture who has been trying so hard (without much success). It is almost like the "light bulb over the head" in the comics; it really comes on just that suddenly sometimes. From then on, the landings really begin to work.

There is a point in flight training where many students make up all kinds of excuses about why they didn't have time to do their homework. If this continues for too many more hours, the student finds that flight training stops and ground instruction sessions begin. Your flight instructor may find your excuses fascinating, but the instructor still needs to see results. There are certain areas of knowledge that you simply must be proficient in, or your instructor can't turn you loose on an unsuspecting public. See you in the kitchen simulator: MAKE time—show some results, not excuses.

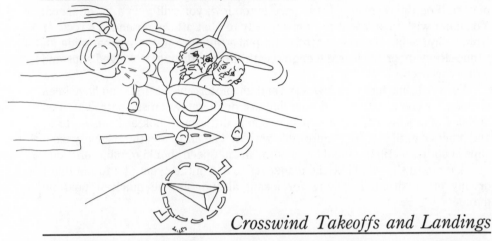

Crosswind Takeoffs and Landings

An approach to a crosswind landing is a side slip. Therefore we will discuss side slips and throw in forward slips for good measure.

The difference between a forward slip and a side slip is another one of those factors that seems designed to confuse us; as far as the airplane is concerned, it can't tell the difference either. Although you may lower either the left wing or the right wing, there is still only one way to slip an airplane. The different terms merely describe different maneuvers that require a slip.

FORWARD SLIPS

A forward slip is a maneuver designed to help you lose a lot of altitude without gaining airspeed, which will happen if you lower the nose and dive. That sounds exactly like one of the reasons for using flaps. But early airplanes were not equipped with flaps, so a dramatic forward slip was often the only method the pilot had of arriving at the runway.

For a normal landing in an airplane that is equipped with flaps, a violent forward slip to make it down to the runway would have to be looked upon as a confession of gross errors in technique. Some airplanes are even placarded against combining the use of slips with the flaps down because they block the downwash on the elevator. Can you imagine what happens if the elevator stalls? You may combine slips and flaps in most airplanes, but check your owner's manual first. A forward slip is still a great maneuver to have up your sleeve for accuracy landings and off-airport emergencies when you need to lose altitude but aren't yet ready to commit yourself to using flaps.

During a forward slip you are not altering your direction of motion. Roll the aileron fully to the left and hold full right rudder (or vice versa). You are still moving in the same direction, but you are just about going sideways. The relative wind is striking a lot of fuselage, increasing drag without increasing lift. You will sink like a brick. Choose to lower the wing that is into the wind; it will be more effective for altitude loss versus forward distance traveled.

Close the throttle first; there is little point in slipping to lose altitude if you are still carrying power. Pay close attention to pitch attitude. Remember that your airspeed indicator is inaccurate in a slip, and if your nose is too high, you may stall on the recovery. If the nose is too low, you will gain a lot of speed. You don't wish to arrive at the runway only to float off the far end. To recover from a slip, neutralize the controls and place the nose in the normal glide attitude. Remember to clear the engine with throttle during prolonged slips and to use carburetor heat.

Forward slips feel very awkward and uncomfortable at first; you have been striving for coordination, and now you are deliberately cross controlled. You are sitting crooked, and the airplane sounds different. Look at it, listen to it, and practice until you are comfortable with it. The entry and the recovery from slips in both directions should be smooth, and airspeed should remain constant.

A forward slip would be the maneuver to use in the event of a fire in flight or any other situation calling for losing altitude in the quickest possible manner.

SIDE SLIPS

According to the FAA's *Flight Training Handbook*, "a sideslip, as distinguished from a forward slip, is one during which the longitudinal axis remains approximately parallel to the original flightpath, but in which the flight-path changes in direction according to the steepness of the bank assumed."

That means you are slipping into the wind while keeping the nose pointed in the right direction. *Example*: The crosswind track is illustrated in Figure 3.3:

1. Line up with runway 36 in a condition where the wind is straight down the runway (or no wind at all). Hold the 360° heading, and the airplane will arrive over the threshold.

2. If the wind is out of the West and you hold the 360° heading, you are going to drift so that the runway will end up off to your left.

3. Correct the drift by crabbing into the wind (holding a heading of 340°) and your ground track is straight to the threshold. Unfortunately it is not recommended that you touch down while drifting sideways. The wheels don't roll well under these circumstances, and the airplane may try to swap ends on the runway (groundloop). *You must touch down with the nose pointed in the direction of forward motion.* There has to be another method we can use to cancel the drift.

4. Lower the wing into the wind. The wing's lifting force is perpendicular to the wing surface. It is now acting directly into the wind; that is the direction the airplane is actually moving through the air. Yaw the nose with the opposite rudder to keep it pointed in the direction of the desired ground track (prevent the turn). You are slipping sideways into the wind, but your forward motion over the surface is a straight line. The greater the crosswind component, the more pronounced the necessary correction becomes. (Steeper bank, more rudder.)

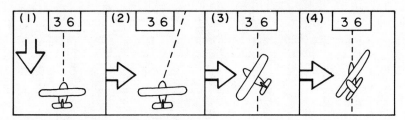

F I G. 3.3. *Crosswind track.*

Full rudder deflection is the factor that determines the "crosswind limitation" for your airplane. When the aileron and rudder controls are fully deflected and the airplane is still drifting off the centerline, you had better find somewhere else to land.

CROSSWIND COMPONENT

One of my favorite things to do with a student returning from a phase check is to let him get the ATIS information and then switch to the tower frequency. As soon as he has changed channels, I ask him innocently, "What did he say the wind was?" They rarely ever know—amazing! They must blithely assume it will be right down the runway, and it seldom ever is.

The surface wind direction is magnetic, and the velocity is in knots. Study the crosswind component chart (Fig. 3.4). To find the crosswind component, you must know the angular difference between the wind and your runway heading.

If we are landing runway 36 and ATIS tells us the wind is 330° at 15 knots, what have we got? A 30° left crosswind. You should have that figured out before you turn downwind, so you can plan your traffic pattern. You also need to know if that exceeds the airplane's crosswind limitation; or more importantly, your own *personal* crosswind limitation. You wouldn't know if you didn't already have some idea of how much crosswind component you have been handling successfully up to now. You may need to be on the alert for a possible go-around. You may even need to divert to another (more favorable) airport while you still have enough fuel to get there.

Obviously you won't always have a crosswind component chart beside you in the airplane, so use this rule of thumb to estimate it: when the wind is 30° off the runway heading, the crosswind component is approximately one-half the wind velocity.

My own personal limitations go something like this: When the wind is within 30° of the runway heading and is under 20 knots, I figure I can handle it. If it is more than 30° off, I listen a lot closer to the velocity. I also pay more attention if there is a gust spread in excess of 10 knots. Don't take my limitations

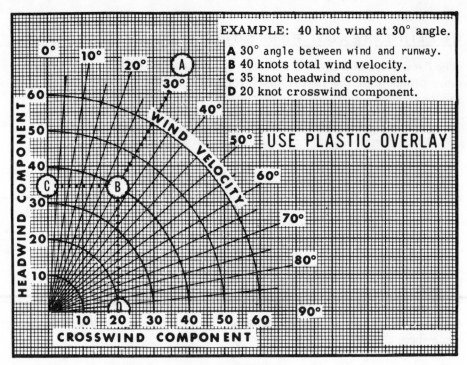

FIG. 3.4. *Crosswind component chart.*

for your own until you have tested them; one of my old stomping grounds was the plains of the Dakotas, where wind was invented.

Gusty winds are one condition that justifies carrying a little extra speed on final. *Example:* The wind is 15 knots gusting to 25 knots; that is a 10-knot gust spread. Add one-half of the gust spread (5 knots) to your normal final approach speed. This is your protection against a phenomenon known as "wind shear." No one knew too much about wind shear until a few years ago when it got to an airliner approaching to land in the vicinity of a thunderstorm. A brisk head-wind component on final approach suddenly became a tail wind, and the airliner developed a rapid sink rate and had insufficient altitude in which to recover. We will discuss wind shear further in the weather section.

CROSSWIND LANDING

Finally, after all this preparation, we are ready to enter downwind. We have estimated a left-crosswind component of 8 knots, and we are flying left traffic (Fig. 3.5). Plan the downwind slightly wider than normal, and crab away from the runway. The downwind heading may be about 200° instead of the

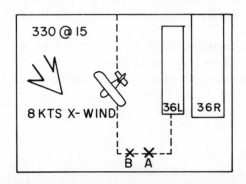

FIG. 3.5. *Crosswind traffic pattern.*

usual 180° (right correction). We are wider because of the tail-wind component we will have on base. Start the turn to final at point B instead of the usual point A; there is a parallel runway to consider, so this is no time to overshoot the final. Roll out on final on a heading of approximately 340°. There is really no need to figure out numbers, so long as we anticipate the fact that we are going to crab to the left in order to maintain the ground track.

Sooner or later it will become necessary to convert from the crab to the side slip, but there is no point in holding a slip throughout the final approach. It is much easier to establish the crab and hold that until we get the picture of how far off the track the nose is pointed. With that picture to work with, it feels much easier and more natural to rudder the nose around so that it is straight *as* you roll in just the right amount of aileron. This is another technique that requires practice.

First common error: Do not level the wings just prior to touchdown. As soon as you do, you will start to drift. Go ahead and let the upwind wheel land first; the other one will come down soon enough. Touch down while still holding the airplane in the slip.

Second common error: Neutral aileron. As soon as the mains are down on the runway, roll the aileron full into the wind. This will be your greatest aid to maintaining directional control on the rollout.

The wind is striking the tail on the left side, and the airplane wants to weather vane. Hold upwind aileron and downwind rudder. Remember the aileron positions for taxiing in a quartering head wind? Be sure that you retract the flaps immediately.

In summary, the procedures for a crosswind landing are as follows:

1. Determine the crosswind component, left or right.
2. Plan the pattern to compensate for drift.
3. Establish the necessary crab on final.
4. Establish the sideslip in the keyhole.
5. Maintain the slip through the touchdown.
6. Roll the aileron full into the wind *immediately* on the rollout and retract flaps.

The use of full flaps for crosswind landings is a matter open to debate. Many pilots hold the position that ALL landings should be full-flap landings. I agree completely with their reasoning, but I still don't always advocate the use of full flaps in a crosswind. There are three reasons why it is good practice to land with full flaps:

1. You will find that wear and tear on tires, brakes, and landing gear components is less at lower speeds.
2. You will be grabbed by centrifugal force (start of a ground loop) if you swerve on the rollout. This force increases by mathematical leaps and bounds the faster you are going (ground loop in progress). Centrifugal force increases "as the square of the speed" at which the swerve started.
3. You are going to have to slow through the speed at which the airplane quits flying at some time. Why prolong the agony?

All of these are good and valid arguments for using full flaps. My reservations about full flaps during crosswind landings involve the proficiency of student pilots in light trainers and the difficulty of executing the go-around in a crosswind. I also advocate that a student pilot be fully proficient in executing a go-around from the full-flap configuration prior to solo. Even so, most students still have their hands full in this situation. If we add gusty crosswind conditions to the load, the problems multiply.

Most primary flight trainers don't have enough guts under the cowling to climb with full flaps, and they sink further when the flaps are retracted. Even on the rollout, students are likely to be a little slower remembering to bring the flaps up, and the wind really reacts on them once the airplane is on the ground. Until you have demonstrated marked proficiency in both crosswind technique and full-flap go-arounds, your instructor may request that you use something less than full flaps for crosswind landings.

CROSSWIND TAKEOFFS

Let us now depart with the same crosswind condition we had on the approach. Begin the takeoff roll holding the aileron full into the wind. As speed builds and the aileron comes alive, relax the pressure somewhat, but continue holding it so that you can feel *some* pressure. Right rudder is always needed on a normal takeoff, but this time it may really seem exaggerated, due to the "weather vaning" tendency. If the crosswind is from the right, you will find the need for right rudder reduced or even completely canceled.

Allow the airplane to remain on the runway until you are assured of adequate climb speed to avoid settling back down drifting. Avoid a tendency to hold forward elevator pressure on the takeoff roll. As the wings take the load off the mains, you are placing that weight on the nosewheel. This results in a very unstable condition known as "wheelbarrowing."

Immediately after liftoff, we will be climbing in a slip; the aileron and rudder controls are in the same position they were when we touched down. This will maintain the track, but it is an inefficient way to gain altitude. Coordinate the controls, and turn to establish a crab that will maintain the desired track.

In summary, the procedures for a crosswind takeoff are as follows:

1. Hold full aileron into the wind and relax the pressure slightly as resistance builds.

2. Rotate after climb speed is assured.

3. Establish a positive rate of climb, coordinate the controls, and establish a crab to maintain ground track.

Crosswind operations are a fact of life in airplanes. They happen when you aren't ready for them, and they are never around when you need them for training purposes. Proficiency is a by-product of practice. After you have been certificated for awhile and you realize that it has been some time since you have encountered a really good crosswind, choose a brisk day and head for the airport. Renew your acquaintance with your old flight instructor and bounce around the patch for an hour; you will both be ahead.

Airspace

Gather together your copies of AIM, FAR Part 91, and your local sectional chart and prepare to spend some time on airspace. This is a very important area, and you won't be able to complete the oral portion of your flight check if you don't understand it thoroughly. Prior to exercising solo flight privileges, your flight instructor will require that you demonstrate a working knowledge of airspace, either through an oral or written quiz. Be sure to mark the references in your copies of the regulations and AIM—they will skip around. If you have not yet read the chapter of AIM entitled "Airspace," NOW is the time.

There are basically two kinds of airspace—controlled airspace and uncontrolled airspace (Fig. 3.6). There are three questions concerning controlled

FIG. 3.6. *Airspace.*

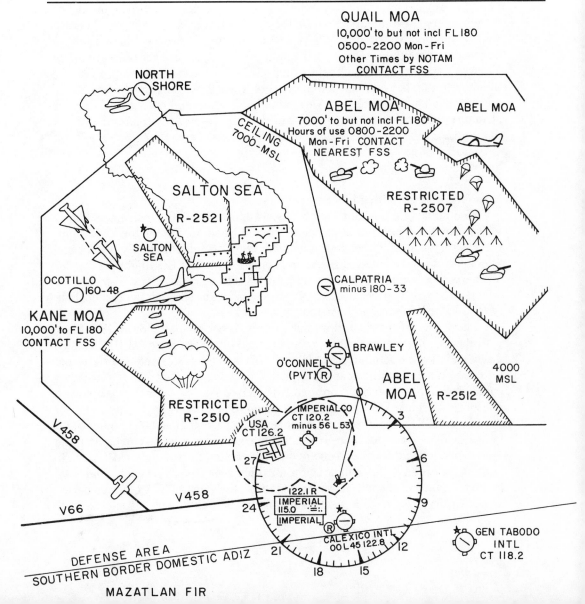

and uncontrolled airspace that are vital to your safe and legal operation: (1) What is the difference between the two? (2) How can I tell which kind I am in? (3) What are the legal requirements for operating here?

You are probably operating in controlled airspace in your local practice area, as there is very little uncontrolled airspace left in the continental United States. So who is controlling you? You are out there practicing stalls, steep turns, loops, spins, and you are not talking to anyone on the radio. You are not even required to *have* a radio; at least not until you return to the airport traffic area, which is also controlled airspace. It is a very confusing situation. The determining factor is WEATHER. Visibility and cloud separation requirements differ between controlled and uncontrolled airspace. You can tell which is which by the markings on the sectional chart; the equipment requirements are all in the regulations.

Numerous changes in the airspace structure have recently been proposed. Most of the proposals involve lowering the floor of Positive Control Airspace (PCA) and adding equipment requirements, such as altitude reporting transponders, to some areas where they are not presently required. There is also a lengthy list of new TCAs in our future. However, the wheels of bureaucracy grind exceedingly slow, and the changes may yet be years away. We won't attempt to deal with the proposals here because they will probably be altered any number of times before they become law. When they do, we'll learn the new regulations together. Meanwhile, let's examine our present airspace structure and the regulations that specify the equipment requirements for operating within it. Come back to us after you have completed reading AIM, "Airspace."

VFR WEATHER MINIMUMS

VFR stands for Visual Flight Rules, as opposed to IFR, Instrument Flight Rules. Any time the weather is below the published minimums for VFR flight, the weather is designated Instrument Meteorological Conditions (IMC), and pilots *must* operate under IFR. Aircraft operating on an IFR flight plan under VFR weather conditions are bound by *both* sets of rules. They may have to adhere to a fairly complicated set of clearances while retaining the responsibility for VFR traffic separation, namely, "see and avoid."

I have an instrument rating, but I'm not about to fool with an IFR flight plan during the daytime when weather conditions are good VFR. I can go direct and have no computerized delays. This is much faster and therefore cost efficient. When conditions are marginal, I'm going to file IFR. The weather could go either way, and if it does go IFR, I am probably safer than if it stayed marginal: Marginal VFR conditions are dangerous for *everybody*.

Marginal VFR weather consists of ceilings of 1,000–3,000 feet, and visibility of 3–5 miles. I am out there IFR, staying right side up while coping with the system and looking for you. You are out there trying to stay right side up while hunting for the airport and looking for me. I hope we never find each other. I've heard marginal VFR conditions referred to as DLE (Death Lurks Everywhere).

The reference for VFR weather minimums is FAR 91.105—memorize it. If you study it until you can reproduce it exactly on a clean sheet of paper, you still won't *really* know what it means. When you find yourself in an airplane going 2 miles per minute with 1 mile visibility and dodging scattered clouds, you will begin to get the picture. Review the FARs as they appear, and you might get a handle on how to operate in the system *legally*. You may want to establish somewhat higher personal minimums in the interests of *safety*.

Take a look at the cloud separation rule: 500 below, 1,000 above, and 2,000 from clouds. You could be up there with someone on an IFR flight plan; that pilot doesn't go around the clouds, but goes right on through them. How close do you want to be when that airplane pops out on your side? Give yourself enough distance to "see and avoid" surprises.

Notice that above 10,000 feet the visibility increases to 5 miles, and cloud separation becomes 1,000 feet above and below, and 1 mile from, and it is the same for both controlled and uncontrolled airspace. FAR 91.70 imposes an airspeed limitation of 250 knots below 10,000 feet. Above that, you can do Mach 3 if your airplane is capable of it, so stay farther away from clouds.

Refer to Figure 3.7 and start at the top and work down. From 60,000 feet (flight level six zero-zero) down to flight level one eight zero (18,000 feet pressure altitude) you are in PCA. Within these limits you must be on an IFR

F I G. 3.7. *Airspace structure.*

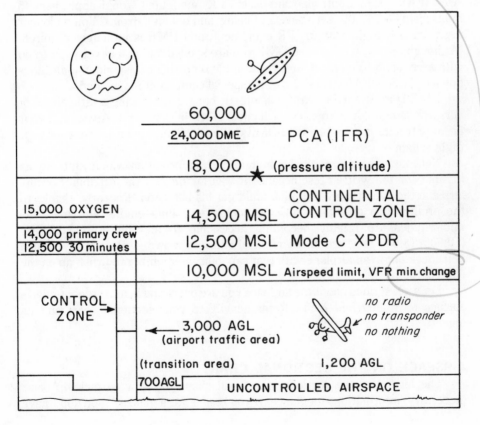

flight plan, and you will be under positive radar control. Your airplane must have all the instruments and navigational aids required by the IFR equipment regulations, and in addition you must have an altitude reporting transponder (FAR 91.24). DME (Distance Measuring Equipment) is required above 24,000 feet (FAR 91.33e).

Pressure altitude means your altimeter is set to standard barometric pressure (29.92) so that everyone is relieved of the responsibility for resetting the altimeter every 100 miles (FAR 91.81). Oxygen equipment would also be nice to have.

The altitudes for the oxygen requirements specified in FAR 91.32 are indicated in Figure 3.7 (*left*). Simplified for our airplane's capabilities, it says that you may operate between 12,500 and 14,000 feet for no longer than 30 minutes without supplemental oxygen; above 14,000 feet primary crew members (you) must use oxygen at all times; and above 15,000 feet you must provide oxygen for all passengers.

I don't care what the minimums are, you probably need an occasional whiff of oxygen above 10,000 feet, especially if you are a smoker. At night, lower that limit to 5,000; night vision really suffers at altitude. Make a point to discuss hypoxia—and conversely, hyperventilation—with your instructor. Refer to the chapter on "Medical Facts for Pilots" in AIM.

Descending to 14,500 feet, you reach the floor of the Continental Control Area (FAR 71.9). Controlled airspace VFR minimums would apply here (5 miles visibility, 1,000 feet above and below and one mile from). You no longer need the IFR flight plan or IFR equipment, and DME is no longer required. (Although once you have used DME you are spoiled and you never want to do without it again.) You must have the altitude reporting transponder at altitudes down to 12,500 (FAR 91.24). No other special equipment is specified.

DME is mentioned in AIM, Chapter 1, but we are getting a little ahead of ourselves going into it now. We will cover DME in Chapter 4. Anyway, if your primary trainer is equipped with DME, call me collect; I want to work for your flight school.

Not many years ago, all this high altitude information was useful only as "cram" for the written test because it was far beyond the capability of any airplane the average private pilot could get his hands on. Recently, thanks to the proliferation of superb little turbocharged, single-engine airplanes, the midaltitudes are rapidly becoming accessible to all. These midaltitudes (10,000–18,000 feet) are an economical and less crowded place to fly. When you check out in an airplane with that capability, remember to brush up on the rules of the road.

Let's get serious about the airspace you are operating in as a student pilot—surface to 10,000 feet MSL. Refer heavily to your sectional chart and its legend.

AIRSPACE ON THE SECTIONAL CHART

The legend of the sectional chart will show you how to pick up basic (necessary) information at a glance. If you *need* it "at a glance," you don't have time to hunt it up in the legend. Thoroughly familiarize yourself with all the symbols on that portion of the chart; when in doubt, read the directions.

Locate an area on the sectional chart where a fuzzy blue line backs up to a fuzzy pink line. Try to find a place where the blue line has one sharp edge. The area bounded by the sharp blue edge is uncontrolled airspace. Inside this area, from the surface to 1,200 AGL, you may operate with 1 mile visibility and clear of clouds. If you climb above 1,200 up to 10,000 MSL, you still need only 1 mile visibility, but the cloud separation rule of 500 below, 1,000 above, and 2,000 from clouds applies. From now on, refer to those numbers as "standard cloud separation."

The fuzzy side of the blue line encloses an area in which the floor of controlled airspace is 1,200 feet AGL. Translation: From the surface to 1,200 AGL, you are in uncontrolled airspace and you may fly with 1 mile visibility and clear of clouds; if you climb above 1,200 AGL up to 10,000 MSL, you need 3 miles visibility and standard cloud separation. Exception: If 10,000 feet MSL is still within 1,200 feet of the surface of the earth (like on top of a mountain), it is still uncontrolled. If you are going to fool around with minimum visibility, I hope your terrain is very flat and free of towers and other obstructions or you stand a good chance of becoming an accident statistic.

Crossing the fuzzy blue line to the area enclosed by fuzzy pink, you have entered a transition area. All this does is lower the floor of controlled airspace from 1,200 to 700 feet AGL. You will find that transition areas coincide with locations that have a heavy concentration of busy airports. More IFR traffic is departing these fields or descending to land; therefore the higher visibility is necessary in order to "see and avoid."

Inside the transition area you will find one or more places enclosed by dashed blue lines. These lines may be circular, or they may have extensions making them resemble keyholes. These are control zones, which extend controlled airspace from the base of the Continental Control Area (14,500 feet MSL) down to the surface. The dashed blue lines lower the floor of controlled airspace from the transition area (700 feet AGL) to the ground. If you have 3 miles visibility and cloud separation, ignore it; the control zone goes away. It was only there to protect IFR airplanes making instrument approaches and departures. You do not have to talk to anyone to enter a control zone so long as you are in VFR conditions. This seems to be an area of monumental confusion to most pilots. Go over it with your instructor until you are sure you have it straight.

The airport in the center of the control zone *may* or *may not* have a control tower. If there is a tower, the airport will be colored blue and the tower frequency will appear in the information block following the letters CT (Control Tower). A nontower airport will be colored pink. PAY ATTENTION: *Do not confuse a control zone with an airport traffic area*—they have nothing to do with one another. The confusion between control zones and airport traffic areas arises because they are usually co-located. I can think of numerous airports that have a control zone but do not have a tower. There are probably a few tower airports around that do not have control zones, but I've never met up with one. STUDY THESE SITUATIONS:

In the control zone on top in Figure 3.8, everybody is VFR. In the other two situations, the airport traffic area is IFR because it occupies the lower portion of the control zone. The portion of the control zone that is above the restricted visibility is still VFR; our friend on top need not talk to anyone. If the pilot down low intends to enter the control zone, a special VFR clearance (discussed later) will be needed very shortly.

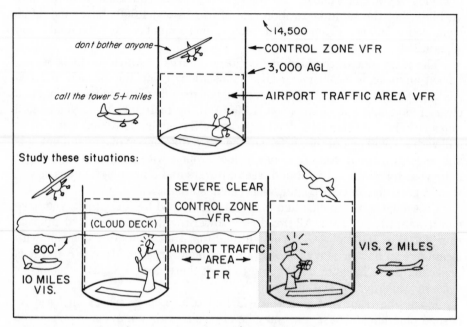

F I G.   3.8.   *Airport traffic area—VFR and IFR.*

The other information in the airport information block on the sectional chart concerns field elevation, lighting, runway length, facilities available, etc. This is explained in the legend; be sure you know what it all means.

For other special use airspace, review AIM. Prohibited, Restricted, Warning, and Alert areas are marked on the chart and numbered. Locate the corresponding number on the edge of the chart to find the controlling authority, hours of operation, and affected altitudes. MOAs (Military Operation Areas) are explained on the chart. Wildlife conservation areas have a requested altitude restriction of 2,000 feet AGL. If any course you plan is going to put you in the vicinity of a symbol you don't recognize, research it before you go, or stay away from it.

Comply with the hemispheric rule when flying more than 3,000 feet AGL; the reference is FAR 91.109. This is designed to assure you at least 500 feet of vertical separation from oncoming traffic. This rule will work if the altimeter is properly set and if you are conscientious about maintaining altitude. Easterly (magnetic) headings are odd numbers plus 500 (3500, 5500, 7500). Westerly headings are even numbers plus 500 (4500, 6500 8500). Stay away from round numbers (3000, 4000, 5000); these are reserved for IFR traffic. Review "Altimeter Setting Procedures" in AIM.

The blue lines you see on the sectional chart connecting one VOR station to another are Victor airways. Airplanes on an IFR flight plan must follow computerized routes, and these routes involve going directly from one radio navigation aid to another because the pilot possibly can't see the ground; Victor airways are the routes they follow. VFR airplanes may also use these depicted routes, and they will make sense to you after you have progressed to VOR navigation.

The floor of a low-level Victor airway is 1,200 feet AGL, and the ceiling is flight level 180. If your planned route takes you along one of these "highways in the sky," avoid climbing to your planned altitude right on the centerline of the airway. Offset to the right until you reach your planned altitude, so you won't bungle through someone else's altitude with your nose too high to see him coming.

There is a wealth of information in the sectional chart, some of it seemingly well hidden. Studying the legend thoroughly should explain it all, but it probably won't. I would make a bet with you that if you studied the chart completely on your own until you were convinced you really knew that legend, I could ask you some questions about chart features that would stump you, even with the legend in front of you. Ask your instructor to try out his favorite chart questions on you and see.

AIRPORT TRAFFIC AREA

An airport traffic area exists only at an airport with an operating control tower. The buzzword is "operating." If the tower is closed, the airport traffic area ceases to exist. Its dimensions include a radius of 5 statute miles from the center of the airport, from the surface up to (but not including) 3,000 feet AGL. Within this area you must be in two-way radio communication with the tower. FAR 91.77 tells you how to get clearance to land (or depart) if you have experienced radio failure. This clearance is obtained through light signals flashed from the tower. Memorize the signals; they are no good to you if you don't know what they mean.

I generally avoid approaching a tower airport when NORDO (No Radio) without making prior arrangements by phone. If you call them before departing, they can brief you about the wind, the active runway, and the barometric pressure. You can tell them what time to expect you and from what direction you will be dropping in. You still have to get a green light before you can land. Should you lose the radio en route, consider stopping at a convenient nontower airport and calling ahead. If that is impractical, comply with the suggestions in "Communications with Tower When Aircraft Transmitter/Receiver or Both Are Inoperative" in AIM under "Radio Communications Phraseology and Techniques." There is more information on lost communication procedures in the "Emergency Procedures" portion of AIM.

If the tower is closed, it is good practice (but not a regulation) to monitor the published tower frequency and use it to broadcast your position and intentions, just as you would on Unicom at a nontower airport. You should also refer to FAR 91.85, operations in the vicinity of an airport; FAR 91.87, operations at airports without control towers; and the "Airport Operations" section in AIM. It has become doubly important to be knowledgeable in this area since the air traffic controllers' strike occurred. Many published towers (shown on current charts) may not be in operation, either because of reduced operating hours or permanent closure.

Once again, VFR weather minimums in an airport traffic area that is in a control zone are: ceiling 1,000 feet, visibility 3 miles. If either the ceiling or the visibility requirement is not met, the field is below basic VFR minimums and you cannot operate there.

Situation: You are out practicing (fooling around) when you notice that the fog is rolling in. You beat it back as fast as you can, but when you call (more than) 5 miles out, you are told, "Homefield visibility is now 2 miles in fog; say your intentions." You smoothly request a special VFR clearance.

The reference for special VFR is FAR 91.107, and it will not be offered to you; you must request it. You are a student pilot operating in an IFR environment, and you are way over your head. This is an emergency exit for an unforeseen situation only. Discuss it thoroughly with your flight instructor, even though you are going to be cautious enough not to get caught in this crack. Special VFR can be a useful tool in the hands of an experienced pilot. In the area where I live, in the summertime our weather is often "clear and 1 mile." By 2,000 feet, you are above the smog and can see forever. But don't forget that a special VFR clearance is good for the *control zone only.* There is no such thing as "special VFR en route." If you haven't reached VFR conditions within 5 miles after takeoff, you've got a problem; and air traffic may not be able to let you back in without filing for an IFR approach. Use your "special" privileges very carefully. Remember that special VFR at night requires an instrument rating and an instrument airplane.

A regulation that seems to cause confusion in communication is 91.85*b.* There are many uncontrolled airports that are located within 5 miles of a tower airport. It is permissible to take off and land at the small airfield without communicating with the tower at the controlled field, even though you are actually in its airport traffic area. Use good judgment, and get in and out in the most direct manner possible. If you are flying through without stopping or if you are landing at the tower airport, communication with the tower is mandatory. Further confusion ensues when you discover that it may be IFR at the tower airfield and still legally VFR at the smaller field, 2 or 3 miles away. Sensible practice would be to treat it as if both fields were IFR. Fooling around with minimums is asking for trouble.

Place yourself in the following two situations:

1. Marginal VFR (MVFR), 1000 feet and 3 miles, airport traffic area, control zone. You are in the pattern, shooting touch-and-goes, and talking to the tower. I am on an instrument approach and will also be talking to the tower before I am close enough to be a factor. The tower will inform us of each other's position.

2. MVFR, 1000 feet and 3 miles, control zone, no tower. You are in the pattern, shooting touch-and-goes. I am on an instrument approach. I will be breaking out of that overcast without the faintest idea that you are there. Think about it—we are *both* right.

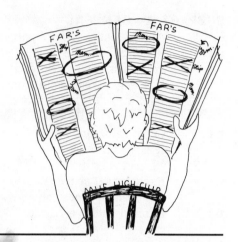

FARs and AIM

FARs are the legal rules by which we fly. They were written by lawyers; trying to study them will put you to sleep faster than anything I know. If you have looked at your copies of FARs and AIM, you are probably somewhat awed by the task of taking in all this information. We can break them down into manageable segments if you will follow directions.

FARs are cursed as being "restrictions" and referred to as "the DON'T book." Partly because they are boring to read, and partly because they impose restrictions upon us, some pilots go at them with a resigned, if not openly negative, attitude. I hope you will come away from this discussion with the same respect for the regulations that I have. Some of the regs will keep you out of jail—others may save your neck! You will find that in most cases the legal minimums are far lower than you feel safe with. It may sound overly dramatic to say that "the regulations are written in blood." The fact is, a great many of them were imposed as a result of accidents.

If you read legal language as poorly as I do, you may struggle all the way through a regulation before you realize that most or all of it doesn't apply to you as private pilot—airplane. Information pertaining to commercial pilots, flight instructors, airline transport pilots, and instrument ratings may also be included in a regulation; part of it may apply to aircraft other than airplanes. As we go through the regulations together, use a marker on your copy to highlight the information you need to memorize (for the times in flight when you can't look it up). Cross out the portions that don't apply to you. Most of us had to go through the regulations more than once to memorize the essential information. You will be surprised how quickly and easily you can review the applicable regulations after you have marked up your book. Gather up your copy of the regs (and your marker pen) and let's go to work.

Explanatory comments appear in parentheses.

FAR Part 61—Certification: Pilots and Flight Instructors

SUBPART A—GENERAL

61.1   Applicability. (Review paragraph *a* and cross out *b*.)

61.3   Requirements for certificates, ratings, and authorizations. (Paragraph *a* says you must carry your pilot certificate; *b* says you may fly U.S.-registered aircraft only; *c* requires you to carry your medical certificate. Paragraphs *d, e, f,* and *g* do not apply. In paragraph *h*, if these people ask, you must produce.)

61.5   Certificates and ratings issued under this part. (Is merely a list; review and cross out.)

61.7   Obsolete certificates and ratings. (Does not apply. Cross out.)

61.9   Exchange of obsolete certificates and ratings for current certificates and ratings. (Does not apply. Cross out.)

61.11   Expired pilot certificates and reissuance. (Does not apply. Cross out.)

61.13   Application and qualification. (Need not be a memory item. It gives the guidelines for application, issuance, suspension, and revocation of pilot certificates. Review and cross out.)

61.15   Offenses involving narcotic drugs, marihuana, and depressant or stimulant drugs or substances. (Render a pilot ineligible to fly for one year, and any certificate held could be revoked. Be aware, and BEWARE.)

61.17   Temporary certificate. (Be aware of the expiration date of your temporary certificate. It may be altered by your examiner to expire in 180 days, instead of 120. An expired temporary is no certificate at all, so don't fly until you obtain a replacement.)

61.19   Duration of pilot and flight instructor certificates. Only paragraphs *a* and *b* apply; cross out the rest. Paragraph *d* may apply someday, and you will stay out of trouble and avoid *e* and *f*.)

61.21   Duration of Category II pilot authorization. (Does not apply; cross out.)

61.23   Duration of medical certificates. (Translates as follows: a class 1 medical is valid as a class 1 for 6 months, as a class 2 for 1 year, and as a class 3 for 2 years. A private pilot only needs a class 3 medical. You can take any class physical exam you choose, and it will be valid for 24 *calendar* months. Start the count the month *after* the month in which you took the physical. The medical expires at midnight on the last day of the 24th month for the exercise of private pilot privileges.)

61.25   Change of name. (Review if you are engaged to be married; cross out unless you are afraid the marriage won't last.)

61.27   Voluntary surrender or exchange of certificate. (Review, and cross out.)

61.29 Replacement of lost or destroyed certificate. (Remember this reg when you wash your pants with your certificates in your pocket. You are grounded until they are replaced.)

61.31 General limitations. (Paragraphs *a, b, c,* and *d* will not apply to you at this time. Highlight paragraph *e* because it will apply to you as soon as you check out in complex airplanes. Make sure you get your logbook endorsement. Cross out paragraph *f* at this time.)

Pause a moment for a definition of category, class, and type. Category is the broadest area, examples being airplane, rotorcraft, glider, and lighter-than-air free balloon. All of these meet the definition of "aircraft." Class means single/multiengine or land/sea. Type is basic make and model (C-150, C-172, PA28-151). Official definitions are found in FAR, Part 1.

61.33 Tests: general procedure. (Places written tests and flight tests under the authority of the administrator.)

61.35 Written test: prerequisites and passing grades. (Bring written authorization from your flight instructor or make an appointment with an FAA inspector for an oral exam—and bring all your home study materials with you. Expiration of the written test is found in 61.39, and is 24 *calendar* months, just like the medical.)

61.37 Written tests: cheating or other unauthorized conduct. (Review and beware.)

61.39 Prerequisites for flight tests. (Your instructor will help you with this because he has to recommend you. Your application [FAA Form 8710-1] should be complete and neat, preferably typed. You will also have endorsements from your instructor in your logbook that you are ready for the flight check and that you have been given ground instruction in the areas you missed on the written exam.)

61.41 Flight instruction received from flight instructors not certificated by FAA. (Probably does not apply.)

61.43 Flight tests: general procedures. (Should be reviewed prior to flight check.)

61.45 Flight tests: required aircraft and equipment. (Should be reviewed prior to flight check.)

61.47 Flight tests: status of FAA inspectors and other authorized flight examiners. (Should be reviewed prior to flight check.)

61.49 Retesting after failure. (Will surely not apply to you.)

61.51 Pilot logbooks. (Translates as follows: You do not *have* to log a flight if you don't want to. However, you *must* log all time that you plan to present as your required time toward a certificate or rating, or evidence of recent experience to meet requirements for passenger-carrying privileges. After you are certificated, some flight time may be logged *both* dual and Pilot In Command (PIC). One example would be if you are sole manipulator of the controls in an aircraft for which you are rated, even though your instructor is on board giving you a checkout in type. Paragraph *d*1 says you must present your logbook for inspection when asked nicely. Emphasize *d*2 and carry your logbook with you on all cross-country flights as a student pilot. My students were always reminded to also carry a dime for the phone. (Wait until you have been stranded at an empty airport with a flat tire and a pay phone—and nothing but a $20 bill.)

61.53 Operations during medical deficiency. (Judgment is yours; exercise it.)

61.55 Second in command qualifications; operation of large airplanes or turbojet-powered multiengine airplanes. (Is a reg to look forward to.)

61.57 Recent flight experience: pilot in command. (Will be a guiding factor during your entire flying career. Memorize it now. Paragraph *a*, Biennial Flight Review (BFR) tells you that to operate as pilot in command, *even solo*, you must have a BFR and have your logbook so endorsed. The BFR is valid for 24 months from the *date* of the *flight*, unlike the medical. A flight check for a new certificate or rating will fulfill the BFR requirement. Paragraph *b* is self-explanatory. Highlight paragraph *c*. In order to carry passengers, you must have logged 3 takeoffs and landings in category and class Airplane Single Engine Land [ASEL] in the preceeding 90 days. If the airplane has the third wheel in the back, the 3 landings must be to a full stop in any tail dragger. Night requirements under paragraph *d* require that in the preceding 90 days you have logged 3 full stop landings [ASEL]. After you are multiengine rated, don't forget category *and* class apply to both night and day. Note that night begins one hour after official sunset and ends one hour before official sunrise. You can't log night unless it is dark. This is being pointed out so you won't confuse it with the time that the aircraft position lights must be on from sunset to sunrise. Paragraph *e* does not apply yet.)

61.58 Pilot-in-command proficiency check: operation of aircraft requiring more than one required pilot. (Does not apply.)

61.59 Falsification, reproduction or alteration of applications, certificates, logbooks, reports, or records. (Review, and BEWARE. This is a hanging offense.)

61.60 Change of address. (Is easily overlooked in the confusion of moving, but don't forget to drop them a note. If you had an accident and Oklahoma City [OKC] didn't have your current address, your biggest problem might be collecting your insurance because you operated in violation of FARs.)

SUBPART B—AIRCRAFT RATINGS AND SPECIAL CERTIFICATES

61.61 Applicability. (Review and cross out.)

61.63 Additional aircraft ratings (other than airline transport pilot). (Will become of interest to you when you wish to add a multiengine class rating, or category ratings [glider, helicopter, balloon] or get your B-17 type.)

61.65 Instrument rating requirements. (Can be crossed out for now.)

61.67 Category II pilot authorization requirements. (Comes after the instrument rating.)

61.69 Glider towing: experience and instruction requirements. (A private pilot may tow gliders if the experience requirements and endorsements listed here are met—but he still can't get paid for it.)

61.71 Graduates of certificated flying schools: special rules. (Flight time requirements for Part 141 approved schools differ slightly from Part 61 requirements. If you have graduated from a Part 141 school, you must take your flight check within 60 days, or else you must go back and make up the difference in flight time. Cross out.)

61.73 Military pilots or former military pilots: special rules. (Unless this applies to you, cross it out.)

61.75 Pilot certificate issued on basis of a foreign pilot license. (Should not apply; cross out.)

61.77 Special purpose pilot certificate: operation of U.S.-registered civil airplanes leased by a person not a U.S. citizen. (Does not apply.)

SUBPART C—STUDENT PILOTS

61.81 Applicability. (Review and cross out.)

61.83 Eligibility requirements: general. (Must have already been met. Review and cross out.)

61.85 Application. (Has been made and accepted. Cross out.)

61.87 Requirements for solo flight, (Should be of interest to you. Review paragraphs *a, b,* and *c*1. Cross out paragraphs *c*2, 3, 4, 5, and 6. Pay attention to paragraph *d* and remind your instructor that you need a fresh solo endorsement if yours has gone over 90 days.)

61.89 General limitations. (Is important. Read it carefully.)

61.91 Aircraft limitations: pilot in command. (Does not apply.)

61.93 Cross-country flight requirements. (Looks complicated and needs emphasis. This might at first appear to be your instructor's responsibility, but read it carefully. "A student pilot may not . . ." and that is *you*. From the very beginning, you are responsible for your operation of an airplane. Remain within 25 nautical miles of Homefield, and land only at airports for which you are specifically endorsed. Review paragraph *b*1 and cross out 2, 3, 4, and 5. Paragraph *c* may come down on both you and your instructor if you run afoul of the law. You must have the solo cross-country endorsement on your student pilot certificate. You must also have a separate endorsement in your logbook for *each individual* solo cross-country flight, and "known circumstances" only exist on the day of that flight. Don't ask to stay overnight. You earn that kind of privilege with your private certificate. The exception mentioned is very specific and fairly rare. Your instructor will only authorize it if you are based on your farm and have to fly to Homefield for your dual instruction.)

SUBPART D—PRIVATE PILOTS

61.101 Applicability. (Review and cross out.)

61.103 Eligibility requirements: general. (Review and cross out.)

61.105 Aeronautical knowledge. (Paragraph *a* applies; cross out paragraphs *b, c, d,* and *e.*)

61.107 Flight proficiency. (Paragraph *a* applies; cross out *b, c, d, e,* and *f.*)

61.109 Airplane rating: aeronautical experience. (Was quoted in Chapter 1. Note that the cross-countries count toward certification only if they are *more than 50 nautical* miles. The long triangle is worth discussing further. Do not plan a landing in the middle of a [more than] 100-nautical-mile leg. In the case of a malfunction or unforecast weather conditions that force you to make a decision to land en route, you will be granted an exception so you don't have to repeat the entire flight; but *plan* as specified, and plan to leave early.)

61.111 Cross-country flights: pilots based on small islands. (If this applies to you, study it carefully and discuss it with your flight instructor.)

61.113 Rotorcraft rating: aeronautical experience. (Cross out.)

61.115 Glider rating: aeronautical experience. (Cross out.)

61.117 Lighter-than-air rating: aeronautical experience. (Cross out.)

61.118 Private pilot privileges and limitations: pilot in command. (Should be thoroughly understood. If any doubt arises about the legality of some future situation, return to this reg and/or call your local GADO for clarification.)

The remainder of FAR Part 61 does not apply to Private Pilot—Airplane. Your copy of a commercial publication of FARs may include Part 71 next. This is the legal description of the federal airways and airspace. Rather than attempting to memorize these regulations, the chapter in AIM on "Airspace" presents this information in a format better designed for pilot comprehension and retention. Your copy of the regs may also include FAR Part 135. Private pilots may skip this part too, as it governs the operations of commercial pilots for hire. Save Part 135 to look forward to. Take a break and come back ready to tackle FAR Part 91.

FAR Part 91—General Operating and Flight Rules

SUBPART A—GENERAL

91.1 Applicability. (Review paragraph *a*; for paragraphs *b* and *c*, if you plan a future flight to a foreign country get some very specific advice from someone who has been there.)

91.2 Certificate of authorization for certain Category II operations. (Can be crossed out.)

91.3 Responsibility and authority of the pilot in command. (Is important.)

91.4 Pilot in command of aircraft requiring more than one required pilot. (Does not apply; cross out.)

91.5   Preflight action. (Is important.)

91.6   Category II and III operations; general operating rules. (Does not apply; cross out.)

91.7   Flight crewmembers at stations. (Required crew [you] must keep your seatbelt fastened. If a shoulder harness is installed, you must fasten it for takeoffs and landings.)

91.8   Prohibition against interference with crewmembers. (You are PIC. Nobody is allowed to push *you* around.)

91.9   Careless or reckless operation. (Don't do it in flight.)

91.10   Careless or reckless operation other than for the purpose of air navigation. (Don't do it on the ground.)

91.11   Liquor and drugs. (This reg is urgent. Memorize "8 hours." If you really tied one on, 8 hours will not be enough, will it?)

91.12   Carriage of narcotic drugs, marihuana, and depressant or stimulant drugs or substances. (FAA will take away your pilot certificate. You can't use it in jail.)

91.13   Dropping objects. (You may, but be very careful what you drop and where you drop it.)

91.14   Use of safety belts. (States that you as pilot in command are responsible to assure that everyone on board over the age of 2 years occupies a seat with a seatbelt, properly secured for takeoffs and landings. You must brief each occupant on how to unfasten the belt and notify each person when it is time to buckle up.)

91.15   Parachutes and parachuting. (In paragraph *a*, parachutes come equipped with a "logbook" showing the name and certificate number of the rigger and the date they were packed. Most of us don't carry parachutes very often, and we need to review this reg when the situation arises. If you get involved with dropping jumpers under paragraph *b* [not for hire] you will need to study FAR 105. Paragraph *c* says don't bank steeper than 60° or pitch steeper than 30° while carrying passengers unless you are all wearing parachutes. Under paragraph *d*, flight instruction given by a CFI or maneuvers during a flight check are exceptions to the parachute requirement.)

91.17   Towing: gliders. (If you are going to tow gliders, review this reg thoroughly, and also FAR 61.69. If you are going to take some glider instruction and be towed yourself, review them also.)

91.18   Towing: other than under 91.17. (Banner towing becomes somewhat specialized, and the FAA wants to know what you are doing and when and where you are doing it. Apply for a waiver from your local GADO.)

91.19   Portable electronic devices. (Applies to air carrier and commercial operators, or to any aircraft operating under IFR. Review and cross out.)

91.20   Operations within the North Atlantic Minimum Navigation Performance Specifications airspace. (Unless you plan to fly over the North Pole above flight level 275, cross out.)

91.21   Flight instruction; simulated instrument flight and certain flight tests. (Paragraph *a* allows the instructor the choice of giving instrument dual in an aircraft with a throw-over yoke—Bonanza, for example. The pilot must be rated in the airplane, *not* a student pilot. Paragraph *b* is important. After you have your private pilot certificate and wish to practice hood work, you must have a safety pilot who is appropriately rated to act as pilot in command of the aircraft. If you accept clearances and hard altitudes from Air Traffic Control (ATC), the safety pilot must be instrument rated and current. If you are in a multiengine airplane, the safety pilot must have a multiengine rating on his private certificate. Your friend who has a student pilot certificate is *not qualified* to act as safety pilot while you wear a hood. Paragraph *c* does not apply.)

91.22   Fuel requirements for flight under VFR. (Is important. Highlight and memorize 30 minutes—day and 45 minutes—night. Cross out paragraph *b*.)

91.23   Fuel requirements for flight in IFR conditions. (Can be crossed out.)

91.24   ATC transponder and altitude reporting equipment and use. (Translates as follows: a Mode C transponder is one which has altitude reporting capability. You must have Mode C to operate above 12,500 feet MSL and to enter Group I TCAs. ATC can authorize deviations if your transponder fails en route; or if you know it isn't working and you need to bring it to a TCA airport for repairs, you may make a reservation with ATC four hours in advance of your Estimated Time of Arrival [ETA].)

91.25   VOR equipment check for IFR operations. (Does not apply, but you may wish to review it and discuss it with your instructor. It never hurts to know the accuracy of your equipment, even in VFR conditions.)

91.27   Civil aircraft: certifications required. (This reg requires that the aircraft contain a current airworthiness certificate and a registration certificate *issued to its owner*, displayed to be visible to passengers and crew. Do you take it for granted that these are in a rented airplane? You may be in violation if you do. An airworthiness certificate does not expire, although it may have to be changed if the aircraft is substantially altered. The registration must change whenever the aircraft is sold. It may carry a temporary (pink) copy for 90 days. If you spot a pink slip in the pocket, check the expiration date. The radio permit is not mentioned because it is an FCC rule, but it should be in the pocket with the others.)

91.28   Special flight authorizations for foreign civil aircraft. (Can be crossed out.)

91.29   Civil aircraft airworthiness. (Is a matter of common sense and self-preservation. Preflight carefully and review inflight emergency procedures.)

91.30   Inoperable instruments and equipment for multiengine aircraft. (Has been suspended. It presently applies only to FAR 135 operations, so cross it out.)

91.31   Civil aircraft operating limitations and marking requirements. (May require the assistance of a good mechanic. In reasonably new airplanes, carrying your owner's manual and weight and balance data for that airplane, you should be in compliance. If you are considering buying *any* airplane, especially an antique, enlist the expert help of a certified mechanic.)

91.32   Supplemental oxygen. (In paragraph *a* highlight and memorize 12,500 to 14,000 for 30 minutes; 14,000 for crew; 15,000 for everybody. Review and cross out paragraph *b*.)

91.33   Powered civil aircraft with standard category U.S. airworthiness certificates; instrument and equipment requirements. (Paragraph *a* says be advised that these items are required, and if they are not installed and operating the aircraft is unairworthy. Review paragraphs *b* and *c* carefully. A commonly overlooked item is item 3, the compass correction card. I recall once climbing into a new student's airplane and noting that the compass was 70° off the taxiway heading [and had no correction card]. As we taxied back I explained that this was probably a factor in his getting lost on his last cross-country flight. In item 9, even though you looked in the gas tank, the fuel gauges must be operating. Item 12 is the newest addition to this reg, and some airplanes may still be operating with the old "lap strap" installed; they are illegal. Item 13 states that if the airplane is newer than 1978, it must have a shoulder harness installed for each front seat. At night, make sure the lights work, the alternator shows a charge, and you have spare fuses on board. Cross out paragraphs *d, e,* and *f*.)

91.34   Category II manual. (Does not apply.)

91.35   Flight recorders and cockpit voice recorders. (Does not apply.)

91.36   Data correspondence between automatically reported pressure altitude data and the pilot's altitude reference. (Before departing, you will check the aircraft logbook to see that the transponder inspection is current [24 calendar months] and that is all you can do. If ATC tells you to turn off your altitude, do so.)

91.37   Transport category civil airplane weight limitations. (Does not apply.)

91.38   Increased maximum certificated weights for certain airplanes operated in Alaska. (Does not apply.)

The next four regulations will not apply to normal operations. Remember that they are here if you get involved with (other than) standard category operations.

91.39   Restricted category civil aircraft; operating limitations. (Review and cross out.)

91.40   Limited category civil aircraft; operating limitations. (Review and cross out.)

91.41   Provisionally certificated civil aircraft; operating limitations. (Review and cross out.)

91.42   Aircraft having experimental certificates; operating limitations. (Should be studied carefully if you are building your own; otherwise review and cross out.)

91.43	Special rules for foreign civil aircraft. (Review and cross out.)
91.45	Authorization for ferry flight with one engine inoperative by air carriers and commercial operators of large aircraft. (How would you like to do that? Cross it out.)
91.47	Emergency exits for airplanes carrying passengers for hire. (Does not apply. Cross out.)
91.49	Aural speed warning device. (Does not apply. Cross out.)
91.51	Altitude alerting system or device; turbojet-powered civil airplanes. (Does not apply. Cross out.)
91.52	Emergency locator transmitters. (Is long and complicated. Paragraph *b*4 is the first part that applies to you. Paragraph *c* tells you the Emergency Locator Transmitter [ELT] must be attached to the airplane, and the deployable type must be as far aft as practicable. Highlight the times in paragraph *d* for battery life, one cumulative hour of use, or 50% of their useful life. Note that the expiration date of the ELT batteries must be logged in *two* places—on the ELT case and in the aircraft maintenance log. Paragraphs *e* and *f* are the exceptions to this reg. If you encounter an airplane for which you can't find an ELT entry in the logbook, be sure you check for compliance with these operations. In item 10i and ii the aircraft must have a placard on the panel, and it must be less than 90 days old.)
91.54	Truth in leasing clause requirement in leases and conditional sales contracts. (Does not apply.)
91.55	Civil aircraft sonic boom? (Wow!)
91.56	Agricultural and fire fighting airplanes; noise operating limitations. (Does not apply.)
91.57	Aviation Safety Reporting Program; prohibition against use of reports for enforcement purpose. (If you encounter an ongoing situation that you feel creates a hazard for others, call your local flight service for information about this program.)
91.58	Materials for compartment interiors. (Does not apply.)
91.59	Carriage of candidates in Federal elections. (Might come up later; review and cross out.)

SUBPART B—FLIGHT RULES

We are going to take a slightly different approach to this portion of the FARs. The clue to this subpart is in the title, "Flight Rules." These you may need when you do not have time for research. The words and phrases listed here are key terms only. Read each listed regulation carefully, highlighting these key words as you go.

91.61	Applicability. (This means you.)
91.63	Waivers.

    a) Issue waiver authorizing deviation

    b) (None)

    c) (None)

91.65 Operating near other aircraft.

    a) Collision hazard

    b) Formation flight except by arrangement

    c) For hire, in formation flight

    d) Any clearance issued to another aircraft

(Now glance back over this reg and see how quickly you can review the "don'ts.")

91.67 Right-of-way rules; except water operations.

    a) See and avoid

    b) In distress has right of way

    c) Aircraft to the other's right has right of way

        (1) Balloon

        (2) Glider

        (3) Airship

        Aircraft towing or refueling

    d) Head-on, alter course to the right

    e) Overtaken has right of way, pilot overtaking alter course to the right

    f) Landing have right of way, lower altitude has right of way

    g) (None)

91.69 Right-of-way rules; water operations. (Does not apply.)

91.70 Aircraft speed.

    a) Below 10,000 feet MSL, 250 knots (288 mph)

    b) Within an airport traffic area

        (1) Reciprocating engine, 156 knots (180 mph)

        (2) Turbine-powered aircraft, 200 knots (230 mph)

        (Terminal Control Area 250 knots [288 mph])

    c) Underlying a terminal control area or in a VFR corridor 200 knots (230 mph)

91.71 Acrobatic flight.

    a) Over any congested area

    b) Open air assembly

    c) Control zone or Federal airway

    d) Below 1,500 feet

    e) Visibility less than three

    Intentional maneuver involving abrupt change in attitude, abnormal attitude, abnormal acceleration

91.73 Aircraft lights.

    a) Sunset to sunrise operate unless lighted

    b) Park or move unless the aircraft

        (1) Is clearly illuminated

        (2) Has lighted position lights

        (3) Marked by obstruction lights

    c) (Does not apply)

    d) Anticollision light (strobe), red or white anticollision light, anticollision light (strobe)

91.75   Compliance with ATC clearances and instructions.

    a) No pilot may deviate unless he obtains an amended clearance—uncertain of the meaning, immediately request clarification

    b) Operate contrary to an ATC instruction

    c) Notify ATC of that deviation

    d) If requested submit a detailed report within 48 hours

91.77   ATC light signals. (Memorize the table.)

91.79   Minimum safe altitudes; general. Except when necessary for takeoff or landing.

    a) An altitude allowing an emergency landing without undue hazard

    b) Congested area or open air assembly, 1,000 feet above the highest obstacle within a horizontal radius of 2,000 feet

    c) 500 feet above the surface, closer than 500 feet to any person, vessel, vehicle, or structure

    d) (Does not apply)

91.81   Altimeter settings.

    a) Maintain the cruising altitude by an altimeter that is set, when operating—

      (1) Below 18,000 feet MSL

        i) A station along the route within 100 nautical miles

        ii) Appropriate available station

        iii) No radio, elevation of departure airport

      (2) At or above 18,000 feet MSL, to 29.92 Hg (Standard barometric pressure)

    b) (Does not apply)

    c) (Does not apply—familiarize for later)

91.83   Flight plan; information required.

    a) (Refer to Chapter 4 on the flight service station)

    b) (Does not apply)

    c) (Does not apply)

    d) Cancellation. Completing the flight shall notify FAA

91.84   Flights between Mexico or Canada and the United States. IFR or VFR flight plan.

91.85   Operating on or in the vicinity of an airport; general rules.

    a) Comply

    b) (Requires a translation; refer to Chapter 3 on airspace and highlight the first sentence)

    c) (Does not apply)

91.87   Operating at airports with operating control towers.

    a) To, from, or on

    b) Two-way radio communications are maintained—radio fails, maintains visual contact and receives clearance (light signals)

    c) Other control towers, to, from, or on

      (1) two-way radio communications are maintained

      (2) tower's frequency monitored

    d) Minimum altitudes
      (1) (Applies to turbine-powered and large airplanes—they fly the traffic pattern at 1,500 feet AGL)
      (2) (Applies to turbine-powered and large airplanes)
      (3) An (any) airplane served by a visual approach slope indicator shall maintain at or above glide slope until necessary
    e) Approaches
      (1) Each pilot shall circle to the left
      (2) (Helicopters may come from anywhere)
    f) Departures
      (1) Comply with procedures established
      (2) Turbine-powered and large airplanes, 1,500 feet
    g) Turbine-powered and large airplanes
    h) No person may operate on a runway or taxiway, or takeoff or land, unless clearance is received. "Taxi to" the takeoff runway is clearance to cross other runways en route. "Taxi to" any point other than an assigned takeoff runway is clearance to cross runways that intersect the taxi route to that other point

91.89 Operation at airports without control towers.
    a) (1) Make all turns to the left unless displays indicate that turns should be made to the right
      (2) (Watch out for helicopters)
      (3) Departing, comply with FAA traffic pattern

91.90 Terminal control areas.
    a) Group I
      (1) Operating rules
        i) Authorization from ATC prior
        ii) Large turbine engine (Does not apply)
      (2) At least a private pilot certificate
      (3) Unless authorized in the case of in-flight failure (radios) or transponder failure, an aircraft within a Group I terminal control area is (must be) equipped with—
        i) Operable VOR or TACAN
        ii) Two-way radio
        iii) 91.24 (Mode C transponder)
    b) Group II (This subparagraph is identical to Group I operation with two exceptions: the private pilot only limitation, and Mode C altitude reporting capability of the transponder are deleted)
    c) (Does not apply—there aren't any)

91.91 Temporary flight restrictions.
    a) Notice to Airmen will be issued designating temporary flight restrictions
    b) No person may operate within the designated area unless—
      (1) Participating and under the direction
      (2) Operated to or from an airport (under *a*)
      (3) Specific IFR clearance
      (4) VFR flight (requires) prior notice

(5) Carrying accredited news representatives, official business; operation conducted above the altitudes being used by relief aircraft; and prior to entering the area has filed a flight plan

91.93   Flight test areas. (Flight test an airplane, not flight check a pilot.)

91.95   Restricted and prohibited areas.

   a) (Requires) permission of the using or controlling agency

91.97   Positive control areas and route segments. (Requires IFR equipment and qualifications.)

91.100   Emergency air traffic rules.

   a) (Administrative instructions—do not apply)

   b) (Administrative instructions—do not apply)

   c) (Highlight the entire paragraph)

91.101   Operations to Cuba. (Return to this reg as necessary.)

91.102   Flight limitation in the proximity of space flight recovery operations. (Stay out of the way.)

91.103   Operation of civil aircraft of Cuban registry. (Return to this reg as necessary.)

91.104   Flight restrictions in the proximity of the presidential and other parties. (Keep away.)

Visual Flight Rules

91.105   Basic VFR weather minimums.

   a) (Memorize the table)

   b) Helicopter (Does not apply)

   c) VFR, within a control zone beneath the ceiling when the ceiling is less than 1,000 feet

   d) VFR within a control zone unless

   (1) ground visibility is three statute miles

   (2) flight visibility is three statute miles

   e) Operating at the base altitude is considered to be within the airspace directly below

91.107   Special VFR weather minimums.

   a) (You may ask for and receive a special VFR clearance)

   b) Clear of clouds

   c) Flight visibility is at least one statute mile

   d) Take off or land unless visibility is at least one statute mile

   e) (Special VFR between sunset and sunrise)

   (1) Pilot is instrument rated and current)

   (2) Aircraft is equipped and inspected as required for IFR operations)

91.109   VFR cruising altitude or flight level. More than 3,000 feet above the surface.

   a) Below 18,000 feet MSL

   (1) Magnetic zero through 179 (East), odd thousand + 500

   (2) Magnetic 180 through 359, even thousand + 500

   b) (Omit until you go pressurized)

   c) (Omit until you go airline)

Instrument Flight Rules. (Omit 91.115 through 91.129)

SUBPART C—MAINTENANCE, PREVENTIVE MAINTENANCE, AND ALTERATIONS

91.161   Applicability. (I think that pilots look at this subpart topic and decide it only applies to mechanics and skip the whole thing. Do not do that. It applies to you. Most of us probably fall into the habit of taking the word of the flight school that the required inspections are met. Sit down with your instructor and go over the airplane's aircraft and engine logs. Some mechanics seem to be in competition with doctors for the most illegible handwriting, but locate the required entries and determine whether they are current. It is your body that you are placing in that machine.)

91.163   General.
   a) Owner or operator
   b) No person may perform other than as prescribed
   c) No person may operate unless the mandatory replacement times, inspection intervals, have been complied with.

91.165   Maintenance required. Inspected as prescribed [and] between required inspections, have defects repaired as prescribed [and] make appropriate entries in the maintenance records.

91.167   Carrying persons other than crewmembers after repairs or alterations.
   a) No person may carry (other than crewmembers) private pilot's certificate, flies, makes check, and logs flight.
   b) Ground tests show conclusively, flight characteristics, or substantially affected flight operation

91.169   Inspections.
   a) Preceding 12 calendar months
      (1) Annual inspection (or)
      (2) Inspection for the issue of an airworthiness certificate person authorized to perform annual inspections, entered as an "annual" inspection in the required maintenance records. (The holder of an Airframe and Powerplane [A&P] mechanic certificate may perform and sign off 100-hour inspections. To sign off an annual, the mechanic must also be an Authorized Inspector [AI].)
   b) For hire, 100 hours (since) annual or 100-hour inspection exceeded by not more than 10 hours if necessary, is included in computing the next 100 hours of time in service
   c) Do not apply
      (1) Progressive inspection
      (2) Special, experimental, provisional
      (3) Air travel club (under) Part 123
      (4) Approved under Part 135
      (5) Large airplanes under Subpart D

91.170   Altimeter tests and inspections.
          a) Under IFR, preceding 24 calendar months
          c) Under IFR at an altitude above

91.171   Progressive inspection.
          a) Written request (Unless you plan to buy an airplane for lease-back or otherwise go into the aviation business, skip this)

91.173   Maintenance records. (This regulation and the two following regs will probably sound to you like they do not apply. If you fly the airplane and these required records do not exist, you are in violation. *Review your airplane's logbooks with your flight instructor.*)

91.174   Transfer of maintenance records.

91.175   Rebuilt engine maintenance records.

91.177   ATC transponder tests and inspections.
          a) No person may use unless within the preceding 24 calendar months, tested and inspected
          b) (Omit, but look for the inspection entry in the aircraft logbook, or don't turn the transponder on)

Subpart D—Large and Turbine-Powered Multiengine Airplanes, and Subpart E—Operating Noise Limits, do not apply to light aircraft.

You have just covered a lot of information, and you have very little experience to relate it to. That is why we took the time to highlight the regulations. Throughout the text we will refer to the reg, as well as other references that pertain to a given situation. One such important reference will be your local sectional chart. Another will be your copy of AIM entitled *Basic Flight Information and ATC Procedures.* AIM is the pilot's Bible. If you knew all of the material that is in AIM, you would be doing the teaching! We will be referring to chapters and sections of AIM by title. Mark that up too. By the time we are through, I want you to cover the whole VFR portion of AIM. The information it contains is too valuable to miss.

First Solo—What to Expect

I sincerely hope for your sake that your instructor is not of the old school that believes early solo is the mark of a real daredevil aviator. Before you get your back up over that statement, give me a chance to explain.

In the early days of aviation, flight training started with several hours of crash-and-goes in some cow pasture. When the instructor had enough of this, he got out and let the student try it alone. If the student (and the airplane) survived, the instructor took him out to the practice area and showed him a few loops and spins and perhaps taught him a few things about flying an airplane. Personally, I was a lot happier knowing a little more about it before my instructor got out—such as, what to do in an emergency.

Our modern airplanes are a lot more reliable but also a lot more complicated. Certainly the air traffic control system we operate in has changed enormously. Solo means a great deal more than being able to get the machine off and back on the ground in one piece. Before I turn you loose with an airplane, I want you to be knowledgeable about your equipment and the system you must operate in and to be prepared to cope with any foreseeable emergency situation. In other words, I want you SAFE.

Your first solo will begin as an ordinary dual flight. You may be feeling suspicious that "today is the day," but I doubt if your instructor will tell you ahead of time. He probably isn't really certain himself at this point whether he will get out or not. He just knows you are close to being ready, and you know it too.

You will probably review maneuvers and emergency procedures and shoot a few dual landings. If the wind and traffic conditions are favorable, he will tell you this is it. You had better have your medical certificate with you; you can't go without it. Your instructor will sign the back of your medical certificate and transform it into a student pilot certificate. He will then stand on the ramp or run up to the tower (and sweat) while you make three (or more) takeoffs and landings. He will brief you before he leaves about how many to make and whether to make full stops or touch-and-goes.

Do not be startled by your initial takeoff. The airplane is lighter without your instructor, and it will seem to leap off the ground (as if it is glad he is finally *out*). Climb performance will also improve slightly, but the traffic pattern and the landing won't feel any different. By the second takeoff, you probably won't even notice the change.

You might get your shirttail cut off after it is all over. I have chopped off quite a few, and I have yet to get hold of one that wasn't soaking wet. If your flight school practices this ritual, you'd better start wearing old clothes when you think the time may be near. I didn't lose my shirttail when I soloed, but they more than made up for it the day my first student soloed. I was waiting for him with the scissors when the rotten kid stepped out of the airplane and doused me with liquid detergent. That was quickly followed by about five buckets of very cold water! I was a tower of billowing, shivering soapsuds.

The process of dual review and supervised solo in the traffic pattern will be repeated one or two more times. Then you will be ready to depart the pattern for the practice area, where you will practice assigned flight maneuvers. PAY ATTENTION—*this is where it's at!* Solo practice is where you really begin to become a pilot.

There is a lot of information you need to know to handle this operation safely, over and above stall recognition and recovery. NOW is the time to learn that information. In between (exciting) sessions of bouncing around the traffic pattern with your instructor, try to absorb the other information (dull stuff) in Chapter 4, so that when the time comes, you will be ready.

Local Solo Phase

WE have said it before, and this is a good time to say it again: Local solo practice is the most important portion of your flight training.

Flight training presents a student pilot with a series of goals. Some of these goals appear so spectacular that other less obvious accomplishments don't seem to get the attention they deserve. During the first portion of flight training, most students are unable to see beyond that dazzling first solo flight. It becomes THE EVENT, and all efforts are directed toward the "Big Day." This is certainly understandable from the student's viewpoint. I have been there myself. Your flight instructor's attitude toward your first solo will be: Thank GOD that is over; now we can get down to some serious flight training.

Flushed with success, many students get the mistaken notion that being able to land the airplane is all that matters. All that is necessary now is to log the required number of hours and the rest will be automatic. I hate to rain on your parade, but nothing could be further from the truth.

Know-How for Local Solo Operations

You are now reasonably safe in the airplane in a carefully controlled and familiar environment with the equipment behaving as it should. You are not yet a pilot. My first solo flight out of the traffic pattern was far more memorable than my first three solo landings. I had never realized how many strange airplane noises are absorbed by the warm body of a flight instructor who is present in the right seat.

The difference between the performance of the student who has practiced stalls and slow flight and the student who merely said he did is so obvious to the flight instructor as to be downright funny. In the local practice area, work really hard on the maneuvers your instructor will assign you. You will need the skills and the self-confidence that you will develop during the course of this solo practice. The next big goal that you should be working toward is your first solo cross-country. This flight is an accomplishment far more memorable and demanding than anything you have done so far.

Your instructor will send you out to practice solo once or twice and then will fly dual with you again. This is to check your progress and to make sure that you aren't teaching yourself bad habits. In between your solo flights, you will be introduced to some more advanced flight maneuvers and hood work. The skills to successfully negotiate an emergency off-airport landing and to operate out of short and/or soft fields will be required prior to solo cross-country operations.

By the time student pilots meet these skill requirements, they have usually used up most of the local solo hours required for private pilot certification. Many students need more than the minimum time to perfect these skills. You should be ready very soon to plan your first dual cross-country flight. Consequently, navigation and weather judgment are next on your agenda. Don't let your flight training stall out for lack of home study. Right after your first dual cross-country, you should be ready to take the written exam. My own personal private pilot applicants do not get endorsed for solo cross-country flight until they have passed the FAA written exam. I believe in setting high standards for safety and knowledge. The rest of this chapter focuses on subjects pertinent to the local solo phase of your training.

Transponders

The section in AIM on "Services Available to Pilots," transponder operation, contains all you really need to know about transponders (Fig. 4.1). You have four numbers on the black box, each one individually tunable from 0 through 7. This gives you 4,096 possible combinations of 4-digit codes. The "ON" knob will stop in a number of positions marked SBY (Standby); ON,

which may have both "low" and "normal"; ALT (Altitude); and TST (Te
green light will flicker when the box is being interrogated by a radar fa
(most of the time). The rheostat dims it at night, or the flickering ligh.
drive you nuts. "Ident" is the button you push *only* when told to by ATC to
verify which bleep you are on the scope.

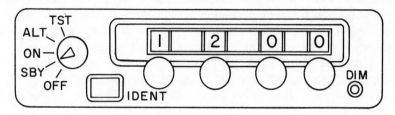

F I G. 4.1. *Transponder unit.*

"Squawk" and "code" mean the same thing, which is the 4-digit code
number you are assigned. If you are into esoteric information, the early
transponder was called an IFF (Identification Friend or Foe). The wartime
code name was "Parrot." Some military genius came up with "squawk."

The ALT feature on your transponder is only there for show unless you
have a special altimeter linked to the transponder. In that case you have "Mode
C" altitude reporting capability, which is required in Group I TCAs and above
12,500 feet MSL.

The state of the art in radar equipment has come a very long way in a very
short time. A few years ago the controller saw your transponder return as
double tracks (like captain's bars) that blossomed with a light when you
squawked "ident" or "emergency." Now there is an alpha-numeric readout on
the scope that gives the controller your "N" number, your transponder code,
your ground speed, and your altitude (if you have Mode C).

Memorize these codes:

>1200—VFR
>7700—Mayday
>7600—Lost Communication
>7500—Hijack
>0000—Reserved for Military Only

Avoid tuning through the last four of these codes on the way to your assigned code; some controller will get very excited. If you have been doing your
outside-reference homework on schedule, you have already covered in AIM the
hijack and lost-communication procedures.

Accept any opportunity to visit a radar facility. It is fascinating, and the
controllers love to have pilots see their side of the system. It's a good idea all
around, and they do a super job.

GROUP I TCA

To contribute to a thorough understanding of operations at large and busy airports, refer to the sections of AIM entitled "ATC Clearance/Separations" and "Pilot/Controller Roles and Responsibilities." That information can save you a lot of confusion and embarrassment. The portion concerning "wake turbulence" might even save your neck. Wing-tip vortices are most pronounced at high angles of attack when the generating aircraft is HEAVY, CLEAN, and SLOW. They descend at 500 fpm until they are 900 feet below the flight path. Carefully plan to remain above the flight path of the "heavies." This very dangerous area will be thoroughly discussed during your oral examination prior to flight check. Cover it with your instructor now.

In Group I TCA, radar service is mandatory, whether landing, departing, or passing through. The equipment requirements for Group I, Group II, and Group III TCAs are listed in FAR 91.90. It is interesting that they list Group III—at the present time there *are* no Group III TCAs.

To operate in a Group I TCA you must have at least a private pilot's certificate, a VOR receiver, a 2-way communication radio, a Mode C transponder, and clearance to enter. The speed limit in a TCA is 250 knots (FAR 91.70), and operating underneath the TCA or in the VFR corridor you may not exceed 200 knots. There is no *minimum* airspeed capability requirement. However, if you are landing at the TCA airport and you find yourself sequenced between two 747s, it helps to be able to manage 160 knots or so—at least downhill. You will also have the effects of wing-tip vortices uppermost in your mind.

Training flights are prohibited in a Group I TCA, and the heavy "Ts" on the chart around the primary airport prohibit special VFR for fixed-wing aircraft (Fig. 4.2). The heavy blue lines on the sectional chart depict the altitude sectors and give the floor and the ceiling in each sector. You may fly over it and in many cases *under* it; to assure that you do not inadvertently fly *through* it when operating at underlying airports, get yourself another chart.

The VFR terminal area chart is worth the investment. It gives you a larger scale and more detailed reference when operating in (or near) a TCA. The example in Figure 4.2 is of Los Angeles International Airport (LAX). Notice that it has a VFR corridor that is explained in the box on the lower left. Consider the problems the pilot of a Cessna 150 would have commuting VFR from Torrance to Santa Monica. How else would you get there? I have done it many times, and I would advise you to keep your head up and on a swivel. You are not required to have *any* special equipment, not even a radio, to transit the corridor.

GROUP II TCA

Operation in a Group II TCA is identical to operation in a Group I TCA, but the requirements are relaxed slightly. A student pilot may enter, if he can get his instructor's permission. If you think you have it tough at Homefield, just remember there are lots of flight schools and student pilots based at TCA airports.

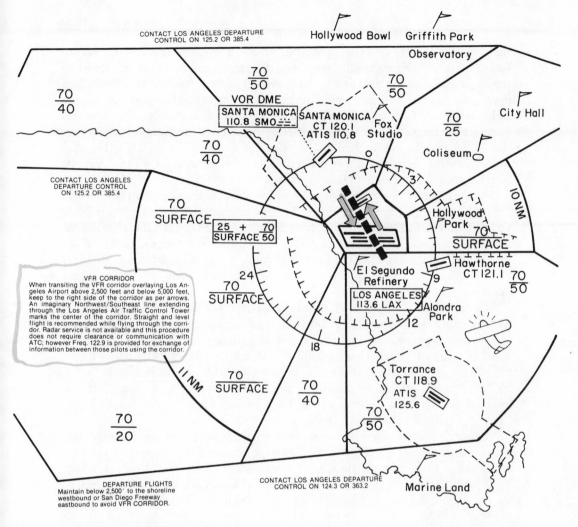

FIG. 4.2.   *Group I, TCA.*

The heavy Ts are missing from the Group II TCA. Thus in theory you might be granted a special VFR clearance. Again, I recommend purchasing a VFR terminal area chart. You still must have 2-way radio, VOR, transponder, and clearance.

I strongly suggest that you plan a dual flight into a TCA, or at least to a TRSA, to see how it is done.

TRSAs AND STAGE III RADAR SERVICE

Read carefully "Services Available to Pilots" in AIM. This is the reference that tells it like it is. Pay special attention to that section before proceeding to the section of the manual entitled "Clearance Delivery."

A TRSA is depicted on the sectional chart in the same manner as a TCA, with the heavy lines colored magenta instead of blue. The floor and ceiling of the different sectors are also printed in magenta. Nearby there is a magenta box that states (abbreviated), "see tower frequency table." This is located on the chart and may list as many as 10 approach control frequencies, depending upon your altitude and magnetic direction from the central airport. Locate the right frequency to start, and you will be handed off and given the new frequency over the radio as necessary. Before departure, information concerning the TRSA may be researched in the "Graphic Notices" portion of AIM. Approach control frequency information may also be included on ATIS: "aircraft North through East contact Ontario approach on 135.05."

Stage III radar service (advisories, sequencing, and separation) is a service I often use, and just as often refuse. If traffic is heavy and/or visibility is poor, you can be certain I'll be calling approach control for Stage III. If traffic is light and the weather is severe clear, I prefer to go direct, no vectors, and mind my own visual separation. Play the game according to the circumstances. Stage III radar service in a TRSA is available and recommended, but it is optional, not mandatory.

En route radar advisory service may also be available to VFR aircraft. Contact approach control and tell them your position, altitude, and heading. They will assign you a squawk, and as you proceed along your route you will be advised of nearby traffic. "Cessna 3567 Victor, traffic 10 o'clock opposite direction, 3 miles." You can spot the military training when a pilot responds "tally-ho" or "no joy." Civilians usually reply "contact" or "no contact." If our military aviator is in a cloud at the time he is warned of traffic, he'll say "Popeye." Civilians just say, "In the clouds."

Using en route radar advisory service is ideal practice for gaining expertise in radio communication procedures. You have plenty of time to listen to others, and you will be able to tell right away which pilots know what they are doing. You also learn to tune your ears for your own call sign and to tune out the chatter when you are busy with some other chore. Do not be lulled into a false sense of security by this service: Airplanes that are not transponder equipped are difficult to spot on radar, and there may be many airplanes not using this service. "See and avoid" is *still your responsibility.*

If you need help to locate an airport, you can call approach control and receive radar vectors. Any Flight Service Station (FSS) can supply the frequency to call for radar service. Many FSSs can also vector you to an airport if you get yourself lost. This is discussed in the FSS section under Direction Finding (DF) Steer. The advantages of having some experience in these areas prior to solo cross-country should be fairly obvious as a back-up, should your budding navigational skills suffer a relapse.

Clearance Delivery

In the light of the lengthy list of additions to the proposed ATC system, let's go back and pick up a link in the radio frequency chain that many pilots are dealing with now—clearance delivery.

This will be encountered in a TCA where positive radar control is mandatory or in a TRSA where Stage III radar service is available on request. Even if you don't have to deal with it at Homefield (yet), TCAs and TRSAs are cropping up all over, and you will encounter them sooner or later, if you plan to make full use of the private pilot certificate you are working so hard for.

Listen to ATIS, then dial in the clearance delivery frequency. The controller will want to know who you are, whether you are VFR, and your direction of departure. Be ready with a pencil and paper because he will come back with a clearance including your assigned departure heading and altitude, the departure control frequency, and a discrete transponder code. It might go something like this:

"Homefield clearance, Cessna 3567 Victor VFR Southbound." He comes back as if you were instrument rated, "Cessna 3567 Victor, after departure fly heading one eight zero, maintain two thousand, expect higher three minutes after departure, contact departure control one one niner point six, squawk zero four six two." This boggles the mind if you aren't ready for it.

You are a student pilot. Swallow your ego and tell him so—in advance. This is recommended and sensible practice on *any* frequency at *any* time. Things happen fast in airplanes, and if you don't understand what is going on, you could get yourself—and others—into trouble. Every pilot listening on the radio was a student once, and they appreciate your situation. The controller will be careful that you don't get handed instructions you aren't equipped to cope with.

Your instructor can show you a simple shorthand system to assist you in copying the clearance. You will acknowledge with a "readback" of your clearance and change to ground control.

"Homefield ground, Cessna 3567 Victor, Mile High Flying Club with Charlie." Proceed normally, with a call to the tower when you are ready to depart. After takeoff, the tower will clear you to the assigned departure control frequency. You will say, "Homefield departure, Cessna 3567 Victor climbing to two." He will direct you as necessary, and turn you loose when you exit his airspace, telling you, "frequency change approved, squawk VFR."

If you are departing a TRSA and elect to decline the Stage III service, simply skip clearance delivery and in your call to ground control politely include, "negative Stage III."

Arriving at a TCA airport, you contact approach control with your position prior to entering their airspace, just as you would contact a tower more than 5 miles out. Entering the TCA, you should include your altitude along with your position report. They will assign you a squawk and vector you clear of traffic. They will NOT vector you to the airport unless you tell them you are lost.

Remain on the approach control frequency until you are told to contact the tower. All you need to tell the tower is your aircraft number. The tower knows where you are, since approach has just handed you off to them.

The "Air Traffic Control" section of AIM is a very important reference for any VFR pilot operating in today's complicated airspace system. This chapter of AIM also covers departure, en route, and arrival—IFR. You can skip the IFR part until you go for your instrument rating.

Advanced Maneuver Practice

This section is designed for use in the kitchen simulator. You are now a solo student, and the time you spend in the practice area perfecting these maneuvers is the most valuable time of all to you; don't waste it sight-seeing. Not only are you polishing up your act for the flight examiner, but you are laying the foundation for your own future flying safety.

The *Flight Test Guide, Private Pilot—Airplane* (AC 61-54A) is a government publication; your flight examiner will have a copy. You should read through it yourself now. It details the subjects to be covered on the oral exam and lists the flight maneuvers you may be asked to perform, complete with objectives, descriptions, and acceptable performance guidelines.

MCA has been covered in detail in Chapter 2, and there is no need to repeat it here. Just because it does not appear in the advanced maneuvers section, don't downgrade it—it is BASIC. MCA is the backbone of your flying skills, and it is the maneuver I would look at the hardest if I were giving you a flight check.

The advanced stalls are presented in a step-by-step, "how to" manner. Remember the method used by the professionals and MEMORIZE PROCEDURES. Until now, the emphasis during your stall practice has been on stall recognition and recovery. The time has come for you to expand your concentration to include precision and smoothness.

We will set you up with an objective and a description, and leave the acceptable performance guidelines up to you. If you set up the maneuver in the manner described, you will have a basis for keeping score on yourself. How much altitude loss would be acceptable to you if you stalled an airplane in the traffic pattern? Begin all stall maneuvers and MCA practice at a minimum of 3,000 feet AGL. Aim for precision and finesse; leave the old "bank and yank" method to the "hamburgers."

APPROACH TO LANDING STALL

OBJECTIVE:

Simulate the conditions of an actual landing approach. Set it up as if you were downwind in the traffic pattern. Practice these turning both to the left and to the right, with recovery initiated at both imminent and full stall conditions and with flap settings from 0° to full flaps.

DESCRIPTION:

Entry:

1. Clear the area.

2. Slow to low cruise, maintaining heading and altitude.

3. Reduce power to approach power setting, maintaining heading and altitude; add flaps as desired.

4. Establish a glide at the airspeed appropriate to the chosen flap setting.

5. Enter a gliding turn with 20° to 30° of bank, maintaining approach airspeed.

6. Select an altitude for level-off.

7. Increase angle of attack (maintaining the constant bank) and smoothly close the throttle. Increase rudder pressure as necessary to prevent yaw. Increase elevator back pressure as necessary to maintain altitude. Attempt to do this smoothly enough so that altitude remains constant as airspeed deteriorates.

Recovery:

1. Add full power, decrease angle of attack, and level the wings (simultaneously).

2. Retract the flaps to the setting used in your airplane on an obstacle clearance takeoff.

3. Accelerate to V_x and maintain that airspeed until a positive rate of climb is established; raise the flaps to 0°.

TAKEOFF AND DEPARTURE STALL

OBJECTIVE:

This maneuver will simulate a takeoff with a turnout to clear an obstacle. Practice turning both left and right, and practice initiating recovery at both imminent and full stall conditions.

DESCRIPTION:

Entry:

1. Clear the area.

2. Reduce power, maintaining heading and altitude while slowing to V_{lo} (normal lift-off speed).

3. Add takeoff power and right rudder as needed to maintain heading, while increasing angle of attack to a pitch attitude slightly steeper than that required to maintain V_x.

4. Enter a shallow banked turn (15° to 20°).

5. Maintain constant pitch and constant bank until the stall.

Recovery:

1. Decrease angle of attack and level the wings.

2. Accelerate to V_x.

3. Maintain V_x until a positive rate of climb is established.

ACCELERATED STALL

OBJECTIVE:

This maneuver will demonstrate the effects of wing loading on stall speed. Practice accelerated stalls turning both left and right, and with recovery initiated at both imminent and full stall conditions.

DESCRIPTION:

Entry:

1. Clear the area.

2. Reduce power (to 1500 rpm), maintaining heading and altitude while slowing to V_{lo}.

3. Reset power to 2000 rpm or low cruise (55% power).

4. Enter a coordinated 45° banked turn.

5. Maintain a constant bank and gradually increase angle of attack until the stall occurs.

Recovery:

1. Add full power, decrease angle of attack, and level the wings (simultaneously).

2. Accelerate to V_x

3. Maintain V_x until a positive rate of climb is established.

Radio Navigation

VOR TRANSMITTER

VOR is the primary navigation aid in today's airway system. Chapter 1 in AIM, "Air Navigation Radio Aids," tells you about it. The explanation in AIM is excellent, but it also contains information that only a radio repair technician needs to know. It is a good idea to read through it and be familiar with what is there; don't let it blow your mind. VOR navigation is really very simple. The VOR consists of only two components: the transmitter (on the ground) and the receiver (in the airplane).

The VOR transmitter is housed in a strange little building resembling an upside down ice cream cone. Locate a VOR station on your local sectional chart—most of them are surrounded by a magnetic compass rose. Consider each degree on the compass rose as the spoke of a wheel, with the station as the hub. These "spokes" are known as "radials."

The compass rose may be left off the chart in high density areas because of chart clutter. If the six-sided symbol in the center of the rose has extensions on or a box around it, the VOR station also has DME capability (see chart legend).

The station transmits two signals. One is constant and omnidirectional. The other radio beam continuously zips around the 360° of the compass. The receiver in the airplane can measure the interval (in microseconds) of the circling beam and translate it into the numbered radial from the station. This is very important to remember. The VOR station is the source of the signals: All course information is magnetic direction FROM the station.

The VOR station also transmits an identifier signal. All VORs have a three-letter identifier, and the station will be broadcasting this identifier in Morse code. No, you do not have to learn to read Morse. The name of the station, the radio frequency, and the three-letter identifier (including the appropriate dots and dashes) are printed on the chart near the station, enclosed in a rectangular box. Shaded corners or heavy lines on the communication box indicate services that are available to you. Refer to the chart legend for their meaning.

Many VOR stations also have voice capability. The identifier may come through as a monotonous recording instead of dots and dashes. Area weather forecasts are broadcast on the VOR frequency at 15 minutes past the hour, and flight service personnel can patch in and talk to you on that frequency. You cannot, however, *transmit* voice to a VOR station. There is nobody there—only a lot of electronic equipment. Your black box is simply a receiver.

The numbers on top of the communication box are the frequencies used to communicate with Flight Service. If one of the numbers is followed by an "R," Flight Service *receives only* on that frequency. You tune that in on the Comm side to transmit and turn up the volume on the Nav side. Flight Service will answer you on the VOR channel.

Always turn up the volume and identify the station before depending on it for VOR navigation. The tuner on your set may have slipped off channel, or the station may have been temporarily shut down for maintenance.

VOR signals are VHF and are within the 108.0 to 117.95 MegaHertz (MHz) frequency band. VORs come in three classes, according to their operational use: T (Terminal), L (Low Altitude), and H (High Altitude). AIM will fill you in on the usable altitudes and distances for each class.

Another important fact to remember about the VOR transmitter is that its signals are "line of sight." Where low frequency radio signals will bend and follow the curvature of the earth, high frequency signals will continue in a straight line. If you let a mountain get between you and the station, you are not going to pick up the signal. If you are going to rely on a VOR station to get where you are going, be sure the weather allows you to fly high enough for reliable reception (Fig. 4.3).

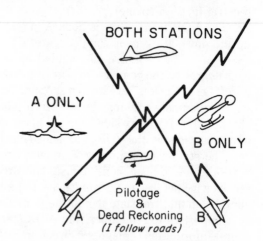

FIG. 4.3. *VOR reception.*

VOR RECEIVER

The VOR receiver (Fig. 4.4) in your airplane is normally housed in the same black box as your communication radio, although the VOR face may be located somewhere else. Most sets have only one on/off knob to activate both sides, but on some makes the Nav side has its own separate switch. Either way, the Nav will have a separate volume knob and a separate tuner, since it is a receiver only and operates on a different frequency band. The Comm side goes from 118.0 through 135.97 MHz. Tune in the frequency and identify the station.

VOR faces will vary somewhat according to age and brand. There is a sophisticated kind of VOR indicator in wide use that is combined with a heading indicator. This marvelous gadget is called a Horizontal Situation In-

FIG. 4.4. *VOR receiver.*

dicator (HSI), and you probably don't have one in your trainer. As with DME and turbocharged engines, most trainers aren't quite so expensively equipped. Here we will discuss a standard VOR face. Yours will have an OBS card (Omni Bearing Selector), which is marked like a rotating compass rose; it is set by twisting the OBS knob. The radial thus set may be read directly at the top of the case, with the reciprocal at the bottom. This might be reversed, depending on the kind of radio you have. The VOR face has an indicator that can read TO, FROM, or OFF. The OFF signal is probably printed on a red background.

The 5 dots on either side of center indicate the amount of course displacement at the rate of 200 feet per dot per nautical mile. If you are 30 nautical miles from the station, 1 dot displacement would indicate that you are 1 nautical mile off the course centerline. Don't panic—you will not need to compute that kind of information. We are just throwing it in, in case you are interested.

The Course Direction Indicator (CDI) or "needle" is attached at the top and swings in an upside-down V through full deflection on either side. When the receiver is located on any radial, the needle will center with a FROM indication when the number of that radial is set on the OBS. The needle will center again with a TO indication if the OBS is rotated to the reciprocal of that bearing.

If you set the OBS so that the needle is right on the edge of a full deflection, an OBS change of 20° (in the appropriate direction) will cause a full needle deflection to the opposite side. Therefore, the CDI will provide course information within 10° either side of the selected bearing.

The OFF indication will show under these five circumstances:
1. Your set is either turned off or broken.
2. The station is either turned off or broken.
3. You are out of range due to distance or obstructions.
4. Your aircraft's position is exactly 90° to the OBS setting.
5. You are passing directly over the station.

The first three are easy enough to deal with. Fall back on pilotage and dead reckoning. In the fourth circumstance the receiver is just a little lost; twist the OBS knob and it will find the transmitter again. In the fifth circumstance the revolving transmitter leaves a cone-shaped hole directly over the station called the "cone of confusion"; no signals are being sent here. As you pass into it, the flag will flip from TO to OFF; it will flip to FROM as you pop out on the departure side.

When the TO/FROM flag and the course needle behave erratically, you are not receiving a strong enough signal for reliable navigation. This can happen even though you are receiving the identifier loud and clear. The situation will probably rectify itself when you get closer to the station or if you climb to a higher altitude.

Whether you are going TO the station or away FROM it, if the needle is centered, you are on track. Should you drift off track, the CDI needle will move off center and will point in the direction of the radial you were tracking. Therefore the rule is: "Correct toward the needle."

This is only part of the story, so don't file it under "Important VOR Rules" yet. Remember that we said the VOR consisted of two components—the transmitter and the receiver. Nothing was said about a compass. "Use the VOR to locate; use the compass to navigate."

There is a vital connection between the airplane's heading and successful VOR navigation, but the connection is not in the equipment. The black box can tell you what radial you are on, but it doesn't care what direction you are going. The compass can tell you what direction you are going, but it can't tell you where you are. There is a connecting factor in there somewhere.

VOR TRACKING

There is one very important rule for VOR tracking: The OBS setting and the airplane's heading must be the same, plus or minus wind correction.

We could present you with a lot of complicated diagrams showing drift and VOR needles, but it all comes down to *holding a heading*. If the OBS needle moves to the left, turn left 20° or so and hold the new heading until the needle centers again. It will not recenter immediately; you have to move back on to the radial, so give it time. If the needle drifted and your heading was accurate, then you have located some wind. After the needle recenters, if you turn back to the original OBS heading you are going to drift off again and end up flying S-turns along a radial.

Flying the original heading allowed you to drift off track, and a 20° correction brought you back. Return to a heading that is 10° left of the original heading and maintain it. Suppose that the needle slowly drifts to the right—we have it bracketed, at least. 10° was too much correction; so recenter the needle and fly the original heading −5° and the needle should stay centered.

The system is only as accurate as the pilot's ability to analyze the situation and then maintain the correct heading. You will get mixed up with TOs and FROMs occasionally until you have seen it in actual practice a few times. The only really gross error you can make is to try to fly the reciprocal of the OBS setting. The needle will be centered at first, but if there is any wind (and there is ALWAYS wind) the CDI will lead you to correct in the wrong direction. This is called "reverse sensing," and it will get you good and lost. Double-check to see that your heading agrees with the OBS, plus or minus the drift correction.

We can now consolidate the "very important VOR rules" into one short list:

1. Identify the station.

2. Verify that the OBS and the airplane's heading agree, plus or minus wind correction.

3. Hold the heading.

In Chapter 5, cross-country section, we will discuss how to use a VOR intersection as a check point, but that should be studied after you have gained some experience in VOR tracking. The time you spend going to and from the practice area on your solo flights need not be wasted. Tune in your VOR and intercept and track a radial. If you cross over a VOR station, be especially alert for other traffic. The chances are good that other airplanes will also be crossing directly over a VOR. Comply with the hemispheric rule for altitude separation.

DME

DME is a very expensive and useful radio. If the VOR you are tracking happens to be a VORTAC, it will have DME capability. VORTAC is a combination of VOR and TACAN (Tactical Air Navigation), which is a military system. Don't worry about it—identify a VOR with DME capability as a VOR-TAC.

The following is the explanation of DME set forth in AIM: "In the operation of DME, paired pulses at a specific spacing are sent out from the aircraft (this is the interrogation) and are received at the ground station. The ground station (transponder) then transmits paired pulses to the aircraft at the same pulse spacing but on a different frequency. The time required for the round trip of this signal exchange is measured in the airborne DME unit and is translated into distance (nautical miles) from the aircraft to the ground station." (See Fig. 4.5.)

For DME information to be accurate, you must be going directly TO or

FIG. 4.5. *DME unit.*

FROM the VORTAC. It will now present you with your correct ground speed (in knots), your distance from the station (in nautical miles), and your time to the station (in minutes). It certainly can make you lazy; then it breaks down, and you have to go back to work.

DME is very accurate with one small deception; the information you receive is "slant-range." If you cross directly above the VORTAC at 6,080 feet AGL, you are still 1 nautical mile away from the station.

ADF

The Automatic Direction Finder (ADF) is not as obsolete as you might think, even though your training aircraft is probably not equipped with one. It is true that ADF predates VOR, but it remains a very valuable radio to an IFR pilot, and you may face a question on the written exam concerning ADF, whether you have ever seen one or not.

The ADF receiver points to a Non-Directional Beacon (NDB), which is covered in AIM. It is the simplest of all radios to navigate by and the most difficult to answer questions about. This is because in actual practice the needle points to the station. If you need to find the station, you turn until the needle is aimed at the nose of the airplane. When the question of heading comes up on paper, it involves arithmetic.

The ADF radio operates from 190 to 1,750 kHz. It can be tuned to commercial broadcasting stations. If you plan to use it for navigation, tune and identify the station, unless you plan to land at the local rock-music station. The disadvantages of the ADF include poor distance reception, static interference, and the other ailments that plague low and medium frequency radio bands. Moreover, ADF needles have a history of confusing daring aviators by deflecting from the desired radio station and pointing unerringly toward large, electrically charged thunderstorms.

The ADF dial is a compass rose (Fig. 4.6). The dial can be manually rotated on some sets, which helps with the arithmetic, but ours has a fixed scale and so will the one on your written test. When you are homing to an NDB, holding a heading becomes even more vital than when tracking a VOR radial. With the ADF, when you move, everything moves. The dial is fixed so that zero is at the top. If the needle is pointing to 330°, that does not indicate a heading. It means you should turn left 30°, so subtract 30° from your present magnetic heading. When you cross over the station, the needle will swing around and point to the tail.

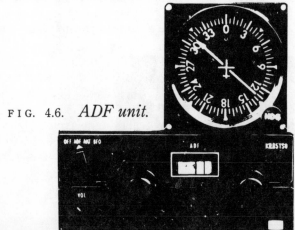

F I G. 4.6. *ADF unit.*

We need to define several terms in ADF language. A "bearing" is simply the direction of a straight line between the aircraft and the station. A "relative bearing" always means relative to the nose of the airplane, measured clockwise. The ADF needle points to relative bearing. "Magnetic bearing" to the station is measured clockwise from Magnetic North. If you need to find the station on paper, you need to know the formula for computing magnetic bearing: $Mb = Rb + Mh$. Translation: Magnetic bearing (to the station) equals relative bearing (the number the needle is pointing to) plus magnetic heading (read your compass). Add your compass heading to the number to which the ADF needle is pointing, and if the total comes to more than 360, you didn't make a mistake; subtract 360, and the answer should be the compass heading that will get you to the station (magnetic bearing).

There is a lot about ADF tracking, homing, intercepting, etc., that we have left out since the ADF will probably never be your primary navigation radio. It is a terrific aid to an instrument pilot on an approach, not only for orientation (since it always points to the station), and it is often used to pinpoint a final approach fix (the point from which the final approach begins).

The formula for computing magnetic bearing should be enough to get you through the written exam, and you will become far more intimate with ADF when you start on your instrument rating.

Flight Service Station

A Flight Service Station (FSS) does just what its name implies—it provides a multitude of services for pilots. It does not pump gas; that is "line service." FSSs are scattered about the country at reasonably spaced locations, so there is one within radio range, and someone is on duty 24 hours a day. This stage in your flight training is a good time to read the chapter on "Preflight" and also the chapter on "Good Operating Practices" in AIM.

To reach the FSS by telephone, look up their number under the listing, United States Government, Department of Transportation. The telephone numbers are also included in AIM, *Airport/Facility Directory*. If you are calling long distance, ask if they have a toll-free number from your town. Many do, but they are usually unlisted. Most airports and FBOs (Fixed Base Operators) provide a direct line to the FSS that is handy to their flight planning facility.

In this chapter (under VOR) we have discussed how to locate the radio frequency to use for contacting Flight Service. Memorize the standard FSS frequency, 122.2. When you call, keep this in mind: The specialist is monitoring three or four radio frequencies and may be busy talking on one that you can't hear. Don't launch immediately into a long-winded request. Give your call sign, repeat the frequency on which you are listening, and wait for their call; then proceed with your request. "San Diego radio, Cessna three five six seven Victor, one twenty-two point four." The specialist will get around to you as soon as possible, and if it takes too long to suit you, repeat it.

Flight Service personnel are federal employees, highly trained for their jobs. They are not weather forecasters, but their facility is linked directly to the National Weather Service computer in Kansas City. The briefer on duty can obtain the weather information you need concerning any location in the country in a matter of minutes. The information is called up on a little TV screen, and it is read off to you. If you are there in person and wish to have a hard copy to carry with you, the computer will print one for you.

FSS can give you the weather forecast, but do not ask them to make your go, no-go decision for you. That is nobody's responsibility but your own. You can help them give you a better briefing if you clue them in on your experience/equipment limitations. If you tell them that this is a cross-country student solo, you won't get quite the same briefing I would get if I told them I'm going IFR; but both briefings would be more valuable to us for gaining the kind of information we both need.

Do not bother them with requests for personal services, such as phoning for a cab, the latest baseball scores, etc. These are items you should contact Unicom for. Flight Service would probably help you out if it were really important or late at night when everything is closed and they are bored silly anyhow. If they are busy, they will have to refuse you; personal services really are not part of their job description.

The major service provided by the FSS is a full weather briefing. You can get the briefing and file your flight plan on the telephone, over the radio, or in person, if you are lucky enough to have an FSS handy. This is the best way because you can look at the weather depiction charts yourself.

Since the vast majority of the serious (fatal) general aviation accidents are weather related, weather is a subject that is important enough to deserve a section all to itself. Right now your instructor is helping you out in the "weather decision" department. Weather, being the most important area you will study, will be saved for last (Chapter 5).

Two other major services provided by the FSS are the VFR flight plan and the DF Steer. You are not very far away from your first dual cross-country flight, so we will cover those two areas now and give you a head start.

VFR FLIGHT PLAN

One of the many flight services provided by the FSS is the VFR flight plan. You can file local flight plans as well as cross-country plans—start now and file a local flight plan or two. You are going to feel loaded down with details when launching your first few cross-country flights. Filing flight plans could be turned into one familiar task you could take in stride.

Call for your weather briefing, figure out the time en route, and fill in the blanks in the form before calling back to file. Follow the numbered blocks when you read it off to the briefer. There is no need to say any more; it will be copied onto an identical form as you go along. This practice will help cut down frequency congestion if you call in the flight plan while en route.

If you file by phone or in person, you will need to contact FSS on the radio after departure to activate the flight plan. Should you fail to call and activate within one hour, they will assume you didn't get off for some reason, and they will throw it away. This also means you don't have to remember to cancel a flight plan that was never activated.

DEPARTMENT OF TRANSPORTATION FEDERAL AVIATION ADMINISTRATION **FLIGHT PLAN**	CIVIL AIRCRAFT PILOTS. FAR Part 91 requires you file an IFR flight plan to operate under instrument flight rules in controlled airspace. Failure to file could result in a civil penalty not to exceed $1,000 for each violation (Section 901 of the Federal Aviation Act of 1958, as amended). Filing of a VFR flight plan is recommended as a good operating practice. See also Part 99 for requirements concerning DVFR flight plans.			

1. TYPE	2. AIRCRAFT IDENTIFICATION	3. AIRCRAFT TYPE/ SPECIAL EQUIPMENT	4. TRUE AIRSPEED	5. DEPARTURE POINT	6. DEPARTURE TIME		7. CRUISING ALTITUDE
☒ VFR					PROPOSED (Z)	ACTUAL (Z)	
IFR	N3567V	C150/T	90 KTS	RAL	1900		7500
DVFR							

8. ROUTE OF FLIGHT

RAL ↛ JLI - V458 IPL

9. DESTINATION (Name of airport and city)	10. EST. TIME ENROUTE		11. REMARKS
	HOURS	MINUTES	
Imperial Co. El Centro	2	10	desert survival gear aboard

12. FUEL ON BOARD		13. ALTERNATE AIRPORT(S)	14. PILOT'S NAME, ADDRESS & TELEPHONE NUMBER & AIRCRAFT HOME BASE	15. NUMBER ABOARD
HOURS	MINUTES		714-787-9596	
4	00	N/A	S. Rambo, Mile High Club Homefield	2

16. COLOR OF AIRCRAFT	
green/white	CLOSE VFR FLIGHT PLAN WITH IPL 122.6 FSS ON ARRIVAL

FAA Form 7233-1 (5-77)

FIG. 4.7. *Flight plan form.*

Look at the sample flight plan form (Fig. 4.7), and let's clarify a few of the information blocks.

Block 3 "Cessna 150 slash tango" means we have a transponder without altitude encoding and negative DME. This is a special equipment suffix code, and it is found in AIM under "Flight Plan." The equipment information it specifies includes whether you have a transponder with or without Mode C, DME, and RNAV, and various combinations of these.

Block 4 is knots, not statute miles.

Block 6 is Zulu time, so convert from local. It is embarrassing when a pilot doesn't know what time it is. Discuss this with your flight instructor. If you can't tell time on a 24-hour clock, shame on you. I will privately admit to some difficulty in converting to local, considering daylight and standard time changes. "Spring forward, Fall back" always drove me up the wall. Find a time conversion table for eastern, central, mountain, and Pacific (both standard and daylight) or copy this one and carry it with you—like I do.

TABLE 4.1. Time conversion table

Convert from	To Greenwich
EST	Add 5 hrs
CST	Add 6 hrs
MST	Add 7 hrs
PST	Add 8 hrs
EDT	Add 4 hrs
CDT	Add 5 hrs
MDT	Add 6 hrs
PDT	Add 7 hrs

Block 8 says, "Riverside direct Julian VOR, then via Victor 458 to Imperial." From this they will know exactly where to search if I turn up missing. Over a long trip, make position reports to en route FSSs. You have to call for an altimeter setting (FAR 91.81), and if you should develop a problem, it would narrow the search considerably.

Block 11 would include information concerning ground time at intermediate stops, oxygen on board, yellow life vests on board, or anything you believe would be pertinent information for someone waiting or searching for you. This information is not teletyped to your destination, but they will send for it if you are overdue.

Block 13 applies only to airplanes on an IFR flight plan; they have to know where you plan on going if your first destination goes completely to zip.

FAR 91.83 tells you what information is required on a flight plan. Oddly enough, the official flight-plan form leaves out one required item—the radio frequencies used. I once tried to list my planned radio frequencies when I filed a VFR flight plan, and the briefer thought I was crazy. In the real world when you use the system (even VFR) you may be handed off to dozens of different approach control frequencies, and there is no way you could list them in advance. On your own copy of the flight plan, list your first departure control frequency and the FSS frequency you will use to activate your flight plan. Also list the appropriate frequencies at your destination (ATIS, tower, and ground control). List the frequency of the FSS where you intend to close your flight plan, if you are planning to close in the air. Of course this information is still available, but you won't have your head down searching for it at arrival time.

You are not required by regulation to file a VFR flight plan, but it is certainly a cheap insurance policy. If you do file and arrive safely, please do not forget to close your flight plan. This *is* a regulation, FAR 91.83 *d*. If you file a flight plan and run into trouble, many dedicated people are going to come looking for you. This is what happens when you are overdue:

Thirty minutes after your filed ETA, FSS at your destination calls your departure point for the rest of the flight-plan information. Thirty minutes later (you are now one hour overdue) they activate an "information search." This involves sending someone at your destination out to search the parking ramp and also contacting every FSS along your route to see if you talked to anyone. Flight Service personnel always log your "N" number and the time whenever you call them for anything; this is one of the reasons why.

Another thirty minutes later (you are now one and one-half hours late) they call Search and Rescue, and people—many of them trained Civil Air Patrol volunteers in their own private aircraft—start burning up fuel looking for you. This would be a comforting thought if you were in trouble, but if it happened while you were in some cozy bar, you would probably wish you had been camping on the desert waiting for them! If you find that you are going to be overdue, call up the nearest FSS and extend your ETA. The VFR flight plan is the greatest free safety device available to a pilot, so USE it.

Visit a FSS in person at your earliest opportunity. Introduce yourself as a student pilot, and they will be happy to answer your questions and give you a guided tour of the facility. No appointment is necessary, but if you want to take a whole group, give them some notice; you might be in for a real lecture tour.

DF STEER

The DF steer is a means by which the FSS can locate a lost pilot, pinpoint his position, and direct him to an airport. No special equipment is required to be installed in your airplane, such as a transponder for radar service. Your microphone is all that is necessary.

There is a visual display in the FSS that is fairly similar in appearance to a radar scope. When this is activated by transmitting over your communication radio (keying your mike), a strobe light appears on the DF scope in the form of a line radiating from the center of the scope to the edge. Your aircraft is located somewhere on that line. Rather than have you carry on a running conversation with the DF operator, you may be asked periodically to give a "short count" (key the mike for five seconds) or a "long count" (key for ten seconds). Follow this count with the last three digits of your "N" number. In this way your progress can be plotted without the necessity for a constant return on the set. It wouldn't work to have you hold the mike button down constantly; you couldn't receive instructions that way.

Contact the FSS in the usual manner, and confess your predicament: You are lost and require assistance to locate an airport before you run out of gas. You will be asked a number of questions. During this process of information exchange, the specialist has already begun charting the location of your return on the scope and figuring out your position. Random questions are not asked; a printed checklist is followed. You will be asked to give the following information:

1. Your aircraft identification.

2. Nature of your request (whether it is for practice or an actual emergency).

3. Your requested destination (for practice, you may have a preference; if you are really lost, just ask for the nearest airport).

4. Your transponder equipment (or lack thereof). If this is a real emergency, you will be reminded to squawk 7700 and identify, and you may be switched to 121.5 for communication.

5. Your type aircraft (make and model), and you will be given the current weather at your destination.

6. Your fuel on board, in hours (or minutes). You had better know the answer!

7. You will be given the current altimeter setting and be requested to report your present heading and altitude. You will be reminded to set your HI with reference to the magnetic compass. This may be why you were lost in the first place.

8. You will be assigned a heading to fly and requested to report when you are established on that heading. Your direction from the station is now known.

9. You are now read your rights: "Cessna 3567 Victor, fly heading zero niner zero, maintain at or above three thousand five hundred, and advise changes necessary to maintain VFR." He is giving you a minimum safe altitude for terrain clearance and a start in the right direction; but you are expected to deviate from the assigned heading (or altitude) if that will put you in a cloud. If you make any such changes, the FSS operator would appreciate being told about it.

10. "67 Victor, transmit." This means they have run out of questions, and you should key the mike for a slow (silent) five count, followed by "67 Victor." They need to verify your position.

11. Information concerning weather conditions in your vicinity may be requested. Your equipment and experience would have a definite effect on the manner in which you are handled if weather conditions are marginal VFR or IFR.

12. "Do you have an operating OMNI on board?" Say "affirmative" if you have a VOR and it is working. You will be given a VOR frequency to tune in, with instructions to rotate the OMNI-bearing selector until the CDI centers and to read off that bearing. A line will be drawn on the chart from the VOR station, and you will possibly be given another frequency and be directed to repeat the performance. In this manner your position can be triangulated relative to the VOR stations and your exact position verified on the scope.

You must agree that this sounds like a relatively simple procedure, once it has been explained. It is simple—that is the beauty of it. If you can hold an assigned heading, you can be directed to an airport. Nevertheless, if you add the unaccustomed communication load to the stress factors already underway during an actual lost, low-fuel situation and throw in approaching darkness or marginal VFR conditions, you would be very glad you practiced the DF steer procedures before. The DF steer is only as good as your ability to maintain assigned headings. A private pilot applicant should be able to accomplish a successful DF steer by reference to instruments (under the hood). Try it with your instructor on board. All of my students experience a practice DF steer (under the hood) on one of their night flights, prior to solo cross-country.

Flight service personnel are required to log time and experience in this area, just as pilots must log time for passenger-carrying privileges. Flight service personnel are happy to oblige a practice DF steer anytime the normal work load permits it. It would be especially interesting should a DF steer be in progress during your visit to the FSS. Believe it or not, one night when I was in the FSS showing a student around, we heard a Lear jet ask for a practice DF steer. He was refused, due to a heavy work load. He came back, "Well, er, uh, can I have one for real?" He got it.

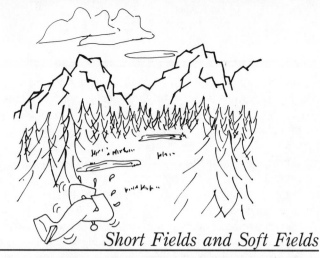

Short Fields and Soft Fields

Before proceeding to a discussion of short- and soft-field operations, we need to return to your aircraft owner's manual and the performance section. There you will find a bewildering array of charts and graphs. No pilot in his right mind launches himself down a short (or soft) runway with any doubt in his mind about whether or not he has enough room to get airborne and stay that way.

AIRCRAFT PERFORMANCE CHARTS AND WEIGHT AND BALANCE

Your manufacturer has his own method of depicting the performance figures graphically, and you need to be sure you know how to pick out the essential information. The graphs in the aircraft owner's manual are usually pretty simple and self-explanatory, but you should run through a trial situation on each one so that you know what information is available and how to get it when you need it. For example, figure out the distance required to clear a 50-foot obstacle at sea level (gross weight) on a standard day with a 10-knot head-wind component. Then compare it with the distance required with a 6,000-foot field elevation when the temperature is 80° and the wind is calm; the difference is impressive. Go on to the next step and find out what your climb performance would be under the same two circumstances. Also check out the charts that apply to the distance you require to get down and stopped without frying the brakes.

Listen to an additional word of caution (as usual). Those figures in the book are accurate as far as they go; the performance was tested and verified by that type airplane, or it wouldn't be in the manual. There is one hitch. The manufacturer built a fine airplane, and he is in the business of selling it; good performance figures will help. Business is business, after all. So he hired a highly proficient professional pilot, put him in a brand new airplane, and waited for perfect weather conditions. Then he tested the airplane. You had better allow yourself some additional margin for error. I am not implying that your technique won't be perfect; just that your airplane is not new anymore.

Your technique for making short- and soft-field takeoffs and landings won't vary much from one type airplane to the next, but the *procedure* involved may be a different story. For example, almost every model Piper I have flown recommends two notches of flaps (25°) for a short-field takeoff. The Cessna 150 manual warns that using any amount of flaps for obstacle clearance will be detrimental to climb performance. Read the owner's manual and abide by their recommendations if you want your performance to match the graphs.

Notice that the obstacle clearance performance graphs assume a dry, hard-surface runway. Also observe that the technique involved for a short-field effort and the technique recommended for a soft field may be somewhat contradictory—as if the two situations will never coincide. In the real world, it seems that the softest fields are also the shortest. Right now don't worry about trying to combine the two techniques; but keep it in mind after you are off doing your own thing.

A discussion of weight and balance follows because it has a decisive effect not only on short- and/or soft-field and high–density altitude operations, but on every aspect of flight. An improperly loaded airplane does not conform to any of the manufacturer's carefully computed performance figures. It has become an experimental aircraft. Furthermore, it may develop some highly undesirable and possibly unpredictable flight characteristics. Other test pilots wear parachutes and have sophisticated ejection systems.

It is the responsibility of the PIC (FAR 91.5, Preflight Action) to determine that the airplane is loaded within the manufacturer's published (and tested) limits. It is quite possible to be under maximum allowable gross weight and still have that weight centered too far forward or too far aft.

An airplane with a forward CG will feel very stable in flight, but it will have a higher stall speed and a lower cruise airspeed. As if that weren't enough, it may run out of elevator when you try to flare; remember the porpoise?

The opposite condition is potentially even more serious, and most airplanes are easier to overload in the back, where the baggage usually goes. An aft CG will lower the stall speed and increase the cruise airspeed. This sounds desirable, until you attempt to trim for level flight and you feel like you are trying to stack ball bearings. The airplane becomes highly unstable around the pitch axis. Assuming you successfully negotiated the takeoff, if you should later enter into an inadvertent stall spin (much easier to do under these circumstances), centrifugal force will pull the tail outside and into a "flat spin." This maneuver, once established, is impossible to recover.

Check the manual to determine how much weight the floor of the baggage compartment is stressed to support. Remember that the weight of the airplane and everything in it doubles at 2 Gs, triples at 3Gs, etc. This was taken into consideration when your manufacturer placed your airplane in the normal or utility category and advertised that it could support that specified number of G forces. You would hate to encounter some turbulence and have your suitcases depart through the floorboards.

Speaking of turbulence and G forces, this is a good time to discuss maneuvering speed (V_a). The definition of maneuvering speed is: the speed at which full, sudden deflection of the controls will not result in structural damage. (The airplane may stall, but you won't tear the wings off.) It is the speed at which you want to fly in rough air.

V_a is determined by the manufacturer, and must be in the owner's manual and placarded on the panel. In your utility category trainer, you probably cruise below V_a. When you step up to a speedier normal category aircraft, you may cruise well above it. V_a is determined at gross weight. If the aircraft is lightly loaded, V_a will decrease to a lower airspeed. This seems backwards to most people, but it can be proven by mathematical computations involving lift coefficient, wing loading, and gust loads. Leave that to the aeronautical engineers and memorize the basic fact—the lighter the airplane is loaded, the more you need to slow down in turbulence. Don't overdo the slowing down. Accelerated stalls are possible with high gust loads. In turbulent conditions, you are better off flying at or slightly below V_a.

Work a sample weight and balance problem with just your flight instructor and yourself on board. Then work one with full fuel and all seats occupied; see how much luggage (if any) you can carry or how much fuel (if any) you need to drain. Most trainers (carrying no baggage) are difficult to overload, provided the people are standard size—standard people being 170 pounds. But higher performance airplanes generally offer more opportunities to make mistakes in the weight and balance department. They were designed to allow you a choice between carrying a heavy load or flying a longer distance. You may have to choose between fuel and passengers. Include a thorough weight and balance workup when checking out in any new airplane.

Now that you have computed weight and balance and takeoff distance, let's try it on a soft field.

SOFT-FIELD TAKEOFFS AND LANDINGS

We should begin with a discussion of the phenomenon known as "ground effect," since the understanding and use of this aerodynamic fact will play an important role in the success of your soft-field takeoff and landing effort.

The wing developing lift is forcing air down behind it. It is also creating wing-tip vortices, which are descending behind you. Up at altitude, this downwashing air is gone and forgotten; don't forget it when the airplane is close to the ground. The three dimensional airflow pattern around the wing is now restricted by the ground surface. Ground effect will cause your airplane to float right along, even though it is below normal stall speed. For that reason, it can get you into trouble by prolonging your touchdown or if you climb above it before reaching a safe airspeed.

Ground effect is a factor up to approximately a wingspan above the surface. If you should balloon out of it before a safe climb speed is established, you will come back down—hard. We will use this phenomenon to our advantage to get us unstuck from a soft surface.

Even taxiing on a soft surface is going to require a slightly different technique. A tricycle-gear airplane really does not care too much for swamps and marshes. There is a heavy engine sitting on top of the nosewheel, and it wants to dig in and fold under. Lighten the load as much as possible by holding full up-elevator while you taxi. If practical, taxi slightly faster than normal so you don't bog down. Keep the wind in mind, though. Up-elevator and a strong tail wind might stand you on your nose as well.

Consider the problem you face: Tall grass, mud, slush, a rough or uphill surface—even puddles of water on a paved runway—would justify the use of a soft-field takeoff technique. All of the above-mentioned conditions are going to slow your ability to accelerate to lift-off speed. As early as possible in the takeoff roll, you need to transfer the weight of the airplane from the wheels to the wings. Once completely free of the ground, the airplane will accelerate much more rapidly; but you must be sure to remain in ground effect until you arrive at V_x.

After completing your run up, set the flaps at the recommended position and clear the approach path. You will try to avoid coming to a full stop on the runway and sinking in again. Taxi onto the runway with flaps set and holding full up-elevator, apply takeoff power, and go.

As speed increases and you can feel the nose becoming lighter, relax the back pressure slightly. Try to hold the nosewheel just clear of the surface. A very high angle of attack on a takeoff roll is going to cause aerodynamic drag that will work against you, and it is possible to bang the tail skid on the ground.

Lift the airplane off the runway below power-off stall speed, and immediately decrease the angle of attack to the level-flight attitude. Maintain level flight just inches above the runway until you accelerate to V_x; then rotate and climb at V_x.

Climbing out, wait to retract the flaps until you are well clear of obstacles. The airplane will sink as the flaps come up. Don't forget that airplanes also stall at a higher speed with the flaps up, so make certain your airspeed is adequate.

This technique will not come to you overnight—it will take some practice. Get your instructor's okay before you practice solo. You will lift off at too high an airspeed at first, until you get the feel of it. The first few times you try it, your directional control will probably be nonexistent.

We suggested making a rolling start; this could have been bad advice in your airplane. Some airplanes are placarded against takeoffs immediately following a tight, taxiing turn, especially with partially filled fuel tanks. The fuel sloshes away and uncovers the vent port inside the tank. Check the manual for your model.

For the soft-field landing, keep this objective in mind: Prevent the airplane from nosing over. This is best accomplished by touching down at a minimum rate of descent and with a minimum forward speed; just *roll* it on. Give yourself a little longer final than normal and make a very shallow approach—use full flaps and carry power through the touchdown. Some power helps hold the nosewheel off the ground longer. As you roll out, bring in full up-elevator and close the throttle. Avoid any use of brakes.

Memorize these procedures for soft-field takeoffs and landings:
Takeoff:

1. Hold full up-elevator (wind permitting) and avoid braking and full stops.

2. Set flaps and hold up-elevator as you move into position for takeoff.

3. Apply takeoff power and hold the nosewheel clear of the surface.

4. Lift off below power-off stall speed, lower the nose, and accelerate in ground effect to V_x.

5. Climb at V_x to an adequate altitude, accelerate to V_y, and retract flaps.
Landing:

1. Establish a shallow approach profile, carrying power.

2. Touch down at a minimum airspeed and rate of descent, carrying power.

3. Apply full up-elevator slowly as you close the throttle, keeping the nosewheel clear as long as possible.

4. Avoid any use of brakes.

SHORT-FIELD TAKEOFFS AND LANDINGS

Time and again I hear student pilots complaining about their confusion between short- and soft-field technique. That makes no sense. They can't be considering the objective of the exercise, the problem they face, and the aerodynamic activity that will solve it.

The term "short field" right away implies minimum available runway. It may further imply obstacles somewhere off the departure and/or approach end. The objective of a short-field takeoff has got to be: Accelerate in the shortest possible distance to the best angle-of-climb speed; maintain that speed until the obstacles are cleared.

How this is best accomplished is largely a matter of the procedure recommended by your particular airplane's manufacturer for that specific airplane. One recommendation applies in all types of airplanes departing a short field: Use all of the runway that is available to you; taxi to the very end before you begin. Now the manufacturer's recommended procedure takes over.

For some models the owner's manual recommends standing on the brakes until full power is applied, and some say not to. Some manuals state that it doesn't matter either way. The manual may tell you to put some amount of flaps down prior to starting the takeoff roll; or it may say to yank the flaps in as you rotate, or it may tell you not to use any flaps at all for the takeoff and climb. Do whatever the owner's manual recommends; once the obstacle is cleared, accelerate from V_x to V_y, retract flaps, accelerate to cruise climb, and have a good trip.

For the short-field landing, there are not *quite* as many conflicts between different airplanes, but there may be a few. Generally speaking, the approach is a steep one, made with full flaps and carrying power. It still pays to know YOUR airplane.

The following procedures should apply to any airplane making a short-field approach over an obstacle: Carrying full flaps, set up a steeper than normal approach at the recommended short-field approach airspeed; keep the rate of descent constant after the obstacle is cleared. If you were carrying power, don't chop it over the obstacle. After touchdown, slowly apply up-elevator, not only to save the nosegear, but to add aerodynamic drag to further assist in slowing the airplane. Retract the flaps to allow the weight to transfer from the wings to the wheels (where the brakes are). Apply brakes as necessary.

Memorize these procedures for short-field takeoffs and landings:
Takeoff:

1. Use all available runway.

2. Set flaps as required, use brakes as required.

3. Accelerate to and climb at V_x.

4. Accelerate to V_y and retract flaps after obstacles are cleared.

Landing: The objective is to clear the obstacle and touch down with minimum floating.

1. Establish a steep descent profile, carrying power.

2. Maintain a constant airspeed to the touchdown point, carrying power. Airspeed will usually be 5–8 knots less than normal (recommended by the manufacturer).

3. Close the throttle in the flare.

4. Apply full up-elevator slowly, retract flaps, and apply brakes.

You may question one statement I have made here—"do not chop power over the obstacle." Yes, the airplane will come down faster if you cut the power. It may also come down a lot faster than you bargained for. Keep in mind that your airplane can get down and stopped in a far shorter distance than it requires to get up and out. If the field is that short, forget it—unless you want to turn your airplane into a monument.

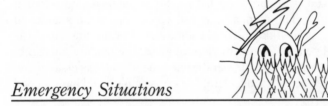

Emergency Situations

Electrical fire in flight is a rousing emergency to start with. Your instructor has probably simulated this one with you already. The trouble with any simulation of this nature is that the old "pucker factor" is missing. You know all the time it isn't real. Even without the stress you would be under if the cockpit were filling with real smoke, you would probably still have to spend some time thinking out the proper actions to take.

If you were sitting in your kitchen and flames suddenly started shooting out of the toaster, I doubt very much that you would grab the family and run out in the yard and watch the house burn down. You would quickly and calmly reach over and unplug the toaster. You have dealt with enough faulty appliances in your time that you know the quickest solution to the problem without having to reason it out: YOU UNDERSTAND THE SYSTEM. You could defuel your aircraft's electrical fire just as quickly and efficiently by merely shutting off the master switch. There is still no reason to wreck a perfectly good airplane attempting an *unnecessary* off-airport landing.

Won't the engine quit with the master switch off? Of course not. You have lost some equipment, though. Can you list the items that use battery power? What is now reliable and what is not? Wouldn't you rather work out the answers in the kitchen simulator, instead of during a real emergency situation?

A student pilot recently demolished an airplane (fortunately not himself) landing in a plowed field. The airplane was making horrible noises, and he really thought he was taking the prudent action. An examination of the wreckage revealed that the end of a seat belt had been hanging out the door— bang, bang, bang. *Trouble-shoot!!* There is a difference between prudence and panic.

The first and most necessary aid in dealing with the unexpected is a cool head. Panic is your worst enemy in an airplane. The best advice I ever got for dealing with fear was to "talk out loud." When thoughts turn into emotions, panic takes over and reason is no longer possible. The simple act of verbalizing your thoughts forces a racing brain to slow down and helps restore reasoning power. Babble out loud and listen to yourself. See if what you are saying makes any sense; you will soon have yourself back under control.

The next best thing to have is a PLAN. You know how to keep from pushing the panic button; the confidence that comes from knowing you are taking all the correct actions as quickly as possible will help *keep* the head cool. To KNOW you are doing everything right, you must be thoroughly knowledgeable about your airplane's systems. I can't imagine operating such a piece of equipment as an airplane without feeling relatively secure about how everything works.

Indulge yourself in a few flying fantasies. In your kitchen simulator, place yourself in every emergency situation you can imagine, and solve them practically and efficiently (heroically).

The following questions will help you get started:

1. What would you do if the engine began running rough?

2. What possible causes can you think of for a rough-running engine?

3. What would be the most probable cause if the engine suddenly quit without warning?

4. What immediate actions would you take?

5. What action would you take if you noticed the alternator was reading a minus?

6. What instruments and/or gauges will you lose if the battery fails?

7. What would you do if the oil pressure is fluctuating and the cylinder head temperature is climbing?

8. What instruments would be affected by failure of the vacuum pump?

9. Which instruments would fail if the pitot tube became plugged or if the static source became plugged?

10. What are the first indications of carburetor icing?

11. Will the airplane stall if a door pops open on takeoff?

12. What is the emergency radio frequency and the emergency transponder code?

13. What is the best glide speed for your airplane?

14. What would you do if you encountered moderate to severe turbulence en route?

15. What is V_a?

Discuss your solutions to these questions with your instructor. I sincerely hope none of the above ever happens to you; at least if it does, it won't catch you unprepared. Above all, if anything goes wrong, "THIMK".

Off-Airport Landings

> *Okay, it has finally happened. The engine has quit. I can't restart it, in spite of all I have tried. It isn't a fuel pump failure. I turned on the electric boost pump, and it didn't restore power. I didn't run the tank dry; I switched the tank selector immediately after turning on the boost pump. Carburetor heat On has produced no results. The mixture is still full rich, so the engine didn't starve. The primer is in and locked, so that didn't flood it out. I have tried priming and restarting, but nothing works. I wonder if I had monitored the oil pressure and the other engine gauges more closely, if they would have given me some warning?*
>
> *I am trimmed for best glide speed; that field down there looks pretty good. The wind should be out of the West, so I'll try to land that way. I'll call Homefield Tower and tell them I am going down in the South practice area. I've already set 7700 on the transponder; tower wants me to switch to 121.5 and they will work with me there. It is good to know they already have me on radar.*

Let's examine what has gone on so far. We have remained calm and evaluated the situation, troubleshooting the possibilities and attempting to restart the engine. There are several actions we have taken (or failed to take) that warrant further discussion. These concern the way we made the radio call and the possibility of stopping the prop.

I've been told that a windmilling prop creates more drag than one that has been stopped; so can't I glide farther if I stop the prop? Probably so, but I won't do that for these four reasons:

1. To stop the prop from windmilling, I would have to slow down almost to stall speed.

2. I am going to choose a field I'm sure I can glide to under ANY circumstances.

3. All my practice has been done with the propeller windmilling, and my judgment has been formed on that basis.

4. The engine may have quit due to carburetor ice, and may yet restart as I descend to warmer air. I will leave the carburetor heat on, the mixture rich, and the prop windmilling until the field is made.

I called Homefield Tower instead of switching immediately to 121.5. I already had them tuned in, and I knew somebody would hear me at once. If I had been off in the boondocks somewhere, with no radio contact I was really certain of, I would have made the Mayday call on the international distress frequency (also known as Guard) of 121.5. In our little piece of fiction, the tower told us to change frequencies. In an actual emergency they probably wouldn't risk adding to the problems of an already overloaded pilot. The point to stress is that help is where you can reach it the fastest; don't switch off somebody you already know is listening. In this case, Homefield Tower will evaluate the situation and work with you on their frequency or tell you to switch, as necessary. Next we should evaluate our choice of landing sites.

"A good landing is any landing you can walk away from." That old joke may be funny when you bounce one off of a paved runway, but it contains an element of truth concerning off-airport landings. You are probably about to "ding" an airplane. Don't worry about that. Airplanes can be replaced; it is the people that count. You can put an airplane down in some unbelievable places and still walk away. Even a tree-covered hillside is a survivable landing site, provided you FLY the airplane in—don't DROP it in. You can steer between trees so the wings take the impact and the cockpit remains intact. You may have to choose to land downwind and uphill, which is preferable to the other way around. I would rather choose a large plowed field over a smaller, firmer strip. I realize I may nose over and wreck the airplane, but I am nervous. I could misjudge a smaller field and end up with some *real* damage. That choice has to be made based on my own proficiency and the state of my nerves. Roads often look more attractive from altitude than they do closer up, as the telephone poles and power lines become visible.

Put your forward slip practice to good use if you are too high; don't commit yourself to using flaps until you are certain you have the field made. Forward slips were discussed in detail in Chapter 3. You can always discontinue a slip when you see that you are overdoing it; but with no power available, once the flaps are down you are stuck with them. Retracting flaps will cost you MORE altitude. DO select full flaps prior to touchdown. You want to make contact at the slowest possible forward speed. Double-check that seat belts and shoulder harnesses are securely fastened. Your shoulder harness may make the difference between getting somewhat shaken up or being very seriously killed. Brief your passengers as necessary.

To minimize the chance of fire, shut off the fuel selector at the tank prior to touchdown. Turn off the master switch as well, but don't forget that it will take your radios (transponder) and possibly your flaps with it, so you may want to leave it on until the last minute. Be ready to hit the ground running; get everyone clear until you determine if there is going to be fire.

There is always more than one way to accomplish anything, and your flight instructor probably has his own method for planning the approach to an off-air-port landing. This is the one that works best for me. In your mind's eye, superimpose a runway on your chosen landing site. From 5,000 feet AGL at best glide speed, you have as long as 10 minutes to get ready. That is plenty of time—so USE it! Don't pick some place 10 miles away. Decide on a nearby spot, and stick with your decision. Work to turn an unfamiliar situation into something you have practiced many times before—a normal traffic pattern. Begin a gliding spiral over the touchdown point. If you maintain best glide speed, you will lose approximately 1,000 feet of altitude per 360° turn. Plan your turns so that you roll out 1,500 feet over your touchdown point (point A, Fig. 4.8). Still maintaining best glide speed, maneuver to position yourself at point B.

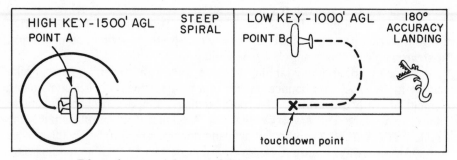

F I G. 4.8. *Planning and key positions.*

In Figure 4.8, point A is the "high key" position, which is 1,500 feet above the point of intended touchdown. Arrive there lined up as if to land. Point B is the "low key" position, directly abeam the touchdown point on a downwind leg. This approach gives you the advantage of being able to study your "run-way" more closely and, more important, NEVER putting you too far away to reach it. From point B you are set up so that you can adjust your remaining downwind, base, and final as necessary to make the planned touchdown point. This method allows you to make a few mistakes and still gives you another chance to correct them. If your off-airport landing is going to be a splashdown, you will be glad you have read the ditching procedures in the chapter on "Emergency Procedures" in AIM.

STEEP SPIRALS

The technique just discussed for setting up an emergency off-airport land-ing involves two maneuvers that are not included in the private pilot flight-test guide. One maneuver is a steep spiral, which appears in the commercial pilot flight-test guide. The other is the 180° accuracy landing, which used to be a commercial maneuver but has been dropped from that flight-test guide. Ob-viously, training at this stage for these maneuvers would be "training to exceed minimum standards." Or would you rather call it "training to assure personal safety?" Insist on some *dual instruction* in steep spirals and 180° accuracy landings. They are not only your best protection if an emergency happens, they are also great fun. The explanation sounds easy, but the performance requires proficiency and practice.

A steep spiral is nothing more than a gliding turn about a point. Airspeed control and bank control are the secrets to success. Remember the graveyard spiral and shallow the bank before applying back pressure if your airspeed starts to build. You are also doing these power "Off." Thus your airspeed is much closer to your stall speed than it was in the steep turn with power. Remember FAR 91.71, Acrobatic Flight, and complete the recovery more than 1,500 feet AGL.

180° ACCURACY LANDING

For the 180° accuracy landing, select an easily identifiable point on the runway that is some distance from the threshold, in case you touch down short. Pretend that your touchdown point is the first solid surface on the far side of a ditch full of snapping alligators. There is another ditch at the far end, so you must touch down within 200 feet beyond your point.

On downwind, slow to best glide speed, and at point B (low key position) close the throttle; now make the runway. You can maneuver, slip, or add flaps, but you *may not add power.* Once again, success will elude you without perfect airspeed control.

WARNING: *Do not attempt to practice these solo,* and certainly not off-airport. Even your flight instructor doesn't do that. It takes two pairs of eyes to look for obstructions, and it is easy to get so wrapped up in making the touchdown point that you fail to plan for the go-around. Somebody also has to remember to clear the engine once in a while; it can load up and quit. More than one embarrassed flight instructor has watched a simulated off-airport emergency suddenly turn into the real thing.

Get your instructor out of bed early enough some morning so that you will have an uncontrolled airport all to yourselves, and do your simulating there. Announce your intentions over the radio at regular intervals, and keep your head up for other traffic. Challenge your instructor to a "spot landing" contest; a little practice wouldn't hurt him or her either.

Attitude Instrument Flying

Instrument flying is a science. It requires a high degree of knowledge and proficiency. The instrument training given to private pilot applicants is sufficient to enable them to cope with the degree of precision flying required in today's airspace system UNDER VFR CONDITIONS, and it is hoped, to sustain them under IFR conditions for long enough to turn around and get out of a cloud if they should be careless enough to blunder into one. Pay attention: THIS MINIMAL INSTRUMENT TRAINING DOES NOT PREPARE YOU TO COPE WITH ACTUAL IFR WEATHER CONDITIONS. The new, low-time private pilot generally understands this. The danger in this area appears to come with time and experience (and overconfidence).

When flying under the hood, it is sometimes hard to avoid getting an occasional glimpse of the ground around the edge of the panel. This is an enormous aid to attitude control, but it completely destroys the objective. Play fair, and try to plug up all the holes with a chart or something. There is also extra *psychological* help in knowing that you can always recover the situation by simply raising your head. It would be a valuable experience if you and your instructor have the opportunity (and the equipment) to allow you to see firsthand what it is like inside an honest-to-goodness cloud.

The flight-test guide outlines the instrument maneuvers a private pilot applicant is expected to perform. The basic maneuvers are simple enough. The problems usually start when navigation and communication duties are added to the work load. Since a pilot caught in an adverse weather situation would definitely be required to cope with these added tasks, it makes sense to include them in the training programs.

Three fundamental skills are necessary for successful attitude instrument flying: instrument cross-check, instrument interpretation, and aircraft control.

1. Instrument cross-check, or instrument scan, involves a continuous visual sweep of the instrument panel; no one single instrument provides sufficient information for successful aircraft control. When the scan breaks down, it is most likely due to fixation (staring at a single instrument). The worst culprit is usually the AI. This will be the central instrument in your cross-check and the one referred to most often; but staring at it exclusively (or at any other instrument) will allow everything else to get out of hand. Having to talk on the radio or tune in a new radio frequency is another time when you need to make an extra effort to keep your scan going. Keep repeating to yourself silently, "cross-check, cross-check, cross-check—"

2. Instrument interpretation requires that you thoroughly understand each instrument and what it is indicating. You must know at a glance what control movement is necessary to produce the desired result.

3. Aircraft control by instrument reference applies the identical principles as control by outside reference, but it becomes a very delicate operation. It requires that you thoroughly understand the airplane and its reaction to airspeed, power, flap, and bank changes. The key to successful aircraft control by reference to instruments is clearly explained in the FAA's *Instrument Flying Handbook*:

> TRIM is used to relieve all possible control pressures held after a desired attitude has been attained. An improperly trimmed aircraft requires constant control pressures, produces tension, distracts your attention from cross-checking, and contributes to abrupt and erratic attitude control. The pressures you feel on the controls must be those YOU apply while controlling a planned change in aircraft attitude, not pressures held because you let the aircraft control YOU.

The primary flight instruments may be placed in three groups: those that give pitch information, those that give bank information, and those that give power information. The term "primary" is used to describe the instrument that is basic to the desired task; the value read on this primary instrument would be constant. For example, if the objective is to maintain an altitude and a heading (straight and level flight), the altimeter would be the primary pitch instrument, supported by the other pitch instruments. The HI would be the primary bank instrument, supported by the other bank instruments. The cross-check would include the two primary instruments most often, with glances at the supporting instruments for verification.

Entering a constant altitude, standard-rate turn, make the entry by reference to the AI, since it gives both pitch and bank information simultaneously. Once established in the turn, the altimeter remains primary for pitch, but the turn needle has now become primary for bank information. The pattern of your cross-check will alter to include these two primary instruments most often. Any time you make a pitch, power, or bank change, make it by reference to the AI. Speed up your cross-check until everything is stabilized in the new configuration. Keep the airplane in perfect trim.

In Chapter 2, under "Primary Flight Instruments," there were comments at the close of each instrument discussion concerning operations under the hood. This information is now consolidated in the following list of flight instruments, arranged according to their primary information group. Use the list with Figure 4.9 in your kitchen simulator and practice a scan for climbs, descents, and straight and level flight.

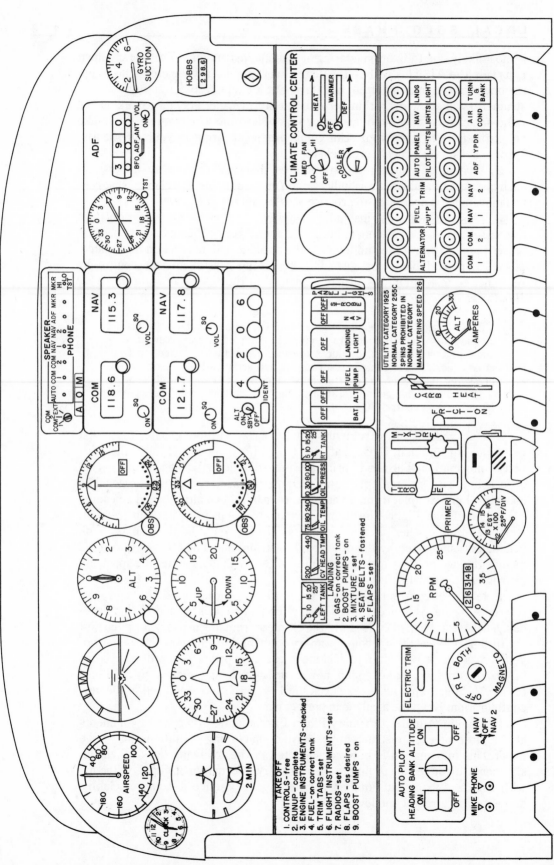

FIG. 4.9. *Instrument panel.*

Pitch instruments:

1. AI—primary during any change in pitch, bank, or power. Supports both pitch and bank in all phases of flight.

2. Altimeter—primary for pitch during level flight and in constant altitude turns. Supported by airspeed, attitude, and vertical speed.

3. ASI—primary for pitch in a constant airspeed climb or descent. Primary for power in constant airspeed flight and supports pitch in level flight and constant altitude turns.

4. VSI—primary for pitch in a constant rate climb or descent, supports pitch in level flight and in constant altitude turns.

Bank instruments:

1. AI—primary during any change in pitch, bank, or power. Supports both pitch and bank in all phases of flight.

2. HI—primary for bank in straight and level flight, and in straight-ahead climbs and descents. Supports bank in turns.

3. Turn and bank—primary for bank in turns. Supports the HI in straight flight.

Power instruments:

1. Tachometer and manifold pressure, if you have it—primary power when a specific power setting is required.

2. ASI—primary power when a specific airspeed is desired.

UNUSUAL ATTITUDES

Unusual attitudes are a device used by sadistic flight instructors to get even with you for all you have put them through. Actually, this is just an incidental side benefit and not the real purpose; but if your instructor cackles gleefully while you are turning green, I would be a little suspicious of the motive. Unusual attitudes do make many students airsick at first; so speak up quickly, before it is too late. In my airplane, the one who does it gets to clean it up.

The true objectives behind unusual attitude practice are:

1. To demonstrate that the sensations of motion that your body is telling you are happening are not to be believed.

2. To show you that the instrument indications are reliable, and that you must believe them absolutely.

3. To show you how quickly and easily you can lose control of an airplane under actual instrument conditions.

4. To teach you how to recover without tearing the wings off if you should get yourself into an unusual attitude while in a cloud.

I usually have students attempt steep turns under the hood. This is a maneuver that is required only for the instrument rating, but it generally introduces them to their first unusual attitude and convinces them to stick with standard-rate turns (or less) while flying by reference to instruments. Then I let them put themselves into their second unusual attitude in the following simple manner: Close your eyes, and maintain straight and level flight. We are usually in a well-developed graveyard spiral within 30 seconds or less if there is even minor turbulence to disturb the trim.

Your instructor will have you put your head down and close your eyes while proceeding with maneuvers to confuse the fluid in your inner ear. You will not know which end is up. Do not be alarmed—it doesn't take much. It may feel like the airplane is being turned every way but loose, when actually the maneuvers are quite mild. Visually, they would not bother you at all; they just seem exaggerated with your eyes closed, and false gravity (centrifugal force) is playing tricks with your senses. When you are convinced that you are about to disintegrate in midair, your instructor will say, "you've got it." Look up at the instrument panel—don't cheat and peek outside—and initiate the recovery. Your instructor will probably be spring loaded to the "go" position; some students' recoveries have been a lot more exciting than my unusual attitudes.

There are only two kinds of unusual attitudes: (1) nose low, high airspeed (Fig. 4.10); and (2) nose high, low airspeed (Fig. 4.11). The first instrument to refer to for information is the airspeed indicator. It tells you immediately what to do with the pitch and the throttle. You had better ignore the AI until you can

F I G.   4.10.   *Unusual attitude, nose low.*

FIG. 4.11. *Unusual attitude, nose high.*

verify that the gyro has not exceeded its limitations and tumbled. The next information you require concerns bank. You can lower the nose in a steep bank without immediate catastrophic results, but you don't want to pull back on the yoke in a high airspeed, steep-bank attitude; you can cause an accelerated stall. In either case, nose high or nose low, you still want to level the wings as soon as possible. So which way is level? Refer to the turn needle for bank information. This gyro doesn't tumble nearly as easily, since it only has one plane of rotation, whereas the AI reacts also to pitch. Your HI is useless; if that gyro didn't tumble, your instructor just wasn't trying.

Do not overcorrect. Smoothly make the necessary power correction, and place the airplane in the level-flight attitude; then wait for everything to stabilize. Even if the airspeed is very high, it will bleed off to normal if you maintain attitude. Overcorrection (or abrupt control technique) can easily lead to a brand new unusual attitude.

When your AI is out of service, either because the gyro tumbled or because it was covered up by the "no-peekie" that came from your instructor's pocket, you can still determine when the airplane's pitch attitude is level (relative to the horizon). If you look closely at the altimeter, it will pause momentarily and begin to reverse direction. At the moment the altimeter paused, the airplane passed through the level-flight attitude. The airspeed indicator also ceased increasing or decreasing, stabilized momentarily, and began to reverse its direction. Hang on to that attitude and allow the stabilizing process to complete itself.

MEMORIZE THESE PROCEDURES for unusual attitude recovery:

Nose-High, Low Airspeed   Objective: Avoid the stall
    (1) Power   (increase)
    (2) Pitch   (decrease) } simultaneously
    (3) Bank   (level)

Nose-Low, High Airspeed   Objective: Avoid overstressing the airframe
    (1) Power   (decrease)
    (2) Bank   (level)   } simultaneously
    (3) Pitch   (increase)   gently

As you continue the pursuit of perfection in the basic and advanced flight maneuvers, proceed in your home study and in the kitchen simulator to the next phase—cross-country operations.

Cross-Country Phase

5

P L A N N I N G the first dual cross-country flight has always been the area of maximum frustration to me as flight instructor. Even the student who has already learned how to use the navigation plotter and the flight computer in ground school can manage to use up from 2 to 4 hours planning a trip that will take about 1 hour to fly. He will show up at the airport ten minutes ahead of the time he has the airplane scheduled and expect to get his act together with absolutely no preliminary flight planning.

After all, you have hung around the airport long enough to have observed other pilots simply get into airplanes and go places. They didn't draw lines on charts and measure distances and true courses or write down check points and estimated times of arrival. Later on, with more experience, you will handle most of your short cross-country flights the same way; but you have to crawl before you can run. Here are a few reasons why you sometimes see me get in an airplane and go without any visible evidence of flight planning other than a call for weather and winds aloft.

There are not many places within the boundaries of my local sectional chart that I haven't been to before. I already know the distance, the terrain, the altitude I need to use, and the approximate magnetic heading that will get me there. I know what the owner's manual says my true airspeed and fuel consumption will be at the power setting and altitude I intend to use. Having checked on the winds aloft for my intended altitude, I can also make a pretty good guess at the ground speed I'm going to make, and I can therefore estimate very close to the time and fuel required for the trip.

You would see a lot more visible evidence of flight planning if the estimated time en route (ETE) was going to come anywhere close to the airplane's endurance, or if it would take me into unfamiliar territory, or if the weather wasn't too great. En route, if you don't see me frantically spinning the computer around to figure ground speed, it is because I can do it without it. I already know it is 15 miles from the freeway to the lake, and if it took me 8 minutes then I'm making close to 120 knots. I will be more careful with the estimates on a 3½ hour trip with 4 hours of fuel on board. You will NOT catch me unaware of exactly where I am every minute of the flight.

Pilotage and Dead Reckoning

Pilotage is navigating by visual reference (following highways and railroad tracks). Dead reckoning is a simple arithmetic problem involving time, speed, and distance while maintaining a constant heading from a known point. Weather permitting, you could navigate from New York to Los Angeles using nothing but pilotage; continuing from Los Angeles to Honolulu would require dead reckoning. The old navigator joke would apply: "Reckon right, or—you're dead."

It is true that the amount of flight planning and checkpoint marking that we are about to do is out of proportion to the length of the trip we are taking, but this is training. After all, we didn't set the airplane on fire to simulate an emergency, either. You will probably fly your first solo cross-country along the same route you are taking today; at least it will certainly be to someplace you have been before on another dual flight. You will find that nothing simplifies cross-country navigation more than having been there before. Don't let that stop you from proceeding with your plotter and computer and your written course log as if you had never been that route before. You will get out of your cross-country flight training exactly what you put into it: 3 hours of dual instruction in cross-country procedures is a mighty short time to touch all the areas that you need to cover.

One of the objectives of this book has been to save you money by helping you cut down on the amount of dual- and ground-instruction sessions you may require. Cross-country is the area of flight training where you can do the most on your own, and the part you do yourself is generally the part you remember best. Ask your instructor to give you the route he intends to use on your first dual cross-country flight and some copies of the course log he uses, as there are many styles of course logs.

The objective of preparing a cross-country flight plan is to ensure that the flight will be safely accomplished. One main consideration is weather; the other is the fuel supply. To determine that the fuel supply is adequate, you must determine the total time required for the flight and that you will be able to locate (and land) at the destination without wandering around lost while you burn up your reserve. This is why an experienced pilot in familiar territory, making a flight well within the endurance limits of the airplane, is really cutting no corners by failing to fill out and keep a complicated course log.

The next time you have a chance, examine the flight log on the back of the FAA's official flight-plan form. These flight logs are always available, and they are more than adequate for most cross-country operations. However, the format favors VOR navigation, and it omits the spaces for all the steps you are learning to accomplish in your training. These steps are necessary for a thorough understanding of pilotage and dead reckoning navigation. After you understand the basic steps, you can learn the shortcuts. Figure 5.1 is a sample course log, which will closely resemble the one you will use on your training flights.

STUDENT COURSE LOG

Open Flight Plan With ____________FSS on ________Mhz TIME OFF__________

Close Flight Plan With ____________FSS on ________Mhz at____________(Time or Extend)

CHECKPOINT	Freq Ident	OBS TO/FRM	PWR SETG	FUEL RATE	FUEL TOT.	ALT	TAS	TC	W/V	WCA	TH	VAR	MH	GS	Miles total	ETE total	ETA ATA

ENROUTE WEATHER/ADVISORIES	FORECASTS
AIRPORT INFORMATION/NOTAMS	FUEL LOG

FIG. 5.1. *Student course log.*

Before trying to fill in the course log, let's examine the sample and clarify some of the blanks:

1. Checkpoint—visual references on the surface.

2. Freq-Ident—VOR, if used as a checkpoint or course information.

3. OBS TO/FROM—Headings TO the station, and if it is a turning point, the new heading FROM the station.

4. Selected Power Setting.

5. Fuel Rate—in gph, at the selected power setting.

6. Fuel Total—total fuel required for the leg/trip.

7. Selected Altitude (for each leg).

8. TAS—True Airspeed at the selected altitude and power setting.

9. True Course—True North and Magnetic North are not the same. It is impossible to measure Magnetic North correctly on the chart, and True North cannot be flown by reference to the magnetic compass. So we measure the ground track with reference to True North with the plotter by using the latitude and longitude lines on the chart; then correct it to Magnetic North with reference to the lines of magnetic variation that are printed on the chart in red broken lines.

10. W/V—The forecast Wind direction and Velocity at our selected altitude.

11. WCA—Wind correction angle; the amount of heading correction (crab angle) that will keep you from drifting off the desired ground track.

12. TH—True Heading is True Course, corrected for wind.

13. VAR—Variation, the local angular difference between True North and Magnetic North.

14. MH—Magnetic Heading is True Heading corrected for variation.

15. GS—Ground Speed is True Airspeed corrected for wind.

16. ETE—Estimated Time En route.

17. ETA—Estimated Time of Arrival.

18. ATA—Actual Time of Arrival.

Our next concern is a cross-country flight–planning checklist. Gather up your course log, sectional chart, flight computer, and nav plotter, and see how far you can go on your own toward planning your first dual cross-country flight. One further word of advice: Forget statute miles; they are for cars. Figure your distances and speeds in nautical miles. Winds are always given in knots. Minutes of arc of latitude (read up and down the longitude lines on the chart) are 1 nautical mile each, 30 miles to a block. This makes for easy "eyeball measuring" when the flight is too bumpy to use the plotter easily: There is your first navigational shortcut.

Cross-Country Flight–Planning Checklist

This checklist is presented in outline form, with explanations, so that you can complete each step as you go along. At the end of the section, the outline is reprinted in short form for quick reference when planning your *next* trip. (See summary outline on p. 139.)

A.1. Study the intended route for terrain features, accessibility of alternate airports, restricted areas, nav-aids, etc. If your course is going to take you over some unfriendly looking terrain, it may improve your peace of mind to deviate a longer way around. Since there are so many small airports all over the countryside now, it is not too difficult to plan a course (at a not too unreasonable altitude) that would keep you within gliding distance of an airport on your entire route of flight. (I am not implying that this is necessary, or even desirable, but it may be possible; it would be a definite consideration at night.) If the countryside is devoid of good, definitive checkpoints, you may want to plan a course where you can use your VOR to help keep your position pinpointed. At any rate, you should be familiar with the closest alternate airports along your route, so that (in case problems should develop) you would be prepared to turn immediately in the direction that would take you to the nearest runway. You should know at all times exactly what you would do (and where you would go) if anything unforeseen arises.

A.2. Draw course line. After you have decided which way you want to go, lay the plotter on the chart and mark your ground track (Fig. 5.2).

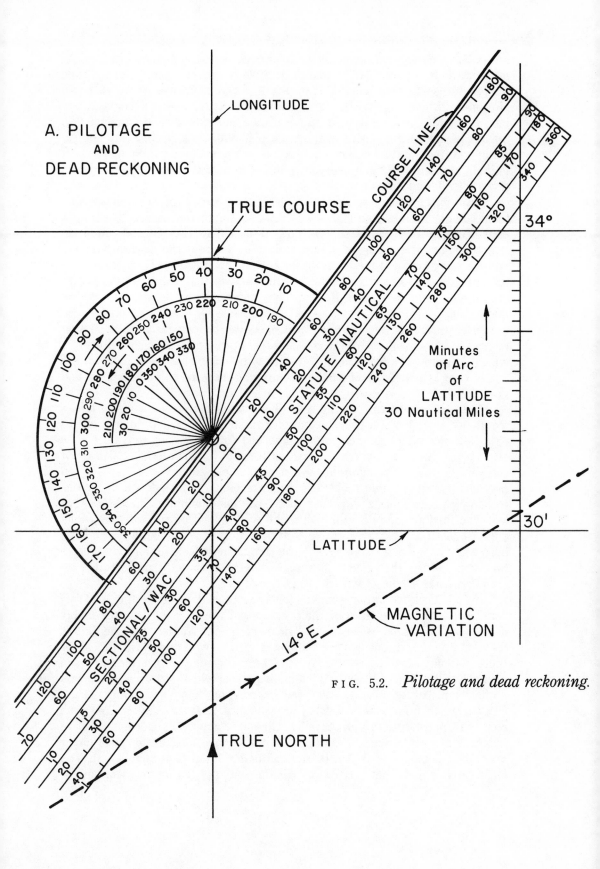

FIG. 5.2. *Pilotage and dead reckoning.*

A.3. Measure and record True Course. Figure 5.2 may help with this. As near the center of your course line as possible, locate a longitude (or latitude) line that bisects your course line. NOTE: If your course is very nearly North/South, you may not be able to position the plotter so that a longitude line bisects the 180° arc; in this case, use a latitude line instead. There is a smaller, 60° arc on the plotter, inside of the large 180° arc. On a North/South course, using a latitude line, read True Course off of the smaller arc. Suggestion: If latitude and longitude confuse you, join the club. LONG-itude goes up and down; FLAT-itude goes across.

Position the plotter so that the hole at the base of the arc is where the longitude line crosses your course line. Line up the plotter so that the straight edge is even with your course line. You can now read True Course where the longitude line bisects the arc. Use your head concerning the general direction you are going, and don't write down the reciprocal. If you are reading the plotter correctly, it should make sense. The instructions that came with the plotter should tell you how to use it. Record the results in the block of the course log under "TC."

SHORTCUT: The alert student will discover he can measure a parallel magnetic course from one of the compass roses printed on the chart. However, winds aloft forecasts are True; if you start with a magnetic course, convert the winds from True to Magnetic before computing the wind correction angle and ground speed.

A.4. Select the en route altitude. This would involve the considerations mentioned in A.1 and a little bit more. You should check approximately 10 nautical miles either side of your course line for the highest terrain and/or obstructions, in case the ceiling turns out to be lower than forecast (How low can you go, without running into something?). Over mountainous terrain you may find it very uncomfortable near the surface, due to turbulence. Whatever terrain clearance you deem proper would be your minimum altitude for that leg. The final altitude decision you make will depend on the forecast winds aloft. Choose the most comfortable altitude with the highest tail-wind (or least head-wind) component. Comply with the Hemispheric Rule for altitude separation; don't forget that if your heading changes en route, it may require an altitude change to comply with the separation rule.

A.5. Check the owner's manual for true airspeed, power setting, and fuel consumption data. Record it on the course log. True airspeed was thoroughly defined and discussed in Chapter 2. The owner's manual gives you the figures for your selected altitude and percent power setting (with fuel consumption) for flight planning purposes. NOTE: We will be doing the distance measuring in nautical miles, and the owner's manual in most older airplanes gives you nothing but statute miles for airspeed information. They are finally getting away from that in newer models, but you may need to convert your true airspeed from statute to nautical miles. On your computer, upper left side, are two little arrows marked "Naut." and "Stat." Place the statute speed under Stat. and read the conversion to nautical under Naut. (and vice versa). You can't mix apples and oranges, whether it be statute/nautical miles,

Magnetic/True headings, or degrees Fahrenheit/Celsius. This is one of the major pitfalls to watch for on the written examination.

A.6. Select and mark checkpoints. On your first dual cross-country flight, you will learn a great deal about selecting a useful visual checkpoint. For these training flights (at our dynamic speed) you should choose a checkpoint APPROXIMATELY every 10–15 miles to give you enough practice. If you choose something directly under your track, you may run over it and never see it; if it is 10 miles abeam and visibility turns out to be 7 miles, you won't see it then, either. Try to select surface features that are easily identifiable and that you can pinpoint as being exactly 90° to your course. When measuring the distances with your plotter make sure you are using the sectional scale, instead of the World Aeronautic Chart (WAC) scale, and the nautical scale, instead of the statute scale. Make a mark across your course line abeam each checkpoint. List the checkpoints on your course log, and measure and record the distance between each one. You need not write down everything you see; you will continue to use the other terrain features in flight to verify that you are still on the course line you drew. En route, use the sectional chart in two ways: (1) find a large object on the chart, and locate it on the ground; (2) find a large object on the ground, and locate it on the chart. Correct back to the track if you have drifted off. Terrain features such as mountain peaks (with the elevations not only printed on, but also color-shaded) appear to be vastly underrated by student pilots; in flight, you will find that they are among the most easily recognizable chart features.

A.7. Estimate and mark the point of level off (top-of-climb). Refer to Chapter 2 and the discussion on primary flight maneuvers for a refresher on figuring top-of-climb. You may want to pick a good visual reference (like a four-lane highway) to follow while you are climbing. Locate another good reference to use to get yourself on track immediately after you level off. Forward visibility is limited in the climb attitude, and cockpit work load is high during the departure. You have more traffic to search for in the vicinity of the airport, and you must maneuver yourself into the direction of departure. You also need to note your takeoff time and contact Flight Service to activate your VFR flight plan. Don't get lost 5 miles out.

A.8. Estimate and mark the time of beginning descent. When approaching an unfamiliar airport, it is good practice to maintain at least 3,000 feet AGL until you are sure you are looking at the right airport. It is very embarrassing to be talking to one tower while landing somewhere else. In the beginning you may want to stay at an altitude where you can safely (and legally) overfly the field and read the name off the runway. At airports with multiple runways, you may want to look down to determine what direction the pattern is, before you get too involved. You will really feel smug about your navigation when you can begin an en route descent and smoothly slide into the downwind leg at the proper altitude without any donkeying around. It will save a lot of stuttering over the radio if you plan your initial call (with position report) in advance.

A.9. Look up the destination airports in AIM's *Airport/Facility Directory* and record pertinent data on the course log. This data would include: radio frequencies, traffic pattern altitude, nonstandard traffic patterns, obstructions, runway numbers, and availability of fuel and services. With this information, now would be the time to check the runway length with the density altitude performance graphs. NOTE: There are a number of outstanding but unofficial publications on the market that give airport information, including a graphic depiction of the runway and taxiway layout. Ask your instructor to recommend the one that is the best for your area. A picture of the airport is really a great aid to orientation if the airport is unfamiliar. Generally, I don't have much trouble in flight, but I surely can get lost among the taxiways. Don't be bashful about asking ground control for directions.

A.10. Study the areas of both departure and destination airports, looking for any special problems you could encounter in avoiding terrain, other airport traffic areas, etc. If there is another tower airport close to your departure field, it may be necessary to communicate with that tower if your direction of departure infringes on its airspace. Plan your departure to avoid it, or plan to call for clearance through the area. This means juggling radios at a very busy time. You should cast a wary eye on the runway direction at these adjacent airports, even if you will remain well clear of their airspace. An arriving 747 may cross your departure path heading for the other airport. These are the kinds of considerations you can't be expected to be on the lookout for without some more experience. Your instructor will check your flight plan and point out any potential problem spots you may have overlooked.

A.11. Plan and mark the point en route at which you begin to listen to ATIS, tune in the tower, and plan the approach. This point should be at least 25 miles from the destination airport; it may or may not coincide with the point of beginning descent. Tune in the airport information frequency as early as you can receive it. The sooner you have the airport and runway information so you can plan the approach (and your radio call), the smoother it will go. I find that students get so involved with navigation they forget they are going to have to land when they locate the airport. That is why I recommend marking on the chart (or on your course log) as a reminder to start listening and/or descending.

There are a few more blanks in the course log that you can fill in before you get the current weather. The compass variation won't change, and neither will the deviation. The broken red lines on the sectional chart depict the lines of magnetic variation; remember "East is least, and West is best" when converting from True to Magnetic. Apply the opposite correction when converting from Magnetic to True; that is how you get the shortcut mentioned earlier. Deviation (found on the compass correction card in the airplane) was discussed in the section on the magnetic compass in Chapter 2. It is usually not more than 2° or 3°, and for practical purposes, forget it. You won't hold a heading accurately enough to notice, anyway. It might get you a wrong answer on the written test, so remember it for at least that long.

The remaining checklist items would necessarily be completed after you call FSS for your weather briefing. You already have enough information concerning the time required for the trip to know whether or not you need to plan a fuel stop. We will press on with the checklist, using fictitious weather information when necessary for examples.

B.1. Check terminal and en route weather. When you call the FSS, tell the briefer that this is a student-dual cross-country flight, your make and model airplane, and your "N" number. He will also need to know your departure and destination airports, your planned departure time, and intended altitude. Assuming (I hope) that there will be no significant weather, you will still write down the forecast winds aloft and their direction and velocity. Winds aloft forecasts are issued with the direction relative to True North, the velocity in knots, and the altitude above MSL. The accompanying temperatures are in degrees Celsius. These forecasts are measured at 3,000, 6,000, 9,000, 12,000, 24,000, 30,000, 34,000, and 39,000 feet. The first level for which winds aloft forecasts are issued is 1,500 feet above the surface; the temperatures start being included at 2,500 feet above station level. You can interpolate the wind direction and velocity for your planned altitude.

B.2. Check Notices to Airmen (NOTAMS). Flight Service probably checked this for you, even if you failed to ask. NOTAMS might include such items as "runway 18/36 closed for construction," or "Destination VOR shut down for maintenance," as well as the times and dates of closure.

B.3. Estimate and record ground speed, True Heading, and time en route, using forecast winds aloft. Whip out your flight computer, study the wind face (the side with the clear plastic window), and work this example: Your true airspeed will be 90 knots (at your chosen altitude and power setting), and your True Course is 330; the winds aloft are forecast from 270 at 20 knots.

   a) Rotate the inner scale and place the wind (270) under the True Index (marked at the top).

   b) Move the slide so that the "grommet" (the little circle in the center of the wind face) is on any one of the heavy black horizontal lines, and leave it there for the next step.

   c) Move up from the grommet (toward True Index), count the wind velocity (20 knots) and place a small x on the clear plastic wind face directly on the vertical centerline. Each "block" represents 10 knots and the smaller lines are 2 knots each.

   d) Rotate the inner scale to place your True Course (330) under the True Index.

   e) Move the slide so that your wind dot (the x you made) is on the true airspeed line (90 knots).

B.4. Correcting True Course for wind gives True Heading; correcting True Heading for variation gives Magnetic Course. Correcting Magnetic Course for deviation gives Magnetic Heading (or compass heading). You are now looking at a picture of the wind direction as it will affect your track. If the grommet is your airplane, and the centerline is your track (330°), you have a quartering head wind from the left (the x is the wind). The wind dot is 12° left of your track; the wind correction angle will be $-12°$. Always subtract a left correction and add a right correction. The ground speed is under the grommet—a dizzy 78 knots. Enter the −12 under WCA, and your True Heading is 318. Subtract (or add) the variation and you have Magnetic Course. The course log we are using has left out a step—the compass deviation. You have to look at the compass correction card in your airplane to get deviation, and it shouldn't be more than ±2° or 3°. We have skipped deviation and pretended that your Magnetic Course and Magnetic Heading will be the same. If you wish to adjust this column before you start your engine, do so.

B.5. Fill in the course log with the estimated time to each checkpoint. Flip over the computer and place the heavy black triangle (the Speed Index) under your ground speed (78 knots). We are now going to compute time, speed, and distance. If you know any two of those three items, the computer will supply you with the third one, free of charge. There are other tricks your flight computer can do, including true airspeed and density altitude computations, time to climb, mach number, etc. It would be very difficult for the average person to learn how to use the flight computer from a book. It is nothing but a round slide rule and is simple to use, but there are a few pitfalls involved in reading the various scales correctly. You will probably need a ground session with your instructor (or a formal ground-school session) to learn all the various uses of the computer, but we will include a few examples here to jog your memory while you are practicing at home.

The outer (fixed) scale is miles, and the inner (rotating) scale is time. The Speed Index is located on 1 hour (60 minutes.) We know the speed and the distance; we are looking for time. We are going 78 miles in one hour (speed); that is set in. You have measured the distance between checkpoints; assume the first one is 14 miles. Locate the 14 on the miles scale and read the minutes underneath it on the time scale. Directly below the 14, it says "almost 11 minutes." Close enough. Enter that information on the ETE column of your course log.

En route, when you note your ATA at each checkpoint and enter it in the course log, you may find that the time was not what you estimated (ETA). Suppose we covered the 14 miles in exactly 10 minutes, instead of 11. Place 10 minutes under 14 miles; we know the distance and the time, and now we are looking for speed. The Speed Index tells us that our ground speed is really 84 knots, so we need to adjust our estimates accordingly. Exercise care with your timing. As close together as these checkpoints are, an error of 15 seconds timing can make a considerable difference in the ground-speed estimate.

B.6. Figure fuel consumption, and plan fuel stops. If we expect to burn 5 gph, place the hour (Speed Index) under the 5. (It actually says 50, but it works the same way). If we expect to fly for 2½ hours, locate the time (2:30) on the inner scale. Above it, read 12.5 gallons of gas. Read your total endurance time under the usable fuel capacity of the airplane (22.5 gal, at 5 gph, equals 4:30, no reserve).

FAR 91.22 states that no pilot may begin a VFR flight unless he has enough fuel to get to the destination and land in the daytime with a 30 minute reserve and a 45-minute reserve at night. This regulation makes sense. Bear in mind that book figures on fuel consumption are at their most optimistic. Extra reserves lend greater peace of mind.

B.7. File your VFR flight plan, noting the FSSs (and the r̶ cies) with which you will open and close. Make an additional note time you filed for, so that you can call and extend your time if nece

B.8. Have a nice flight. In the next section, we will fly th country you have planned in the kitchen simulator.

SUMMARY OUTLINE: CROSS-COUNTRY FLIGHT-PLANNING CHECKLIST

A. Complete the following steps prior to arrival at the airport:
   1. Study the intended route for terrain features, accessibility of alternate airports, restricted areas, nav-aids, etc.
   2. Draw course line.
   3. Measure and record True Course.
   4. Select the en route altitude.
   5. Check the owner's manual for true airspeed, power setting, and fuel consumption data. Record it on the course log.
   6. Select and mark checkpoints.
   7. Estimate and mark the point of level off, TOC.
   8. Estimate and mark the point of beginning descent.
   9. Look up the destination airports in AIM's *Airport/Facility Directory* and record pertinent data on the course log. (Refer to A.9.*a* through *f*.)
   10. Study areas of both departure and destination airports, looking for any special problems you could encounter in avoiding terrain, other airport traffic areas, etc.
   11. Plan and mark the point en route at which you begin to listen to ATIS, tune in the tower, and plan the approach.
B. Complete the following steps just prior to the flight:
   1. Check terminal and en route weather.
   2. Check NOTAMS.
   3. Estimate and record ground speed, True Heading, and time en route, using forecast winds aloft. (Refer to B.3*a* through *e*.)
   4. Correcting True Course for wind gives True Heading; correcting True Heading for variation gives Magnetic Course. Correcting Magnetic Course for Deviation gives Magnetic Heading (or compass Heading).
   5. Fill in the course log with the estimated time to each checkpoint.
   6. Figure fuel consumption, and plan fuel stops.
   7. File a flight plan, noting where to open and close and when to extend (if necessary).
   8. Have a nice flight.

Flying the Cross-Country

The first dual cross-country flight involves so much that is new that a poorly prepared student gains almost nothing from the experience (except an awareness that he was poorly prepared). This first cross-country is mostly pilotage and dead reckoning, with perhaps one leg, or portion of a leg, devoted to VOR navigation. Trying to go to a TCA or a TRSA or deal with en route radar service is too much of a work load at this point. In the cross-country dual time remaining, it would be a shame not to include these experiences. However, if we don't get the pilotage and dead reckoning procedures pretty securely nailed down on this first flight, you won't be ready to add these extra tasks next time, either. Some degree of expertise with the flight computer will lighten your load considerably and free your attention for other aspects of cross-country experience. Another tremendous aid is a well-organized cockpit. Fold the chart so that you can follow your course, and promote some sort of clipboard arrangement so that you can fill in your course log. It is hilarious to watch the airplane turn 90° to the course and dive 400 feet, while the student is groping under the seat for a computer and a pencil. In your kitchen simulator, mentally confine yourself to the space you will have available in the airplane, and organize your supplies accordingly.

Cockpit organized, run up complete, and ready for takeoff—almost. Set radio frequencies and VOR courses to the ones you will need first. Review these items just prior to calling for takeoff:

1. Method of departure (left turn, right turn, downwind departure).
2. Magnetic Heading for the first leg.
3. Any immediate changes of radio frequencies and/or calls.
4. First checkpoint.

You are ready to get off in the right direction smoothly and efficiently. NOTE YOUR TAKEOFF TIME and enter it on the log. Compute (in your head) the ETA to the first checkpoint.

As soon as you are established on course and clear of the airport traffic area, call Flight Service and activate your flight plan. Rehearse the call now, because you will feel pretty busy when the time comes. If your flight calls for changing to another tower for clearance through the area, rehearse those calls as well.

One of the difficulties you must overcome is a very narrow attention span. During your first few dual flights, your hands were so full of airplane that you didn't notice much of what was going on outside—including where you were or other traffic in your vicinity. On the first cross-country, your hands will be full of charts, logs, and computers, and you will have a strong tendency to bury your head in the cockpit, leaving other traffic to look out for itself. You don't really want that! When you need to spend a few seconds studying the chart, raise it to eye level instead of leaving it down in your lap. In this way you can continue to scan outside for other traffic. Trim the airplane for hands off, and turn it loose when you must spend a few moments with your log or your computer. If you continue to hold the yoke, I guarantee you will inadvertently exert enough pressure to cause a turn off course.

Leaning the mixture is necessary to the efficient performance of the airplane. An important point to remember is that the fuel consumption data in your owner's manual is based on a perfectly leaned mixture; if yours is running too rich, you are burning more fuel than you expected. If your airplane is equipped with an Exhaust Gas Temperature (EGT) gauge, leaning to the perfect temperature is easy. Light trainers are usually not equipped with this handy added gadget, so you have to guess. The fuel consumption and range data may also fail to include the amount of fuel needed for taxi, run up, and the full-power climb to altitude. These are valid reasons for the 30-minute fuel reserve.

To lean the mixture, slowly pull the mixture control knob out and listen carefully to the engine noise. When it begins to sound a little rough, advance the mixture control until the engine sound smooths back out. You might see an increase to "peak" on the rpm, but it is so slight that you will do better by listening. Monitor the temperature gauges; if you have overleaned, you will overheat, and this may cause damaging detonation in the cylinders. Don't forget to increase the mixture in the descent. If you were properly leaned for 7,000 feet, it will be too lean when you come down to 5,000 feet.

Lean for the best mixture at ANY altitude if you are cruising below 75% power. Leaning in the climb will also be necessary if you are going very high. As a rule of thumb, begin leaning the mixture in a climb at 5,000 feet (density altitude). Monitor the temperatures—the airflow is not cooling the engine as efficiently at the lower climb airspeed. If the density altitude at your departure airport is over 5,000 feet, *you will need to lean the mixture for takeoff* if you expect to get maximum performance.

There is one additional point I want to emphasize concerning fuel consumption. You have a power setting for best performance (fastest true airspeed), which will be 70–75% power and will burn the most fuel. You also have a power setting for best economy, which will be around 55% power, resulting in a somewhat slower speed and a considerable reduction in fuel consumption.

The percentage of power being developed is what is going to determine fuel consumption. Developing 65% power at 2,500 feet and 65% power at 7,500 feet will result in very nearly the same fuel consumption; but it will not result in the same rpm or true airspeed at those altitudes. Example: The owner's manual for 3567 Victor, the fastest Cessna 150 in the West (vintage 1975), states that we can develop 65% power at 2,500 feet by setting 2,500 on the rpm, resulting in a true airspeed of 110 knots and a fuel rate of 4.8 gph. At 7,500 feet and 65% power, the fuel rate is still 4.8 gph, but the true airspeed is 114 knots and the rpm must advance to 2,600. If I flew with that power setting at 2,500 feet, the "mean green machine's" performance would be: 72% power, 116 knots, and 5.4 gph.

I normally plan to cruise at 65–70% power. Carry the manual in the airplane and refer to it whenever you make a drastic altitude change, adjusting your cruise power setting accordingly. If you know the sea level rpm that will develop 70% (or any other specific percent power), a good rule of thumb to maintain that percent power is: Increase the sea level rpm by 25 rpm for every 1,000 feet of altitude gained. The above example from the manual is a 5,000-foot altitude increase, and it checks out as a 125-rpm power increase. That would be 2,625 (which is probably more than I can get with full throttle at that altitude, anyway).

The following is an example of how to keep your course log while en route: If you pass abeam your first checkpoint at 12 minutes past the hour (clock time), write down :12 in your ATA block. If your ETE to the next checkpoint is 9 minutes, write down the clock time (:21) in the ETA block. When you get there, if you arrive at 21 minutes past the hour, you are right on schedule and your ground-speed estimate was correct. If the ETA and the ATA are different, compute the ground-speed correction and fudge accordingly on your other estimates. If you received a halfway accurate wind forecast, they should be pretty close. Get an accurate ground-speed check as early in the flight as possible, and figure your ETA at the destination. If fuel is going to be no problem, the experienced pilot now puts away his computer, but the student continues to practice. NOTE: You are working with very short distances in the interest of training. Be as accurate as possible because errors in timing will be more significant than on longer legs. Don't let it blow your confidence. A 15-*second* difference in 10 miles will have a noticeable effect on your estimates.

Keep up with your course log, writing down the ETA at the next checkpoint as soon as you have the actual time at the last one. REASON: If you cannot locate a checkpoint in flight, do not panic. You can easily become distracted (or choose a poor checkpoint) and pass one by without seeing it. You planned the flight; now fly the plan. This means continue on your heading and TIME; the next checkpoint can't be far away. The worst mistake you can make is to start flying in circles hunting for a checkpoint, drifting farther off course and losing your timing.

You have the time at the last known position written down, and you know your ground speed. If you have maintained a constant heading, your position on the chart is a matter of simple arithmetic, and you have a computer to do your figuring for you: Time, speed, and distance.

Overrunning one checkpoint en route is one thing; overrunning the destination airport without seeing it is something else again. If you started your descent on schedule, the nose-low attitude will contribute to your search for the field. When you study the destination on the chart, locate a fine outstanding surface feature you can't possibly overlook (such as a major highway or a mountain range) that is just BEYOND your destination. If your ETA runs out on the clock, and this "last ditch" checkpoint shows up below you, now it is time for some circling—but not AIMLESS circling. Circle with a PLAN.

There is bound to be a VOR station within a few miles of your destination airport. *Assuming you have a couple of hours* of fuel remaining, you could try "Plan A," VOR tracking. Tune and identify the station, center the OBS with a TO indication, and track directly to the station. On the way, lay the plotter on the chart and determine the radial that goes directly over the destination airport. Over the VOR station, set that radial on the OBS, turn to that heading, and fly the radial FROM the station. You can eyeball the distance with reference to the minutes of arc of latitude and estimate the time. (This is assuming good weather and an altitude at or above 3,000 feet AGL, in addition to more than adequate fuel.)

If "Plan A" fails, don't hesitate to activate "Plan B"—that is, call for help. You have the frequency on your course log (and also on your chart) over which to contact Flight Service. Confess your predicament, and be directed to the airport with a DF Steer or radar vectors. Ask for a "flight assist." This does not constitute "declaring an emergency." This is why the services are available, and they get used every day. The emergency arises when the initial call is postponed to the point of fuel exhaustion; this requires a word of explanation to the FAA. "Plan B" is still available en route through any FSS or over 121.5.

There are several other tasks involving en route procedures that you can accomplish to fill the idle hours. Regularly monitor your engine gauges; reset the HI to coincide with the magnetic compass; periodically check for carburetor ice, whether you suspect it or not. Have your instructor show you how to figure true airspeed and density altitude on the flight computer. Checking the actual performance against the book's predictions while en route is sensible practice, and you could have some adjustments to make. In an airplane you are constantly checking something and then rechecking it; the pilot who doesn't take his flying seriously is the one who becomes a statistic. Remember Murphy's Law: "If anything can possibly go wrong—."

Now is your chance to practice a skill that you will be asked to demonstrate for the flight examiner. Simulating an en route emergency, you will deviate from your present position to the nearest alternate airport. This is where the shortcuts come in handy. You can turn immediately to the approximate Magnetic Heading by referring to any compass rose printed on the chart. Measure a "quick and dirty" distance by fingering the mileage scale on the longitude line; you already know your groundspeed, so make a reasonable adjustment for the wind direction and come up with an ETA based on "two miles per minute." If you are going 120, your time is exactly half of the distance. If you are closer to 90, the time is half plus half. You don't need a plotter or a computer. In a real emergency, you would be too busy for that anyway. The examiner will certainly be impressed, and you will be well on your way toward simple, easy navigation—the safe kind.

In any airplane with two or more separate fuel-tank selectors, you must keep another careful log en route of the time and endurance on each fuel tank. Fuel mismanagement is second only to weather as a major cause of airplane accidents. This is an aspect that the Cessna 150 drivers don't have to deal with nearly so much, so they had better pay special attention for when they upgrade to a larger airplane.

Burning fuel out of one side only will cause your airplane to become wing heavy on the opposite side after an hour or so; the airplane wants to enter a gentle bank toward the heavy wing whenever you let go of the yoke. ESTABLISH A PROCEDURE for fuel management. How many gallons of gas you have left in a tank is important only as it relates to TIME. Keep your fuel log in minutes (or hours) and always know the amount of time you have used up from each tank, and therefore how much time you have remaining. The simpler the procedure that you establish, the easier it is to keep track of. Example: Depart on the left tank, and remain on it for 1 hour; switch to the right tank, and remain on it for 2 hours. If you are going to fly to the limit of your endurance (with reserve), plan to leave most of the remaining fuel in one tank, instead of evenly split between the two. The fuller tank is the one you will select for the landing, in case you have to execute a go-around.

This method is easy to remember, since you know your takeoff time. When you switch tanks 1 hour out and find the number two tank is clogged at the fuel line, you have enough left in number one to return to where you started. Deliberately running a fuel tank completely dry in flight is stupid; if you fail to get a restart when you switch tanks—you earned it. The simplest of all possible fuel logs consists of a check mark at your position on the chart at the time you made the switch (on the hour after departure). All the information you need to compute it over again is right there if you need it; but if you are thinking as you fly, you probably won't need any more than your established procedure.

While you are en route, think about where you are. I realize that is the object of this exercise and that you can put your finger on your exact position on the chart. If your engine quits and you have to report your position to Search and Rescue, you can't just say, "I'm right here." Verbalize your position occasionally, if only to yourself. Reporting "10 miles Southeast of Sun City," or "the Oceanside 030° radial, 15 miles" would be a lot more helpful.

Now is the time to discuss using a VOR intersection as a checkpoint. Locate a VOR station off to the side of your course line, and use your plotter to draw a line from the station to intersect your course line at the position you wish to pinpoint. Tune and identify the station, and rotate the OBS so that the number of the desired radial is set in; you will have a FROM indication. If the station is to the right of your course line and you have not yet crossed the radial, then you will have a full right needle deflection. If the station is on your left, you will have a full left deflection. MEMORIZE THIS RULE: With a FROM indication, if you have not yet crossed the radial, the needle will point in the direction of the station. As you approach the radial, the needle will move and center at your checkpoint, then continue to a full deflection on the other side, pointing *away* from the station. It may move fairly fast if you are relatively near the station and crossing the radial at close to 90°.

If you have only one VOR receiver in the airplane that you are using to track directly to a station, it is still easy to use the "intersection" procedure to triangulate and pinpoint your position. Maintain the heading you have established to hold the radial you are tracking; tune the intersecting VOR and center the needle with a FROM indication to find your position; then tune the first station back in again. If you held your heading, you should still be on course.

Flying your first genuine cross-country flight plan mile-for-mile in your kitchen simulator will assist you to a degree that you will not realize until AFTER you have actually flown it. Work your simulated computer problems until you can figure them smoothly (and know where to record the solutions). The kitchen simulator is cooperating by *holding still*.

At this point I would like to issue you a personal challenge involving another "goal" in the continuing series of challenges you have met up to this point in your training. The challenge (I dare you):

From a point 25 miles from your destination airport tell your instructor to shut up; accept no further "mouth" from him or her until you are wondering where to park. (Clue your instructor in first; there may be a violent reaction to being gagged.)

YOUR GROUND RULES: It is fair to ask *before takeoff* for specific advice about how to handle communications and the approach. Once that 25-mile mark is reached, no more talk. If you ask a question, you "blew" it.

INSTRUCTOR GROUND RULES: Your instructor is allowed to save you from midair collisions, serious FAA violations, and fuel exhaustion. Your instructor is also allowed to debrief you, so long as it doesn't get too physical. It beats learning solo.

Written Examination

Unless you have done a lot of self-study on the regulations (and weather), you are not quite ready to take the written test.

Turn to the table of contents of your copy of AIM. If you have marked up your copy as you did the FARs, you should find you have covered Chapter 1, "Navigation Aids." You need to read Chapter 2, "Airport, Air Navigation Lighting, and Marking Aids" prior to night operations. You should have done a pretty thorough job of Chapter 3, "Airspace," when we covered it in Chapter 2 of this book. You have also been referred to Chapter 5, "Emergency Procedures."

In Chapter 6, "Safety of Flight," skip section 1 on meteorology; that subject will be studied in the weather section of this chapter. Concentrate on the other sections listed in Chapter 6, as well as Chapter 7, "Medical Facts for Pilots." Chapter 8, "Aeronautical Charts and Related Publications," need not be studied but be aware that this information is available there. Look through the Pilot Controller Glossary in the back of AIM. If you haven't discovered it already, you may find it very interesting.

To help you review the FARs, let me restate some regulations for clarity:

To act as pilot in command of an aircraft—even solo (not carrying passengers) you must have:

1. A current class I, II, or III medical certificate (carried on your person). Any class medical carried for private pilot privileges expires at the end of the twenty-fourth *calendar* month. If you got your medical on January 1, 1982, it will expire on January 31, 1984.

2. Your private pilot certificate, carried with you. This is valid so long as you have a current medical and you keep up notification of name/address changes by writing Oklahoma City within 30 days of the change. When you receive your permanent certificate in the mail, be sure and sign it or it isn't valid.

3. A logbook endorsement by a Certificated Flight Instructor (CFI) that you have satisfactorily completed a BFR. This endorsement expires at the end of 24 months from the actual date of the BFR, not at the end of that month. You cannot operate solo without it. A successful flight check for a new certificate or rating will substitute for the BFR.

You must comply with the following for passenger-carrying privileges:

DAY: within the last 90 days, you must have *logged* 3 takeoffs and landings (either full stops or touch-and-goes) in an airplane of the same category and class. This means any single-engine land airplane, with one exception: If the airplane is a tail dragger, the landings must be in a tail dragger and must be full-stop landings.

NIGHT: during the last 90 days, you must have *logged* 3 takeoffs and landings *to a full stop* in a single-engine land airplane. "Night" starts 1 hour after sunset and ends 1 hour before sunrise.

Miscellaneous review:

1. Allow 8 hours from bottle to throttle.

2. Turn position lights on from sunset to sunrise.

3. Fasten seat belts. Fasten shoulder harnesses (if installed) for takeoffs and landings. Brief your passengers on how to get loose.

4. Review ARROW for aircraft documents (Chapter 1, under Walk-Around Inspection).

5. Check that the airplane is in a current annual inspection and in a 100-hour inspection if operated for hire. It must have an ELT, and the batteries expire after 1 hour of use or 50% of their useful life. Transponder and pitot-static inspections are good for 24 *calendar* months.

6. Observe oxygen requirements: 12,500 to 14,000 for 30 minutes; 14,000 for crew; 15,000 for everybody.

7. Review all of the regulations you highlighted in your FARs.

Consult your copy of *Private Pilot—Airplane: Written Test Guide*. It contains the actual (verbatim) test questions used in the FAA written examination. The first few pages explain the test fully. Refer to the study outline provided in the guide and you should be ready to work your way through the book, with the exception of aviation weather and possibly some of the questions that pertain to complex airplanes and fuel-injection systems.

You are not more than a few (if any) flights away from solo cross-country and (weather permitting) only a few weeks away from flight check. Do not procrastinate; get the written test accomplished. Set yourself a goal of a specific date and stick to it. It's a shame to see a potentially good pilot turn into a "professional student" because he is afraid of the written test. When I took the private pilot written exam, I had not taken a written test in ten years. Dreading it was a lot worse than actually taking it turned out to be.

Work through the test guide and see what you need to review (probably airspace and regulations). Continue with me through the weather section, and complete the test guide. Ask your instructor for an endorsement to take the test, then go get it over with. The relief will be tremendous. You may surprise yourself and ace it.

Night Operations

A night flight can be the most delightful experience you have in an airplane or it can turn into a *nightmare*. There are many pilots who go so far as to say that an instrument rating should be a requirement for night cross-country operations; I wouldn't go quite that far, but there is no doubt that a great deal of extra care in flight planning and weather checking is necessary for a safe night operation, even for a *local* night flight.

Any flight begins with a weather check. Your own minimum standards for weather conditions in the daytime will not be high enough for night operations. A severe clear night with a big bright moon is almost like flying during the day, but an overcast condition (even at 10,000 feet or more) will change that considerably.

At this point some weather definitions should be memorized. A "ceiling" is the lowest *broken* cloud layer not classified as "thin." A "scattered" cloud layer does not constitute a ceiling. As reported in the forecast, the base of the clouds will be AGL; more about that in the weather section. Although a scattered cloud layer is not an "official ceiling," you should consider it one at night (especially if there is a higher overcast) and plan any flight below that layer; you can't see clouds coming at you in the dark. For the same reason, if there is precipitation of ANY kind in the forecast, stay home.

Another major consideration in night weather is ground fog. Essential here is an explanation of another important term, DEW POINT. Based on the present humidity, if the air cools to this mathematically computed temperature, the air will contract enough to squeeze out its moisture. The result is fog. The forecast will include the temperature/dew point spread. If the temperature is 65°F and the dew point is 60°, that means danger and you need to know the "trend." If it is near dawn and the temperature is rising, visibility should be okay; but if it cools down to 60°, it may be "socked in" for miles around. You are asking for trouble at night if the temperature/dew-point spread is within 5°.

We will discuss various types of fog in the weather section in this chapter, but if you are suspicious of fog developing while you are in flight, land immediately. Fog is very tricky. Looking straight down, the lights begin to appear slightly fuzzy, but it doesn't look too bad yet because you are ABOVE it, not IN it. When you descend into the fog, it will look considerably worse, and the world may disappear completely. The worst things about fog are its suddenness and its size. Once fog starts forming, it finishes the job fast and may blanket hundreds of miles; you could run out of gas heading for a clear airfield. Fog is not limited to nighttime, either. But since it is associated with falling temperatures, it is more likely in the dark.

Preflight the airplane with extra care, also checking the position lights and the panel lights. FAR 91.73 states that position lights will be turned on from sunset to sunrise, and FAR 61.57 gives the night landing requirement for carrying passengers. Notice that you can count as nighttime only those hours from 1 hour after official sunset to 1 hour before official sunrise.

Be certain you have a good, reliable flashlight on board. I once took off in the late afternoon in an airplane I had flown many times before, knowing I would arrive at my destination well after dark. The sun had gone down before I realized I had no panel lights whatsoever. They are not bright enough to see if you depart in the daytime.

Night vision is different from day vision. The retina of your eye has two kinds of cells: "cones," which are located in the center of the retina, and "rods," which form a ring around the cones. In the light you are using the cones, and in the dark the rods are doing the work. The cones in the center also determine your color perception, so colors are more difficult to distinguish at night. The main point is, the ring of rods you see with at night leaves you with a blind spot in the center of your gaze; so scan more for traffic and avoid staring fixedly in one spot. The decreasing oxygen supply as you climb will also seriously impair night vision, as will smoking. Avoid long periods above 5,000 feet unless you have supplemental oxygen on board. Smoking doesn't mix well with airplanes anyway.

There are many optical illusions at night—some you almost have to see to believe: a stationary light that moves all over the place; sparse surface lights that cannot be distinguished from the stars; the phenomenon sheepishly (or belligerently) reported by many military and airline crews—UFOs. I would sort of like to believe they aren't all optical illusions!

Choose your route and your altitude, exercising extra care as you consider the terrain. You may want to go a few extra miles to follow a good highway. For your checkpoints, you will have to rely far more heavily on the VOR and the intersection procedure; one batch of lights looks pretty much like any other. Dead reckoning and radio navigation will be more valuable than pilotage. If you memorize radio frequencies and courses, maybe you won't have to fly along with a flashlight in your mouth and wreck your night vision while you hunt on the chart for essential information.

Research the facilities at your destination and any en route stops. Most line-service people pack up and go home for dinner, and they charge extra to return to the airport to gas you up—if they will come at all. Airplanes are great for flying, but they are lousy for sleeping. Don't forget your fuel reserve at night must be 45 minutes.

Check on the kind of lighting at your destination. If there is no rotating beacon, the field will be harder to find. Sometimes runway lights are turned off to save energy and must be activated by keying the mike on a specified frequency. Many tower airports become uncontrolled fields after 10 or 11 o'clock at night, so plan your procedures accordingly. Check the obstructions *very* carefully. I do not like to go into a small airport at night if I have not seen it previously in the daytime. I have done so and been horrified the next morning.

Altitude can be crucial, so make certain that your altimeter is properly set to the current barometric pressure. Rely more on your altimeter in the traffic pattern; depth perception is difficult at night due to the lack of references. A long, straight-in final is especially deceiving. Use a few extra minutes to set up a downwind, base, and final. Visual Approach Slope Indicator (VASI) lights at your destination would be most welcome.

You will log at least 3 hours of night dual, including at least 10 takeoffs and landings (if you are training under Part 61). During these landings, you will find out about depth perception in the dark. You will carry power to the runway and close the throttle slowly. Feel for the pavement with the power; most night touchdowns come as a surprise. Landing lights are very high-powered bulbs, and they burn out regularly; I have lost them any number of times. Be sure to make several of your night landings with the landing light turned off. It isn't difficult; then you won't panic the first time you lose yours solo.

Just as you will rely more heavily on radio navigation for flight in the night, you will also depend more on instruments for attitude control. Don't let the optical illusions put you upside down. If you are taking off toward a very dark area (such as a lake), as soon as you rotate you are on instruments. There may be no visual reference at all; be ready and go on the gauges.

Build night-flying experience with some local flights before tackling anything too ambitious. Make your first night cross-country to some place familiar; or else plan it *from* somewhere, with Homefield as the dark destination. ABOVE ALL, avoid what seems to be a serious problem to some night pilots—booze. They take their friends to dinner at some really neat airport restaurant; many of these are great fun and loaded with flying atmosphere. The pilot ends up loaded as well, and on the way home he kills his friends.

Closely monitor your engine gauges and check for carburetor ice; it is more likely to occur in the cooler night air. An engine failure at night is a terrifying thought. You can do everything in your power to guard against it, but it would be foolish to ignore the possibility. Carefully plan what you would do and accept the risk, or else don't fly single-engine airplanes at night. First, accept the fact that you are likely to wreck the airplane. If it turns out that you don't damage it, you were extremely skillful, planned magnificently, and were extremely lucky.

I have my own plan for how I would react to a total engine failure at night: Squawk 7700 and start calling for help while selecting the likeliest looking spot. Slow the airplane to minimum speed with full flaps while maneuvering to the chosen area; tighten seat belt and shoulder harness; make the decision about the landing light.

If it is a bright, moonlit night, you are better off without the light. I keep the panel lights as dim as possible to protect my night vision. Without the landing light, I can see over a broader area to steer between obstructions, and I want the master "OFF" at the last second to reduce the chance of fire. If it is too dark to see *anything,* I will have to turn the landing light on; but I will have "tunnel vision," completely limited to the area illuminated by the light. I feel I still have an excellent chance of getting by with a few bruises and a phone call to the insurance company.

After those grim words of potential death and destruction, we had better close this section with a *positive* word about night flying. If the weather is right, the flight can be magical. The air is without a ripple; the lights of the city are like diamonds; and the satisfaction of accomplishment is total. Have a happy night flight!

Complex Airplanes

There are usually a few questions on the written exam concerning complex airplanes, and like the ADF, you may never have used one. After solo cross-country and the written exam, your next big goal is the private flight check. After that, for most of us anyway, the goal is to check out in an airplane whose wheels go up and down. This goal is generally stymied for a while by two problems: money and insurance requirements. If you have plenty of the one, you can overcome the other. Otherwise you can go about getting some complex-airplane time by making a nuisance of yourself. Ask to sit in the cockpit and read the owner's manual. Be around to clean the windows when your instructor has a charter and beg to go. I got my first 30 hours of retractable time, and later, my first 30 hours or so of multiengine time in this demeaning manner.

Spend a lot of time and attention on the owner's manual for your first complex airplane. You will find the manual for your second complex model is very similar, and you have only to make note of a few differences. Comparisons are easier to remember once basic procedures are firmly established.

Memorize the same basic airspeeds you learned for your trainer: V_x, V_y, cruise climb; V_a; best glide speed; normal approach speed, with and without flaps; short- and soft-field approach speed; and flap settings and procedures for short- and soft-field takeoffs and landings. Add one new one: V_{le}, maximum landing gear extension speed.

Decipher the performance graphs and work a weight and balance for every conceivable load. Learn the oil capacity and grade, the fuel octane, and the usable capacity of each tank, as well as the average cruise speed and fuel consumption.

Study the schematics of the electrical and fuel systems. Be sure you know whether or not boost pumps are used for takeoffs and landings. Your complex machine probably has a fuel-injected engine instead of a carburetor. Use of the boost pump may flood it, instead of acting as a safety backup. As a general rule, you use the boost pump for takeoffs and landings with a Lycoming engine; leave it off with a Continental engine. If the airplane is equipped with an autopilot, be sure you thoroughly discuss its use with the check pilot. There is more to using an autopilot correctly than just pushing a button. Obviously, the emergency gear extension procedure is one you won't want to search the manual for when the need arises.

Let's compare this larger engine to the one in your trainer. We will stick to a normally aspirated (no turbocharger) fuel-injected engine. There are several new gauges on the panel: one indicates fuel flow in gph; another, the EGT, assists in setting the mixture to maintain the proper temperature. Because this engine is more powerful, it develops more heat and it will take less kindly than your trainer to abrupt throttle usage. Monitor the engine gauges on the ground and in flight. Large engines often load up (foul the plugs) on the ground with a full-rich mixture and need to be leaned for taxi and returned to rich for takeoff. They are also more susceptible to overheating during extended ground operations, so get your checklist procedure organized to minimize ground time. Many complex airplanes have cowl flaps to assist in cooling during ground operations and climbs. Remembering to open and close them at the proper time will be one of the procedures you must establish, not only to protect the engine, but to get maximum performance from it. However, if it is cold, prolong the ground time until the engine is warmed up to the green arc.

You will use this airplane for going places, and that probably means climbing higher than you did for stall practice. Don't forget to monitor the EGT and fuel flow in descents, as well as climbs, and adjust the mixture accordingly.

A fuel-injected engine cannot get carburetor ice since it has no carburetor. It is still susceptible to induction icing, but not unless you are in clouds or freezing rain. Fuel injection also provides more efficient fuel distribution to the cylinders, making it easier to start when the engine is cold and more responsive to throttle changes. The injection system may provide for a vapor-return line, whereby excess fuel and vapors are returned to the fuel tanks. It usually goes back to the inboard tanks, but sometimes it goes to the left main only. In this case, select the left main tank for the first hour of flight, or you may lose fuel through the overflow valve.

If a fuel-injected engine is easier to start when cold, it makes up for it when it is hot. It can be a bear cat, requiring several extra hands and some strong language. Memorize the hot-start procedure because you won't get it going if you stop to read the directions. If you deliberately run a fuel tank dry in flight with a fuel-injected engine, you are out of your mind.

The instrument panel sports a new power gauge, manifold pressure, which is controlled by the throttle. The throttle quadrant has also sprouted a new lever, the prop control, which controls the rpm. Memorize the basic rule for all power changes: Advance the prop control before adding throttle, reduce the throttle before reducing the rpm (prop). Restated: Keep the rpm higher than the manifold pressure. This is not only to protect the engine, but also the oil pressure governor that controls the pitch of the propeller. NOTE: At high altitudes, the recommended cruise-power setting may include a manifold pressure that is higher than the rpm; but up in the thinner air, the prop encounters a lot less resistance.

ONE MORE TIME: The procedure for entering a climb is:

1. Mixture forward.
2. Prop forward.
3. Throttle forward.
4. Cowl flaps open.

The procedure for leveling off is:

1. Cowl flaps closed.
2. Throttle set.
3. Prop set.
4. Mixture set.

During the run up, exercise the prop control three times. The constant-speed prop has a governor that works on oil pressure and counterweights to keep the prop at a constant rpm. The oil in the governor needs to be flushed and warmed prior to takeoff.

On takeoff, you will still apply full power. The proper trim setting for takeoff will be more of a factor. In your trainer (even with full nose-down trim) you were muscular enough to easily hold the necessary pressure until you retrimmed correctly. This airplane is heavier. You will definitely notice the difference if the trim is not properly set for takeoff. An electric trim control on the yoke is usually standard equipment; check that it works and is properly set. You also have more torque working on you, so the left-turning tendency will be greatly increased. There should be rudder trim to relieve your right leg in extended climbs. After you level off, check the ball and retrim for cruise.

Finally, you will learn to check more carefully that the doors are properly secured than you did in your trainer. You still won't stall (or fall out) if one pops open on takeoff, but you won't get it closed in flight, either. Apologize to the passengers for your carelessnesss, and return and land. Secure the miserable door, and take off again.

Get some cockpit time prior to your checkout. Locate all the knobs and switches, and practice your new procedures. Get the avionics sorted out; you probably have more radios than you are used to, and for a while you will transmit on the wrong one if you aren't careful. One complex airplane in particular (which I *love* to fly) is notorious in its older models for having the avionics scattered around in the most unlikely places. You had better be able to put your fingers on everything you need, especially before getting caught in the dark. Sort out the system for fresh air and heat in the cabin. Air conditioners are great, but they usually cost performance if they are turned on during takeoff.

On takeoff, boost pumps as required, the mixture is full rich (depending on density altitude) and the prop control is full forward, apply takeoff power, gear up. PAY ATTENTION: Do not retract the gear until: (1) a positive rate of climb is established, and (2) there is no remaining runway available on which to abort the takeoff. Additionally, you will save a lot of wear and tear on the tires if you tap the toe brakes prior to putting the wheels in the wells. If they fold in spinning, they burn rubber. Delay retracting the gear if it is wet and cold out. Wheels have been known to freeze up in the wells when put away wet.

The next problem will be your climb power setting. In your trainer you needed all the power you had available to gain altitude, and the rpm stayed well below red line in a full-power climb. In this airplane you will probably take off with full power and shortly thereafter reduce the throttle (and *then* the prop) to the manufacturer's recommended climb-power setting, but don't rush it. Full available power is nice to have while obstacles are still a factor. There is a funny thing about aircraft engines: They run like crazy at full throttle, just like they were designed to do. When power is reduced, that is when they break if they are going to. Make an educated decision about when to reduce to climb power.

The manufacturer's recommended climb-power setting in most light airplanes is 25 squared. This is 25 inches of manifold pressure and 2500 rpm. Mixture may remain full rich, or it may be reduced to a specified fuel flow. At this point, when you are busy fiddling with power levers, the tower usually calls you to change to departure control—thanks a lot!

As you climb and the air becomes thinner, the manifold pressure will decrease. Approximately every 1,000 feet, advance the throttle to maintain climb power. The rpm will remain constant, like a good constant-speed prop should. You will probably be using full throttle by 6,000 or 7,000 feet, without a turbocharger. The level-off procedure is: Cowl flaps, throttle, prop, mixture.

For the descent, nose it over and fly faster. The rpm will remain constant, but the manifold pressure will begin to increase as the air becomes more dense. Keep reducing the throttle to maintain the desired manifold pressure, and adjust the mixture as dictated by the EGT. All engine and power gauges require more attention in a complex airplane. Imagine watching two of each, or four, or eight.

The basic difference between this airplane and your trainer is SPEED. En route procedures in this airplane don't change. Aviate, navigate, communicate; check and recheck. This airplane goes faster, and the faster it goes, the farther ahead of it you must be. Get organized, or the airplane will run off and leave you.

Your trainer slowed down immediately as soon as you reduced power. This one is a slick little devil, and takes much longer to slow down. The drag devices (flaps and gear) have maximum airspeed limitations to protect them from structural damage. The airplane cruises well above those limitations. You will need to plan descents and traffic pattern entries farther ahead. Closing the throttle to idle to slow down will cool the engine too rapidly, and you will probably hear the gear-warning horn as further evidence of poor planning. Also, plan to fly a wider traffic pattern; the burden of adjusting to slower traffic is going to fall on *you.*

A twentieth century aviation cliché predicts: "There is the pilot who has landed gear up; and the one who is about to." I don't even like to think about it. Gear-up landings (prop stopped) can be accomplished with very little damage to the airplane; if done unintentionally, imagine the embarrassment. You will probably spoil your first few flights in a retractable airplane by worrying, "Don't forget to put down the wheels."

ESTABLISH A PROCEDURE: The standard procedure is the GUMP check: Gas, Undercarriage, Mixture, Prop. (1) Gas—on the proper tank, boost pump as required; (2) Undercarriage—down and locked; (3) Mixture— rich; (4) Prop— full increase. When you are ready for a go-around, this procedure fills the bill. Even so, once in a while a very experienced pilot still slides one on. He got distracted by a last-minute go-around (or an open door) and properly retracted the gear for the climb; he was frosted by the lost time (and fuel) and *did it.* In addition to the GUMP check, add one more procedure. Inside of the keyhole (on short final), look at the indicator and verify out loud, "THREE GREEN." Confucious never said, "It is better to roll than to slide." He *might* have said it, if he had been a pilot.

During the course of your checkout, go through the actual emergency gear extension procedure. Some are so simple that below a certain speed the gear falls automatically. Some have to be hand cranked as many as 60 turns. The "automatic free-fall wheels" lower the insurance rates, but they offer one disadvantage: they may not retract at V_x on an obstacle-clearance takeoff. A gear override system is provided, and don't forget to engage it if you need to yank the wheels up early. Disengage the override when you accelerate to normal climb speed.

During the checkout, go through minimum controllable airspeed in all configurations and all stalls. Practice short- and soft-field takeoffs and landings. Make a 180° accuracy landing as well, to see the power off glide ratio. It won't glide like your trainer. Your check pilot will see to it that the gear fails to extend as expected at least once. If you discover it on short final, execute a go-around and troubleshoot on downwind. NOTE: If only one of the gear-indicator lights is out, check the bulbs; they are interchangeable.

Most gear-indicator lights dim automatically when the panel lights or the nav lights are turned on. This helps at night, but you can't see them in the sunlight. Check the panel lights and check the circuit breaker. Then go through the emergency gear extension procedure.

Several popular models of complex airplanes carry up to six people. Insist on making several landings with all the seats full; when your airplane is heavy, you will find that you have a different airplane on your hands. Carry power until you are ready to touch down. It may fall out from under you if you close the throttle too soon.

When you are finally allowed to take your friends for an airplane ride, keep in mind how you felt the first time. Fly as smoothly as you know how, and keep the banks shallow. If the passengers are nervous about it, choose a very calm day. This airplane makes several loud noises that will frighten a nonflying passenger who isn't expecting it. The gear thunders, rumbles, and thumps going down; if you mismanage your approach, you may get the gear-warning horn, accompanied by a flashing red light on the panel. Take time to explain such things in advance; it makes a big difference to your passenger. Above all, maintain an air of total confidence. Many pilots deserve an Academy Award for their portrayal of "Joe Cool" when something goes wrong. Such consideration may make the difference in whether or not your passenger ever gets into another light aircraft. The ultimate compliment to your flying skills will come when your (initially nervous) passenger gets out of the airplane with an enthusiastic, "When can we go flying again?"

Weather

It seems appropriate to begin this section with another quotation from the Flying Confucius: "It is better to be on the ground, wishing you were flying, than to be flying, wishing you were on the ground."

Possibly unlike most other training manuals, we have saved this section until rather late in the game. The purpose was to wait until you were experienced enough to relate it to a flight situation and realize the importance of weather knowledge. We have previously dipped into some weather when necessary, but your flight instructor has had the last word on whether or not you went flying. Soon you will be deciding for yourself.

WEATHER JUDGMENT

Reading aviation accident reports is sensible if grim practice if you can learn anything from other pilots' mistakes. It is disheartening, especially to a flight instructor, to see how many of those accident reports include the words, "non-instrument-rated pilot continued VFR flight into adverse weather beyond his experience/ability level." Incredibly, an astonishing percentage of these reports also state, "The weather forecast was substantially correct; no evidence was found that the deceased obtained a weather briefing prior . . ."

Somewhere along the line, those of us whose job it is to teach are just not getting the message across. It is very difficult to "teach" weather; real weather knowledge comes from experience. Gaining the necessary level of experience, while not overstepping the boundary line into real trouble, is a problem, especially when you take the pilot-type personality into consideration. You are a fairly adventurous-type individual to start with, or you would never have come this far. Now you are faced with a choice. Here are the extremes:

1. You can limit your flying to perfect conditions, when there is not one hint of trouble in the forecast. You may never have a weather problem this way, but you will severely limit the versatility of your airplane (and yourself) and virtually stand still as far as learning and skill goes.

2. Bursting with macho (and no sense), you figure you can handle it; you will become a statistic.

The happy medium is reached through two avenues—weather judgment and humility. Weather judgment results from your ability to translate the forecast into the actual conditions, and what those conditions will mean to you in an airplane. Humility is recognizing your own limitations and having the courage to admit them.

You will quickly learn that forecasts are often wrong. I'm glad that I am not a weather predictor. Forecasters try hard, and the knowledge they must have is almost incomprehensible, while the tools they work with are space-age fantastic and they are improving all the time. But dealing with anything as capricious as weather is thankless work. If it seems that the forecast is often gloomier than the actual weather, don't blame it on the poor forecasters. If you have an accident because you didn't believe them when they were right, they won't feel a whole lot better about it. The trap for the pilot can be that conditions ARE often better than forecast. The pilot falls into the old "take a look" syndrome, and it usually works. Once is all it takes, when the forecast was right (or wrong on the bad side). "Take a look" is the pilot's tool for learning weather judgment, but it must be used VERY CAREFULLY. Don't go take a look without being certain the old back door is wide open; the "humility" part comes in when you make the 180° turn. Now you have gained some weather *experience;* the way you turn that into weather *judgment* is by analyzing the forecast after you get on the ground. Compare the charts and graphs to what you saw from the airplane, and store the knowledge for the next time.

Perhaps in the weather training for the private certificate too much emphasis is placed on the charts and symbols and not really enough emphasis on what the forecast may *mean* to the pilot. It is nice to be able to read the weather depiction charts, and reading them accurately should be a requirement for any *professional* in aviation. The private pilot (and the commercial pilot and the ATP) has a trained, professional weather briefer on the other end of the telephone to tell him in plain language what the charts say; it is still up to the *pilot* to figure out what they mean.

WEATHER IN AIM

Refer to the section on meteorology in AIM. If you have been keeping up with the outside reading as directed, this discussion should just about complete your study of AIM, "Basic Flight Information and ATC Procedures." You are aware that this publication is reissued quarterly. They sometimes shuffle the order of topics and add or delete some. Note the heavy black lines down the edge of the page—these mark changes in the issue. This really helps you focus on those changes and maintain your current reading requirements. The topics we discuss here may be out of order if compared to the most recent issue of AIM, but the following explanations should help to clarify the information:

1. GENERAL: How often a forecast is issued and the time of day it is supposed to come out is the forecaster's problem. The pilot cares (a great deal) about how recent the forecast is; "old" weather is useful to determine trends but is not so great for what is happening NOW. You will want to know how to determine the time the forecast was issued. Some of the charts *are* "forecasts," while some are actual reported weather, and you will want to know which is which. Be advised that the Flight Service specialists are "briefers" only. They are very good, but if you want to talk to a weather forecaster, you will have to call the Weather Bureau. The definition of such a term as MVFR and what conditions it implies is good to know.

2. IN-FLIGHT WEATHER ADVISORIES: For the written exam, remember the difference in intensity between Significant Meteorological Information (SIGMET) and Airmen's Meterological Information (AIRMET); in flight, pay close attention to either kind.

3. PREFLIGHT BRIEFING SERVICE: This subject has been covered in Chapter 4, FSS.

4. PILOT'S AUTOMATIC TELEPHONE WEATHER ANSWERING SERVICE (PATWAS): The need for this service annoys me. It is good they have it because it is better than nothing, but there is no real substitute for being able to ask specific questions when you need to. If the forecast is good, this briefing is probably enough; if it is going to be marginal, I want to know more about it.

5. FLIGHT SERVICE STATION PREFLIGHT BRIEFING: Refer to Chapter 4, FSS.

6. EN ROUTE FLIGHT ADVISORY SERVICE (EFAS): Memorize that frequency for Flight Watch, 122.0. Sometime during your cross-countries, tune it in and listen. It is better than a forecast because you may get information passed by a pilot who is actually there. Report good conditions as well as poor ones, especially if better (or worse) than forecast. If I were bracing myself for a rough ride through Banning Pass, it is good news to hear a pilot say he had a smooth trip in a Cessna 182 at 8,000 feet. Note that this frequency is strictly for weather, not flight plans.

7. TRANSCRIBED WEATHER BROADCASTS (TWEB): Listen to the VOR. The communication box in the sectional chart legend shows which stations provide this service.

8. SCHEDULED WEATHER BROADCASTS (SWB): These are broadcast the same as TWEBs.

9. WEATHER RADAR SERVICES: This network is what enables us to obtain avoidance assistance.

10. ATC IN-FLIGHT WEATHER AVOIDANCE ASSISTANCE: An instrument-rated pilot with very sophisticated equipment is grateful for weather radar service. If the weather is such that YOU need radar to locate the cells, you have serious grounds for a "no-go" decision. These sections are slanted more for the IFR pilot who must comply with his computerized clearances or possibly tangle with other IFR traffic, while he would still prefer not to punch into the really dark stuff. Familiarize yourself with it, because if you get yourself into this kind of weather, you will need it too.

11. RUNWAY VISUAL RANGE (RVR): Familiarize yourself with this equipment, but if visibility is so lousy that it needs to be measured by RVR, stay on the ground.

12. REPORTING OF CLOUD HEIGHTS: Be careful of this on the written exam and also in planning your en route altitude. If the cloud bases are reported "6,000 overcast," and the surface elevation is 2,000 feet, your altimeter would read 8,000 when you went in the clouds. Therefore your lowest legal altitude would be 7,500 if you are going East and 6,500 going West (VFR minimums, and the Hemispheric Rule for altitude separation). Cloud *tops* are necessarily reported MSL, so you can go by your altimeter.

13. REPORTING PREVAILING VISIBILITY: This is the criterion the tower uses to determine prevailing visibility and may help to explain why you thought the visibility was better (or worse) than they reported. When you fool around with the legal minimums, be advised it may very well be below those minimums in your quadrant.

14. ESTIMATING THE INTENSITY OF PRECIPITATION/DRIZZLE: If you can see the horizon through the shower, a little water may wash some of the bugs off. If you can't see through it, go around it. The numbers are important only to the weather specialist. NOTE: If the water is falling out of a thunderstorm, go around it anyway!

15. ESTIMATING THE INTENSITY OF SNOW: Note that the visibility in even light snow is well below VFR minimums. Besides, it may stick to the airplane.

16. PILOT WEATHER REPORTS (PIREP): A forecast is what *may* be happening; a PIREP is what is really going on. Join the flying fraternity and put your two bits in. Someday your PIREP may save someone else from getting into trouble. Example: You encounter higher-than-forecast winds aloft, making it necessary to plan an unscheduled fuel stop.

17. PIREPS RELATING TO AIRFRAME ICING: This is very serious stuff, and if you are in it, your first mistake was taking off. They define rime and clear ice here, but they left out the one you are most likely to encounter—frost.

Frost forms when you sit on the ground overnight, and it is a royal pain to remove—but DO IT. It is a real troublemaker. Any kind of ice on the airplane's surface disrupts the laminar flow of air over the wings and will reduce the lifting capability and raise the stall speed. Frost can also form in flight when the airplane flies from subfreezing temperatures into a temperature above freezing with a high relative humidity. It zaps your windows so the pilot who is not instrument rated had better be fast with the windshield defrost. Add the OAT to your list of "check and recheck" items.

This winter, cold weather will get to a predictable number of pilots who never even get off the ground. Some frosty morning the pilot runs the battery down trying to start a cold engine. He attempts to hand-prop it, and it chops him up. Or he is too cold and miserable to remove the frost and stalls on takeoff. Or he pays the fee to have it melted off in a nice warm hangar; then he takes off with water in the nooks and crannies, which promptly freezes and blocks the controls.

Rime ice looks like the ice that forms in your freezer. It is a result of the rapid freezing of small, supercooled water droplets and builds when you are inside of clouds at below-freezing temperatures. Clear ice may be encountered IN clouds or UNDER them, when you run into freezing rain. The larger droplets form a clear (heavy) coating on the airframe, and this can build thick and very fast. As if you didn't have trouble enough at this point, ice has been known to break off in hunks and take radio antennas with it. Avoid any areas of visible moisture when the temperature is below freezing.

18. PIREPS RELATING TO TURBULENCE: Familiarize yourself with the turbulence-reporting-table criteria so you won't confuse people by reporting "occasional intermittent severe light chop." In flight, consider the source. Severe turbulence reported by a student pilot in a Cessna 150 may mean he scared himself when his chart fell to the floor; if reported by a 747 captain, give the area a wide berth.

In conditions of turbulence or chop that you would consider moderate or greater, slow the airplane to V_a. Most (utility category) trainers cruise well below V_a anyway, but a high-performance airplane will have to slow down to prevent possible structural damage. NOTE: Structural airspeed limitations usually have some margin for error, meaning you can probably exceed them somewhat and get by with it. Each time the limitations are exceeded, the airframe may be weakened until someday something will fail, even well *below* the maximum airspeed. Watch those design limitations and abide by them.

19. WIND SHEAR PIREPS: Be on guard if conditions are gusty or if a thunderstorm is nearby. Report any sudden increase or decrease in airspeed on final; you may save the next guy from a rude surprise. An abrupt change from a tail wind to a head wind may give you a jolt as you pass through the layer of friction between opposing air masses. In addition it will slow your ground speed considerably, requiring that you add power to make the runway. An abrupt change from a head wind to a tail wind can leave you momentarily without the necessary airflow over the wing. Approach-to-landing stall recovery technique will come in very handy.

20. CLEAR AIR TURBULENCE (CAT) PIREPS: Probably not a factor for you now, but it may be after you check out in that little turbocharged number you have your eye on. Personally, I have never encountered CAT, but a friend of mine once reported doing a snap roll in a Navajo at 16,000 feet on a clear day.

21. THUNDERSTORMS: *Read carefully.* Thunderstorms come in three stages: (1) cumulus, or "building," characterized by strong updrafts; (2) mature, characterized by both up- and downdrafts, with rain beginning; and (3) dissipating, characterized mostly by downdrafts, with heavy rainfall. In the mature stage, those up- and downdrafts may be making big hunks of ice as the precipitation is carried up and down through the freezing level. Hail is no joke in an airplane, and it may be slung out as far as 20 miles from the storm—usually underneath the anvil-shaped top of the storm. When you go around a thunderstorm, stay out from under the anvil.

In this discussion of thunderstorms in AIM, paragraph *c*, the 20–30 mile space between two granddaddy thunderstorms is what is known in aviation as a "sucker hole." I have only one good thing to say about thunderstorms—they travel slower than airplanes. You can always outrun them, if you have any place to go. If the forecast says "isolated thunderstorms" or even "scattered thunderstorms," you might take a look at it; anything more, forget it. Isolated or scattered thunderstorms that are formed by the normal rising of convection currents (updrafts of heated surface air) are no less potent individually than the ones formed by advancing frontal systems. The difference is they can be seen and circumnavigated, whereas frontal weather may be widespread and deep and offer a mixture of other problems (including low visibility), which makes the cells difficult, if not impossible, to see and avoid. Until you have an instrument rating and a lot more experience, avoid flying in the vicinity of a front of any kind. You can find plenty of excitement while the front is on the way and for several hours after frontal passage.

In paragraph *e* on thunderstorms, you will be advised that it is very uncomfortable to be flying along watching lots of cloud-to-cloud and cloud-to-ground lightning. However, the brave (or crazy) pilots who fly into thunderstorms for a living have reported that lightning very rarely STRIKES airplanes. What happens instead is just as noisy. Static electricity builds up too fast to be dissipated by the static wicks on the airplane. It begins to cast a very eerie glow around the propellers, called "Saint Elmo's Fire." It finally discharges with a loud bang, which may also leave a small hole burned in the airplane's skin somewhere. Being the cautious type, I have seen this happen only once; the experience was very . . . "interesting."

22. THUNDERSTORM FLYING: Avoidance is the policy. THEY ARE NOT KIDDING. The "do's and don'ts" listed here are excellent advice. When flying on top of a broken or solid cloud layer in the summertime, I have watched the tops of thunderstorms shoot up visibly at a most remarkable rate. You can't help wondering if that activity will start from under your present position. Sucker holes happen on top, as well as underneath, when you try to top the "saddle" between buildups. Don't forget that you are already hanging by the prop just to hold altitude, and you are operating much closer to the stall. If you blunder into a thunderstorm, FLY ATTITUDE. Forget altitude; you don't have a chance to maintain it. Don't turn back. Once inside, it is too late for a 180; you will be out faster if you blast on through. Set the power for the airspeed that will maintain V_a and leave it alone; go on the gauges and FLY ATTITUDE. Turn on the panel lights and pitot heat—you may have to become a submarine for a while. Ignore the sights and sounds of World War III going on outside, tighten seatbelts and shoulder harness, and hang on. You are in for the ride of your life.

23. KEY TO AVIATION WEATHER OBSERVATIONS AND FORECASTS: This key, on a yellow card, is available at aviation bookstores. It is the key to deciphering weather reports and forecasts, so study it closely and memorize the symbols. You can never know too much about something as important as weather.

Notice in the "Sky and Ceiling" portion of the key that a Broken Ceiling (BKN) is from 0.6 to 0.9 sky coverage. Many times, even though the ceiling is reported as broken, if it is only six-tenths coverage there may still be plenty of big, blue holes to climb (or descend) through. But they are still calling it broken at nine-tenths, and for all practical (VFR) purposes, it may as well be solid overcast. A lot of VFR pilots have gotten trapped on top and lost control trying to spiral down through a "glory hole." Don't sit up there until you run out of gas or attempt any such spiraling descent. Call someone on the radio and ask for help. The FAA may want to discuss it with you later, but they do not hand out violations when you request a flight assist. Your call will result in getting you identified on radar and vectored to the nearest place where you can make a VFR descent. If your fuel supply doesn't permit that, they will coordinate your IFR descent with the ATC center, so you don't run into anybody. This has become a genuine emergency, since you are not instrument rated. FAA will be quick with a violation for such irresponsible acts as "buzzing," drinking and flying, and taking off deliberately into known IFR conditions. But when forecasts fall apart on you, and you make the right moves to ask for help, you find you have their assistance both in flight and on the ground. NOTE: If you are on top and lost and are without a radio frequency, this is time for 121.5. Furthermore, every FSS monitors the standard FSS frequency, 122.2.

Weather on the Written Exam

I am generally opposed to a common practice known as "teaching the test." Cramming for a written exam may get you a passing grade, but if the material you "crammed" needs to stay with you, I hope your life doesn't depend on remembering it. Keep your *Private Pilot Written Test Guide* handy, and work through the weather questions. Combine the remainder of this section with any other study materials you may have on aviation weather. You will need that added material for a true, scientific approach. Rather than merely getting you through the written exam with a passing grade, I am concerned with launching you into the world as a new private pilot with enough weather SENSE to keep you out of trouble (while you learn).

Let's start with a few definitions and explanations of weather generally. The atmosphere tends to maintain an equal pressure over the entire surface of the earth; but the sun causes unequal heating, with air rising from the equator and conflicting with cold air over the poles. Combined with the Coriolis force (the way the earth turns), in the Northern Hemisphere we get a general weather pattern that moves from West to East. A LOW is a center of pressure surrounded on all sides by areas of higher pressure; it is also called a cyclone. A HIGH is a center of pressure surrounded by areas of lower pressure, or anticyclone. Low pressure areas develop where air lies over surfaces that are warmer than the surrounding areas. The warm air rises, and the surrounding air starts coming in to fill the "vacuum." MEMORIZE: Air circulates clockwise around a HIGH; and counterclockwise around a LOW. A high pressure area usually signals good weather. Watch the lows closely; they are "weather magnets."

Figure 5.3 is a surface analysis weather map. There is also an example in the written test guide. This gives you a general picture of the weather pattern

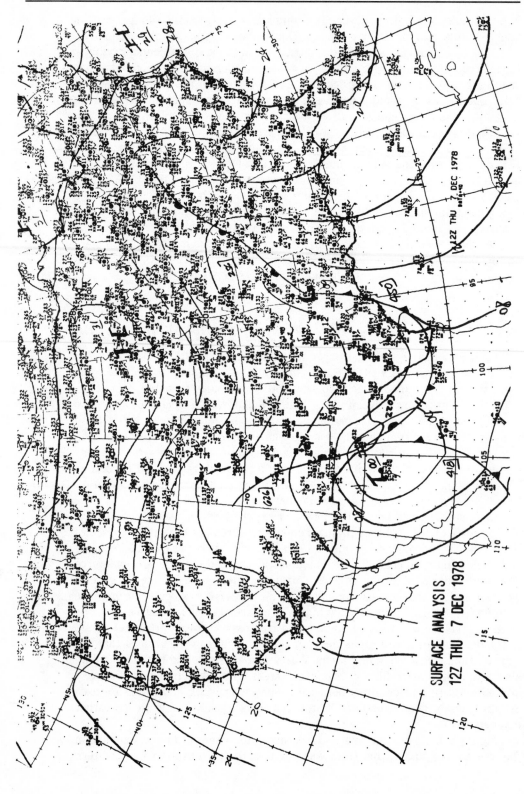

F I G. 5.3. *Surface analysis.*

by showing the position of highs, lows, and fronts. It is the first chart you would study, planning a trip. It is not a forecast, but the actual weather as it was at the time the chart was issued. First check the time of the chart in the lower left corner. The surface analysis also gives you the winds, temperatures, and dew points.

Front symbols are easy; cold-front lines have icicles hanging on them, and warm-front lines have raindrops; occluded fronts have both. The solid lines are "isobars," lines of equal barometric pressure. The winds will blow parallel to the isobars; the closer together the isobars, the stronger the wind. When the isobars are elongated, they squash up against each other like accordion pleats and form "troughs" (lines of low pressure) and "ridges" (lines of high pressure). Listen to weather forecasts for the effects that troughs and ridges can have on advancing fronts. These can strengthen and cause the advancing front to speed up or stall out. When a front stops moving, it becomes "stationary." It may then bend around on itself and become "occluded." At this point you get a real mixed-up mess, with the characteristics of both warm AND cold fronts. To make matters worse, it may hang around for days. Figure 5.4 shows the station model and sky coverage symbols found on surface analysis charts.

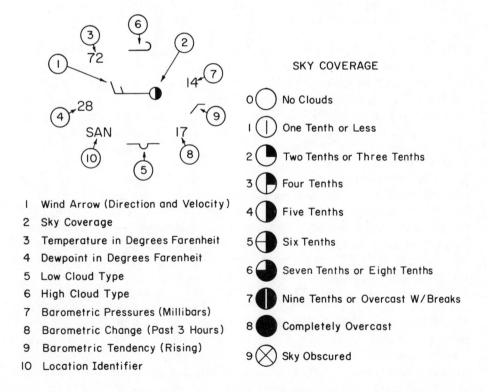

1 Wind Arrow (Direction and Velocity)
2 Sky Coverage
3 Temperature in Degrees Farenheit
4 Dewpoint in Degrees Farenheit
5 Low Cloud Type
6 High Cloud Type
7 Barometric Pressures (Millibars)
8 Barometric Change (Past 3 Hours)
9 Barometric Tendency (Rising)
10 Location Identifier

SKY COVERAGE

0 No Clouds
1 One Tenth or Less
2 Two Tenths or Three Tenths
3 Four Tenths
4 Five Tenths
5 Six Tenths
6 Seven Tenths or Eight Tenths
7 Nine Tenths or Overcast W/Breaks
8 Completely Overcast
9 Sky Obscured

FIG. 5.4. *Station models and sky coverage symbols on surface analysis.*

Barometric pressure in millibars is pretty worthless to a pilot, but the forecaster needs to know. Comparing the changing pressures tells him how fast the front is moving, so he can tell you. He issues a significant weather prognostic chart (Fig. 5.5). This comes out four times a day, every 6 hours. It will depict expected low or middle clouds and the expected position of fronts. These charts appear in pairs to show the expected movement of the fronts and significant weather. These are *forecasts,* not depictions of known facts; but the forecaster's guess is much better than mine. In the old days when FSS used teletypes, you could go in and see these charts pinned all over the walls. Now you must ask to have them called up on the TV.

The weather depiction chart (Fig. 5.6) is not as complicated to read. It plots total sky coverage, cloud or ceiling heights, and visibilities of less than 7 miles. The meaning of the solid and/or scalloped lines is printed on the chart. The weather depiction chart also shows actual weather at the time of issue. Figure 5.7 is a station model for a weather depiction chart.

It is time for a few words about the general characteristics of fronts. Roughly defined, a front is the point where different kinds of air masses have a head-on collision. This is bound to cause some confusion, and the resulting weather will depend on many varying factors. Warm air expands and rises, and cold air contracts and sinks. Already, that spells turbulence and moisture— WEATHER probably not suitable for VFR flight.

When the surface is heated by the sun, the air is warmed from below. As air rises, it also cools off at the "normal lapse rate" of 3.5°F (2°C) per 1,000 feet. Rising DRY air will slow down quicker because it cools off faster. Rising MOIST air retains its warmth longer and keeps going up. Therefore warm, moist air is less stable than dry, cool air. (Stable air is air that maintains its altitude.) Rising air, especially with some moisture in it, is going to cool off to the dew point eventually and create clouds.

Around midmorning in the summertime, little puffy white cumulus clouds begin to form. These are baby cumulonimbus (CBs), which will grow into the afternoon thundershowers. They are (little, as yet) weather factories, and flight below them is very bumpy and uncomfortable. It is tempting to climb on top where the air is smooth. One of the traps for the "VFR ON TOP" pilot is the back side of a warm front. The warm air slides up and over the heavier, cooler air. The flat-looking stratus cloud deck slides upward as well. If the pilot "maintains altitude" by reference to this false visual horizon, he may have been in a shallow climb for some time without realizing it. If hypoxia catches up with him before he notices his altimeter, he may not even care. Euphoric pilots have happily decided they can fly without fuel and other minor details like that.

Conditions such as approaching warm fronts can cause the normal lapse rate to collapse, causing air at altitude to actually be considerably warmer than it is on the surface. This is called an "inversion"; it puts a lid on the pollution particles in the air below, and the people are going to breathe their industrial smog until something comes along to clean it out again. This temperature inversion is a semipermanent condition in the Los Angeles basin in the summertime, thanks to the terrain features. The cool air comes in from the Pacific, and hot air rises off the desert. The basin coughs and cries all summer. Be on the

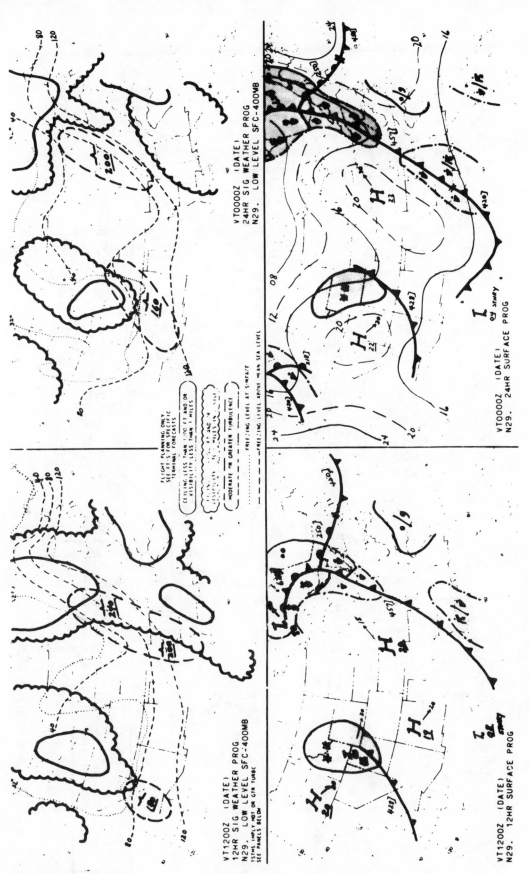

FIG. 5.5. *Significant weather prognostic chart.*

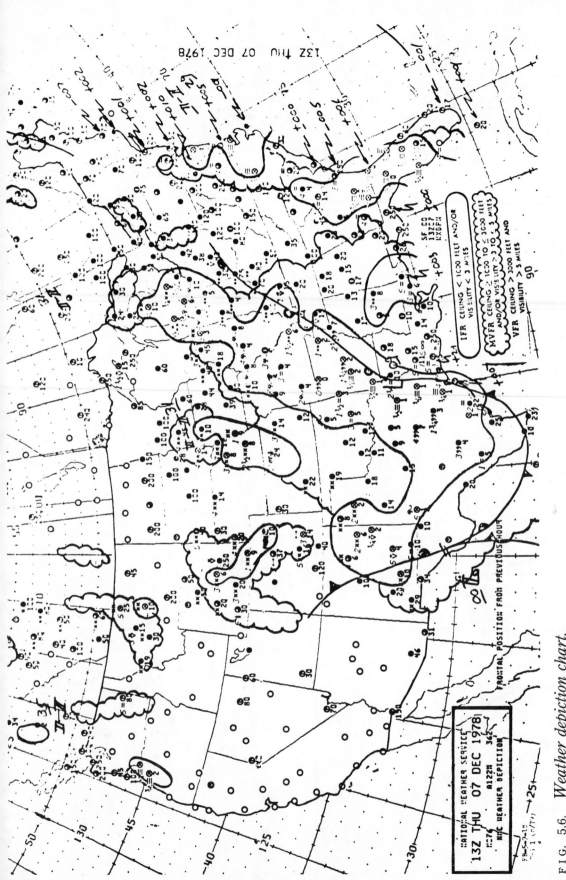

FIG. 5.6. *Weather depiction chart.*

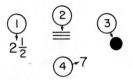

F I G. 5.7. *Station model for weather depiction chart.*

1 Visibility

2 Visibility Restriction

3 Sky Coverage

4 Ceiling Height (Hundreds of Feet)

Visibility Restriction:

∞ Haze	● Rain
⌇⌇ Smoke	✱ Snow
—S— Dust or Sand	▽ Showers
☰ Fog	△ Hail
❮ Drizzle	↰ Thunderstorm

lookout for lower visibilities and possible fog in the vicinity of heavy industrial centers. The pollution particles provide a nucleus on which moisture can form, increasing the chance of fog.

A warm front is usually slow moving at the rate of 10–25 mph. The air will be stable, with possible low clouds, drizzle, and poor visibility covering a very large area. A cold front may be very fast moving, usually 20–25 mph and occasionally up to 60 mph, with unstable, clear air. The areas of precipitation may be the more violent kind (thunderstorms), and these may march along in rows (squall lines) stretching for hundreds of miles. Set the airplane down somewhere, put some good strong ropes on it, and wait it out. Cold fronts may be very exciting; warm fronts may be sneaky. The briefer looks at a radar summary chart (Fig. 5.8) to warn you of the location of heavy weather. A radar summary chart shows the radar echoes of thunderstorms, indicating their location, coverage, movement, and tops, and possible clues about the severity of the cells.

The winds aloft forecast (Fig. 5.9) has been discussed in this chapter under cross-country flights. To decode the forecast, remember that the first two digits plus zero is the True direction; the second two digits are wind velocity in knots; the last two digits are temperature, $\pm\,°C$; and altitudes are MSL. Check the dates and times of the forecast.

An area forecast (Fig. 5.10) is easy to read, since it is in plain language. Area forecasts are issued twice a day and are valid for 18 hours, with a 12-hour outlook. The heading identifies the forecasting station, the day, and the times of issue and coverage; all times are Greenwich. The area forecast also includes the freezing level and will specify any heights that are AGL instead of MSL. There is a brand new addition to the area forecast called a "flight precaution." This is not extreme enough to become an AIRMET and may include local conditions that are just about standard. For example, in my local weather briefing I

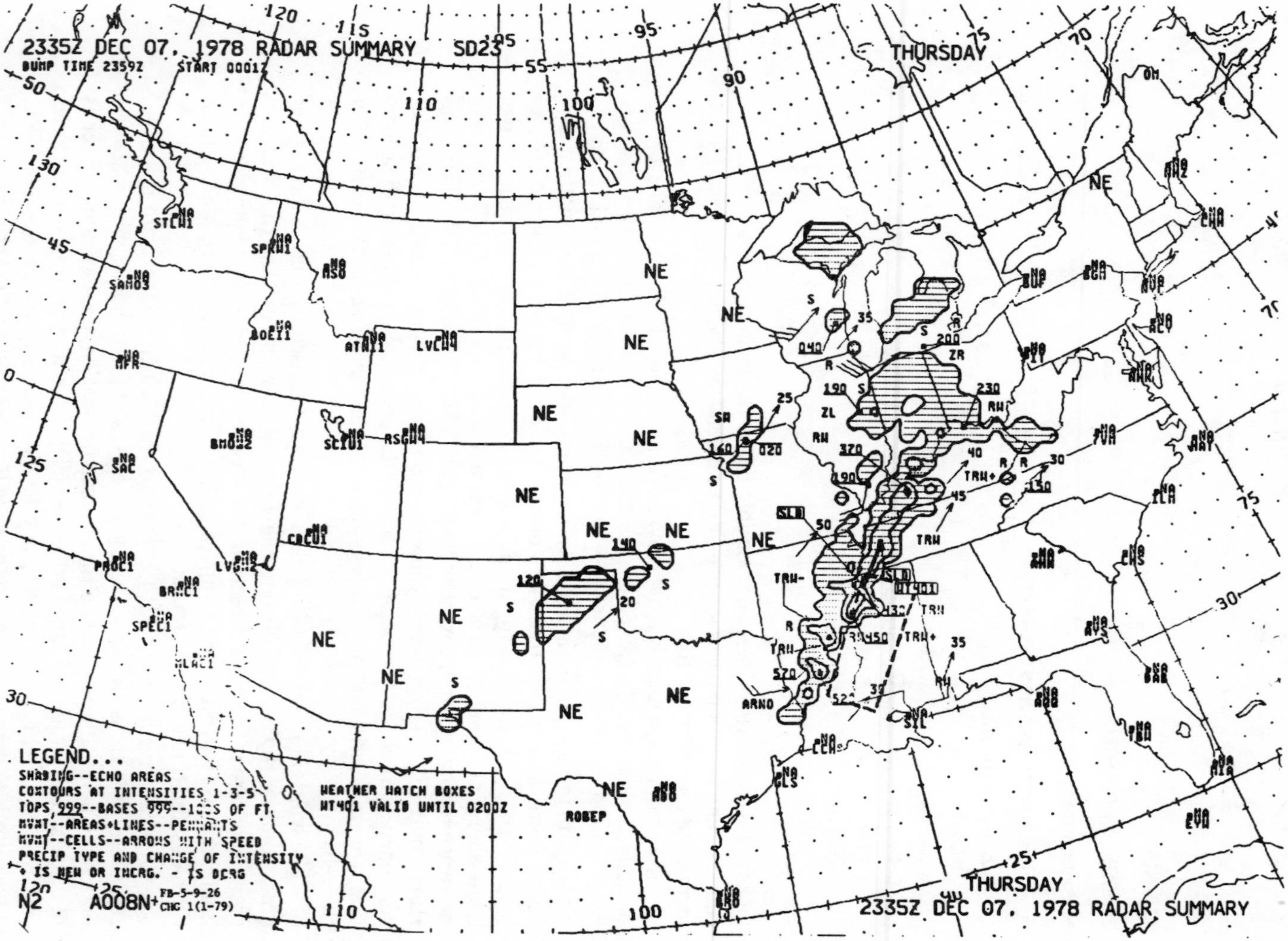

FIG. 5.8. *Radar summary chart.*

```
FDUS1 KWBC Ø 61200Z
DATA BASED ON Ø6120ØZ

VALID Ø70ØØØZ    FOR USE 1800-Ø30ØZ.    TEMPS NEG ABV 24ØØØ

FT(MSL) 30ØØ    60ØØ      9ØØØ     12ØØØ   180ØØ   24ØØØ   30ØØØ   340ØØ  39ØØØ

ABI            2318+Ø5   2329+Ø3  2337-Ø3 2359-16 2386-25 731737  742945 743554
ABQ                      2323-Ø9  2337-15 2369-26 73Ø5-34 734345  732846 730547
AMA            1815      2129-Ø3  2239-Ø9 2367-21 73Ø3-29 734241  735748 732952
ATL     99ØØ  2317+11   2423+Ø7  2428+Ø1 2540-12 2651-25 266340  266549 256859
BNA     1806  2418+Ø7   2428+Ø3  2438-Ø2 2453-14 2560-26 256840  257Ø49 247158
BRO     24Ø8  2614+18   252Ø+11  2425-Ø4 244Ø-11 235Ø-21 236335  236744 247Ø54
```

F I G. 5.9. *Winds aloft forecast.*

```
DFW FA 131240
131300Z-140700Z
OTLK 140700Z-141900Z

NM OK TX AND CSTL WTRS...

HGTS ASL UNLESS NOTE...

FLT PRCTN...E OF PNC-SPS-LRD LN FOR TSTMS AND ICG.  ERN HLF TX FOR
CIGS BLO 10 VSBY BLO 3 TIL ARND 18Z.  PTNS WRN TX SERN NM FOR BD AND
TURBC 17Z-02Z.

SYNS... AT 13Z CDFNT NR A GCK-SPS-DLF LN MOVG EWD ABT 20 KTS TO NR A
SHV-BRO LN BY 07Z.

CLDS AND WX...
OK AND TX ALG AND AHD CDFNT...
WDSPRD CIGS BLO 10 OVC VSBYS LCLY BLO 3L-F OVR TX PTN AND CIGS 15-25
OVC OK PTN.  TOPS LYRD TO 150.  SCT RW OVR AREA WITH ISOLD TRW OK PTN.
CB TOPS 280.  16Z-18Z OVR TX CIGS IPVG TO 15-25 BKN-OVC VSBYS 7 MI OR
BTR WITH RW/TRW INCRG OVR ENTR AREA.  AFT 19Z OVR ERN THIRD TX PSBL
SVR TSTMS TOPS ABV 350.  OTLK...MVFR CIG.

SERN QTR NM RMNDR TX AND OK BHND CDFNT...
MSTLY CLR BCMG AFT 17Z PTCHY CIGS 80-100 BKN 120-150.  ALSO AFT 17Z
VSBYS LCLY 2-4BD IN CDS-ABI-INK-CVS AREA.  D TOPS 100-120 WITH VSBYS
IPVG ARND 02Z.  SFC WIND 3020G35 17Z-02Z.  OTLK...VFR CLR.

WRN AND NRM NM...
PTCHY 80-100 BKN-SCT 120 WRN HLF OTRW MSTLY CLR.  AFT 17Z MSTLY CLR
WRN HLF AND PTCHY 80-100 BKN 150 NERN QTR WITH HIR RDGS OCNLY OBSCD.
OVR NCNTRL MTNS CHC 2SW- 17Z-01Z.  OTLK...VFR.

CSTL WTRS...
10-20 SCT CIG 80-100 BKN TOPS 150 WITH WDLY SCT RW-.  AFT 22Z RW INCRG
WITH SCT TRW.  RW TOPS 180.  CB TOPS 300.  OTLK...MVFR CIG TRW BCMG
VFR 12Z.

ICG AND FRZLVL...MDT MXD ICGICIP ABV FRZLVL AHD CDFNT.  LGT RIME ICGIC
BHND CDFNT.  FRZLVL 70 NRN NM SLPG TO 100 SWRN TX AND 90 NERN OK SLPG
TO 120 SRN TX.

TURBC...OCNL MDT TURBC SERN NM AND OVR WRN TX MAINLY 17Z-02Z.  ELSW
GENLY LGT TURBC.

THIS FA ISSUANCE CANCELS THE FOLLOWING AIRMETS...QUEBEC 1 ROMEO 1.
```

F I G. 5.10.
Area forecast.

STATION IDENTIFIERS

ABI	ABILENE, TX	INK	WINK, TX
BRO	BROWNSVILLE, TX	LRD	LAREDO, TX
CDS	CHILDRESS, TX	PNC	PONCA CITY, OK
CVS	CLOVIS, NM	SHV	SHREVEPORT, LA
DLF	DEL RIO, TX	SPS	WICHITA FALLS, TX
GCK	GARDEN CITY, KS		

expect to hear, "moderate to severe turbulence within 5,000 feet of mountainous terrain." I know the bumps are there, but I'm not going over the mountains today. However, this bugs the eyes of a student pilot getting his first cross-country weather briefing. If there is something in the briefing that you don't like the sound of, ask for clarification or discuss it with a local pilot.

The freezing level is included in the area forecast; this becomes of acute interest to the IFR pilot who will be inside of clouds because this is the altitude at which the clouds begin to stick to the airplane. Watch especially the areas where surface temperatures are below freezing, with warmer air at altitude. These conditions can lead to precipitation-induced fog, or worse yet, clear ice.

Terminal forecasts are issued 3 times a day during the daylight hours when most general aviation activity takes place. Study Figure 5.11 and practice on the other samples in the test guide.

```
FT 18Ø94Ø

RAP  18    1Ø1Ø   1ØØ SCT   25Ø-BKN   1615.   18Z   C8Ø BKN   1815

ØØZ   C5Ø   BKN    3215.   Ø4Z MVFR CIG.
```

F I G. 5.11.   *Terminal forecast.*

Key:
First line: Heading (Forecast Terminal) 18th of month at 09:40 Zulu (GMT).
Second line: Rapid City, Valid from 18th at 1010 Zulu, 10,000 Scattered, 25,000 Thin Broken, Winds 160 at 15 Knots, Time 1800 Zulu, Ceiling 8,000 Broken, Winds 180 at 15 Knots.
Third line: Midnight Zulu, Ceiling 5,000 Broken, Winds 320 at 15 Knots, Time 04 Zulu, Weather on the way.

The surface weather reports (sample in the test guide) may be decoded by use of the key you studied in AIM. These are hourly reports of existing surface weather; you really should be able to read them. It takes a lot of practice to be able to read a string of symbols for content. On the written exam, determine which line is referred to in the question and write it out in plain language on your scratch paper; then you can figure out what they are asking.

Figure 5.12 shows the cloud types and the symbols used for them in the forecasts. Study them very closely. Not nearly enough attention is given by student pilots to the types of clouds and the kind of weather those clouds are associated with. This is much more than a gouge for the written exam; the types of clouds you see from the airplane are better than rheumatism for warning you of what is ahead. It may be the first clue, even before the forecasters get one, that a front has speeded up its activity and will arrive at your destination much earlier than expected. Recognizing cloud types can give you time to make some alternative decisions. If you move your kitchen simulator outdoors and listen to the forecast, you can watch from the ground the types of clouds

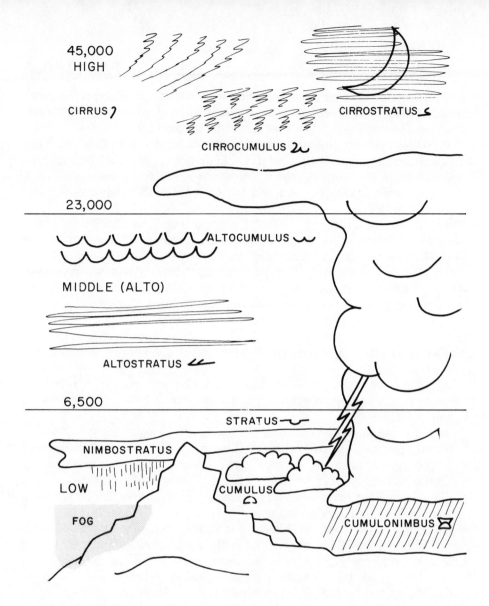

FIG. 5.12. *Clouds.*

that precede the forecast front, and the ones that follow frontal passage as well. Even "weather knowledge" need not ALL be acquired in an airplane.

There are three basic cloud types. Cumulus, meaning "accumulation," are clouds that are heaped-up and billowy in appearance, and are formed by air currents rising vertically. They have bumps in them. Stratus, meaning "stratified" or "layered," are clouds that are formed by the cooling of a layer of stable air and are usually smooth flying. Rain can fall from either cumulus or stratus clouds. The prefix "nimbo" or the suffix "numbus" means rain. "Cumulo-nimbus" is a thunderbumper; "nimbostratus" produces the steady drizzle. If they add the suffix "fractus" to the cloud type, it means the clouds are fractured or broken. Cirrus clouds are composed entirely of ice crystals, instead of water droplets. They appear only in the high-altitude family.

The three cloud types fall into four basic cloud "families": (1) high clouds, (2) middle clouds, (3) low clouds, and (4) clouds with extensive vertical development. Let's look at the families, together with the cloud types:

1. High clouds form with bases from about 16,500 to 45,000 feet. They will all be cirroform clouds because it is cold up there. "Mare's tails" are high cirrus clouds.

a) Cirrocumulus are thin, high, and cottony looking; they may contain some turbulence and icing.

b) Cirrostratus form a thin, whitish layer (like a veil), which will appear as a halo around the sun or the moon. They usually contain no turbulence or icing but produce severe restriction to visibility.

2. Middle clouds have their own prefix, "alto." These are composed primarily of water, but much of it may be supercooled and ready and waiting to stick to the airplane. These cloud bases run from 6,500 to 23,000 feet.

a) Altocumulus may appear in layers or patches and often have a "waved" appearance; the old "buttermilk sky." They contain turbulence and icing. A standing lenticular is an altocumulus cloud, but it deserves its own separate description.

b) Altostratus appears as a bluish layer, possibly merging into cirrostratus. The sun may be dimly visible through it, and it contains little or no turbulence, with moderate icing.

3. Low clouds range from near the surface to bases of about 6,500 feet. These may be stratus or stratocumulus. Low stratocumulus are often referred to as "fair weather cumulus," as they form on clear summer days from convection currents. Both kinds can contain icing if the temperature is right.

4. Clouds with extensive vertical development may be called towering cumulus or CBs; you know about those.

Although not really a cloud itself, you should recognize "virga." This is ragged-looking rain, falling from the base of a cumulus cloud and evaporating without reaching the ground. Look for some turbulence when you see virga. The really scary ones for turbulence are the standing lenticulars, including the accompanying roll, or rotor clouds, and possibly cap clouds.

A lenticular is lens shaped and "standing" because it is constantly forming on one side, due to rising (BLOWING) air, and dissipating on the other side. It forms in a "mountain-wave" condition when wind blows up a mountainside at 30 knots or more and causes trouble. Below the lenticular, there may be a cap cloud (foenwall) sitting right on top of the mountain ridge. Another cloud, the rotor (which does just what it sounds like it would), is located downwind from the ridge and usually parallel to it (on the leeward side). This "horizontal tornado" can produce up and downdrafts in excess of 5,000 fpm. That is turbulence.

You can get a mountain-wave condition without any of the accompanying clouds; but if you see any (or all) of them, either climb to clear the lenticular by several thousand feet, or turn around. With a little imagination, you can almost SEE turbulence in the mountains. If you know the wind direction and velocity, picture water flowing over those rocks; the air will flow the same way. Hug the upslope (windward side), and stay as far as possible from the downslope (leeward side).

These are the cloud types you might see if you were flying toward a warm front:

From about 600 miles ahead of the front's position, you would begin to encounter high cirrus and cirrostratus.

Some 200 miles later, still 400 miles from the front, the sky would be overcast with stratus and altostratus layers; it will be raining soon, if it isn't already.

By 200 miles ahead of the front, which is still coming to meet you, there are nimbostratus clouds and continuous rain. Ceilings are lowering, and visibility is worsening. Passing through the front itself, you will definitely be IFR, with drizzle, possible icing, and imbedded thunderstorms.

Racing a fast-moving cold front head-on to your destination might present this picture:

You are flying under a high overcast, with stratocumulus clouds, smooth air, and VFR visibilities, although possibly on the low side. The leading edge of a cold front is much steeper than a warm front, so you will come upon it more suddenly. These conditions may last until 200 miles or so from the front's position. If the warm air ahead of the cold front is generally stable, it may resemble a warm-front condition; but if it is unstable, there is the potential for meeting up with squall lines and even isolated tornado activity. After the front passes (I assume you landed and waited a few hours) there is usually rapid clearing, it is colder, and you have clear air with gusty surface winds. Watch for the signs, and keep in touch with Flight Watch (or somebody) as to the position of the front. Gambling with weather is idiotic; the odds are stacked in favor of the house.

We discussed the dangers of fog in the section on night operations. Fog is classified by the way in which it forms. Understanding it could put you on guard, based on the forecast. There is no substitute for knowing the local area; ask someone who does.

1. Radiation fog is relatively shallow ground fog. It occurs on land and stays shallow when the wind is calm. Winds up to 5 knots may stir things up enough to deepen the layer considerably. Stronger winds will probably blow it away or deepen it to become a layer of low stratus clouds. Conditions favoring the formation of radiation fog are a clear sky, little or no wind, and high relative humidity. It is usually a late night and early morning situation; it has been known to wait until sunrise to start forming, as the rising sun kicks up a slight breeze.

2. Advection fog can form over land or water when moist air moves over a surface that is colder than the air. It is more of a coastal problem, most prominently our West coast "Marine Layer." It forms offshore and is blown inland. It can come in very fast, but when it finally starts to burn off, it goes away quickly.

3. Upslope fog is predominantly a mountain problem—moist air blows up the sloping terrain and is cooled adiabatically (lapse rate). Upslope fog can form under *cloudy skies* as well as clear conditions; it may be very dense, and the layer may be very deep. It needs wind to move upslope and form. This fog can sneak up on you where the upsloping terrain is gradual; it may look flat from the air, but the elevation is steadily increasing. Again, knowing the area helps.

4. Precipitation-induced fog is caused when warm rain falls through cool air. Most commonly associated with warm fronts, it may extend over large areas. Any fog is bad enough, but this may lower visibilities and mask such hazards as thunderstorms, turbulence, and icing conditions. This is the situation with the potential for clear ice from freezing rain. Monitor the OAT very closely.

5. Ice fog needs extreme cold ($-25°F$ or more). It is cold-weather radiation fog and would be blinding in the sunlight.

Snow can be as weird as fog. It may stick to the airplane, but it probably won't. There is no forward visibility in snow. A snow shower is no place for a VFR pilot. Even if you think you can see through it, wait until you are IN it; snow can glop up on the windscreen and visibility goes to zero-zero. The mere presence of snow on the surface can transform once familiar terrain into brand new territory. Ice and snow on a runway turns takeoffs and landings into a whole new ball game. If you were to have an emergency en route in this kind of weather, you should be prepared with warm clothes. Even if you survived your landing, you could freeze while you waited for Search and Rescue. If your training did not include any experience with ice and snow, get some additional information before blasting off where you will encounter it, or the lessons you learn could be your last.

In summary, there are several points I want to reemphasize, along with a new one or two. Check weather; ask local pilots to interpret conditions for you if there is any question in your mind. Be scrupulously honest with yourself in evaluating your own ability. Set your own personal weather minimums, and don't let any kind of pressures make you deviate from them. For the first couple of trips, I recommend you don't go with less than 3,500 feet and 7 miles. Lower than that requires skillful pilotage and dead reckoning, especially in unfamiliar terrain. I stuck with 3,500 feet as a ceiling minimum long after I was willing to decrease my personal visibility minimum.

Learn to look for weather trends yourself by checking a couple of previous reports. This is the way you will learn if the conditions are improving or worsening. Each time you fly and encounter some weather, go back and analyze it afterwards. Compare the forecast with what you saw from the airplane. You will know better what to expect the next time a similar situation comes up in the preflight weather briefing.

If you feel there is a chance of it being better than forecast, take a look; but don't try it unless you have a sure way out. The 180° turn is often the smartest move a pilot can make; don't leave the decision to turn around until it is too late.

A solo pilot is forced to be his OWN weather teacher. Be sure he doesn't have a fool for a student.

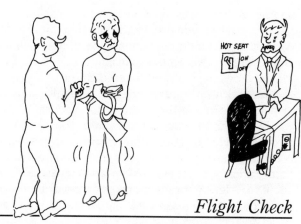

Flight Check

At long last, the Big Day is here. You really should not be nervous (your flight instructor knows you are ready), but you are probably suffering from advanced "checkitus." Your instructor has seen to it that all your logbook endorsements are in order and has furnished you with a (typed) recommendation form that both of you have signed.

Last night before you went to bed you reviewed the *Flight Test Guide,* which supplied you with a suggested checklist for the flight check. Some words of advice: Plan to arrive at the airport far enough ahead of time to run down the aircraft maintenance records and check the tach time, so you can show the examiner that the airplane is airworthy. If the inspections are not current, the flight check will end right there. Be sure your sectional chart is current. If you are unable to produce a current (full set) copy of AIM, the examiner will supply one (by prior arrangement). If you are going to fly with the FAA, you won't have to pay the inspector; a designated examiner will want a check in advance.

With the checklist items organized, present your trembling (neatly groomed) self to the flight examiner—*on time*! He will sit down with you and talk a little bit. In the course of the conversation, the horns and fangs you noticed at the beginning may start to disappear. He should explain to you that he will do nothing to trick you or trap you into doing anything illegal or dangerous.

He realizes that due to nervousness you can normally perform better than you will today. As an evaluator, he can tell the difference between the jitters and a lack of skill or knowledge. He will do everything in his power to put you at ease.

The flight examiner is not supposed to give you ground instruction on the oral or dual instruction on the flight, either; but I would be very surprised if you don't learn a great deal during both phases. If he asks you a question that you don't know the answer to, admit it. I have never met a flight examiner yet who could end an oral in which the applicant answered every question correctly. It would drive him crazy. Some of my best friends are flight examiners, and I know how their minds work.

The oral will consist of direct and specific questions. Asking good questions, and by "good" I mean clearly phrased so that BOTH parties understand the question, is a definite skill; some examiners are better at it than others. If you are not sure you understand a question, say so. The examiner will find another way to phrase it. This is just an oral, not an inquisition. The objective is not to prove that you don't know anything; it is to determine whether you know enough to fly innocent, nonpilot, *passengers* around in airplanes. A flight examiner has an awesome responsibility.

As far as the material covered on the oral goes, I can only advise you about the areas I would cover myself. I might start with your airplane and its systems, including the reasons for density altitude performance graphs. I would also check your knowledge of the recent experience requirements for yourself, and inspection requirements for your equipment. I would bear down especially hard on airspace and VFR minimums. Examiners tend to probe the tender areas when they discover a weakness. Your attitude in that instance will count for a lot. A conscientious pilot, realizing his deficiency, will take steps to correct it. I would make sure that you understand wingtip vortices and that you could correctly evaluate emergencies in various phrases of flight. We would also cover the areas in which you missed questions on the written exam. After you two have talked for awhile (and you have calmed down), the examiner will assign you a couple of problems and leave you alone to work them out. You will do a weight and balance problem and prepare an assigned cross-country flight plan. Including calling for weather, it should take you no longer than 20 minutes to plan a 2-hour flight. Afterwards, you will talk a little about the weather and about your flight plan. Then you and your examiner will go out together to preflight the airplane. You will probably find out things about your airplane that you never heard of before. This *still* keeps happening to me, and I have been around airplanes longer than you have.

There are ten pilot operations in the private pilot flight test guide. Your examiner must test you in each pilot operation. You will not be tested on *every* item in the flight test guide; it would take all day. You will demonstrate the stalls and MCA, at least one ground reference maneuver, short- and soft-field takeoffs and landings, at least one simulated off-airport emergency, some hood work (possibly including VOR tracking), and unusual attitudes. At some point you will depart on the cross-country flight you planned. After you are established well enough to compute an accurate ground speed and ETA, you will be given the emergency diversion like you have practiced.

The minimum acceptable standards are clearly defined in the flight test guide. If you blow a maneuver, you should know it yourself. Just as in the oral, admit you goofed and ask to try it again. You know you can do it right, and this is still not an inquisition. I have mentioned before that I consider MCA the most important maneuver in the flight test guide because you can't handle MCA unless you understand the airplane. If you can handle that well, the rest is easy. I would also be watching very closely to see that you are clearing the area. The objective of the flight check is to determine your safety as a pilot.

Most examiners don't say much in the airplane during a flight check, except to tell you what maneuver they want next. They write little notes on a piece of paper. This silence feels ominous, and it drives me up the wall wondering what is being written. Try not to let it bother you; the notes being made may be complimentary.

You are the pilot in command of this flight; you are not receiving dual instruction. The examiner will not take control of the airplane unless you scare him half to death. The examiner keeps quiet so as not to interfere or influence your performance and makes notes for your debriefing when it is all over. After the examiner is satisfied one way or the other about your performance, he (or she) may take the airplane and show you a thing or two. This can be a very humbling experience; most examiners are good. They like to show off a little and feel they must impress upon you that even though you are a private pilot now, you don't know *everything* yet; good plan.

Please accept my sincere congratulations on earning your private pilot certificate. If you feel that this book has been any help, join me in one last "miscellaneous" section, now that you have pinned on your wings.

Private Pilot—Airplane

There is a phenomenon that attacks many pilots at this point called "postflight-check depression." You put in a lot of time and effort, and all the study and practice culminated in one successful flight. So now what? Booted out of the nest, you feel at loose ends. Flight training has become a way of life, and many of us plunge right in working toward the next certificate or rating, whether it is to be the commercial, the instrument, or the multimotor. Now that you are a private pilot—airplane, consider going for some added class. In just a few hours of the most fun you ever had, you can add a seaplane rating. Added categories are also available to you, and you can find the requirements in FAR, Part 61. You haven't experienced flight until you have been soaring. Consider gliders, hot air balloons, helicopters, gyroplanes—once you have opened the door to the world of flight, the possibilities are endless. Then there are ultralights, hang-gliders, . . .

I will make a statement that may get me boiled in oil by approved-school flight-training salesmen all over the country. Before signing up for a programmed, integrated training course, consider building some experience on your own. The commercial certificate is a professional level of accomplishment; the instrument rating is also, even if it is going on a private ticket. If this is your ambition, you should be willing and able to direct your own training, at least to this extent: You can look up the requirements in the regs; discuss your flying future with a number of qualified people, including your old instructor, your new flying friends, and, yes, the flight-training salesman. You may want to build experience with some long cross-country flights and take a dual ride once in a while to stay sharp. Use the dual rides to be introduced to the commercial flight maneuvers. This will give you something new to play with during your local solo flights. At least you can select the direction that is right for you.

Just because you are a certificated pilot now, you haven't been abandoned. As you tackle more ambitious trips, your old instructor (or any experienced pilot on the field) will be more than happy to answer any questions. One of the greatest rewards in flying is the friends you make. Any time you are in unfamiliar territory and feeling unsure, ask a local pilot. Other pilots are never total strangers, and they usually love to give advice.

If you can possibly swing it, plan a trip from coast to coast. I promise you will be a different pilot when you get home. If you live in the West, you can't avoid getting a little mountain flying experience if you ever leave the state; there is no way "out" except "over." If you are a flatlander planning a trip across the Rockies (or any other mountain range), invest in a mountain flying course before you go. There are techniques involved in flying the mountains and aspects of mountain weather that would fill another entire book. If you can't locate an experienced mountain man in your territory, plan a brief layover just short of the ridge line. A couple of hours with a local instructor could make the difference between a beautiful trip and disaster. The same goes for over-water flights, or if your training includes no experience with ice and snow. Get some sound advice before striking out.

Regulations are going to continue to change, and you are now responsible for keeping up to date. You can get on the mailing list for free FAA advisory circulars by writing:

U.S. Department of Transportation
Distribution Requirements Section, M 482.2
Washington, DC 20590

You will have to specify the subject series you are interested in. For years I received A & P mechanic–type advisories, along with the ones I needed to know about. There are excellent organizations you can join that will be of great value to you in keeping abreast of changes in aviation. There are also numerous magazines on the newsstand that I look forward to every month for information as well as entertainment.

Earlier, we mentioned a few things a pilot can do to be considerate of nervous passengers. It is time to discuss one thing that *unnervous* passengers can do to *pilots*. They can influence them to make dumb decisions concerning weather.

It is not too surprising that nonpilots will press to go ahead when they have prepaid tickets to the Super Bowl game; after all, they haven't the faintest idea what they may be getting into. A few thunderstorms never slowed down a Cadillac. It's incredible that pilots (who SHOULD know better) don't swallow their egos and tell the jerks that the weather is more than they can handle. The pilot, who would never attempt the flight solo, gives in to the circumstances. Do not underestimate the power of "passenger pressure." It can get you in big trouble.

Another pressure is "Get-Home-Itus." This one can get to solo pilots who figure they will risk it this time since they have only themselves to consider. Their families are still going to miss them a lot.

A safe, conscientious pilot checks the weather and learns from every new experience. The old saying that "flying is hours of boredom, punctuated by moments of sheer terror" may be funny because of the grains of truth it contains. If I have emphasized anything in this book, I hope it is the importance of solid procedures—habit patterns to fall back on if the going gets rough—and the good sense to plan ahead and avoid the obvious problems that catch up to so many of us.

Whatever future goals you set for yourself in aviation, I wish you success, enjoyment, satisfaction, and most of all, safety.

"THE BEGINNING"

RECOMMENDED READING

Airman's Information Manual: Basic Flight Information and ATC Procedures. Washington, D.C., USGPO, May 1982.

Aviation Instructor's Handbook. Washington, D.C., USGPO, 1977.

Aviation Weather. Washington, D.C., USGPO, 1975.

Aviation Weather Services. Washington, D.C., USGPO, 1979.

Federal Aviation Regulations. Washington, D.C., USGPO.

Flight Training Handbook. Washington, D.C., USGPO, 1980.

Instrument Flying Handbook. Washington, D.C., USGPO, 1980.

Pilot's Handbook of Aeronautical Knowledge. Washington, D.C., USGPO, 1979.

Private Pilot—Airplane: Flight Test Guide. Washington, D.C., USGPO, 1975.

Private Pilot—Airplane: Written Test Guide. Washington, D.C., USGPO, 1979.

INDEX

Absolute altitude, 33
Accelerated stall, 98
Acceleration error, 31
Accuracy landings, 120
    planning, key positions, 120
Advanced maneuver practice, 96–98
Adverse aileron yaw, 39
Aerodynamics, 22–24
Agonic line, 30–31
AIM (*Airman's Information Manual*),
    71, 86
Airport traffic area, 69–71
Airspace, 63–71
    in AIM, 63–71
    on sectional chart, 66–67
    structure, 65
Airspeed Indicator, 34–35
    calibrated, 34
    indicated, 34
    true, 34–35
Altimeter, 32–34
Altitude, 33–34
    density, 20, 33–34, 112
    indicated, 33
    and medication, 8
    pressure, 33
    true, 33
ANDS (Accelerate North, Decelerate
    South), 31
Angle of attack, 22
Approach to landing stall, 97
Area forecast, 169
Arriving, controlled airport, 18–19
Asymmetric loading, 23
Attitude
    Indicator, 27–28
    instrument flying, 122–28
    unusual, 125–28
Automatic Direction Finder, 104–5
Automatic Terminal Information Serv-
    ice, 17–18
Avgas, 9
Axis, 22
    lateral pitch, 22
    longitudinal roll, 22
    vertical yaw, 22

Barometric pressure, 16, 32–33
Bernoulli's theory, 22

Best glide speed, 37–38
Biennial Flight Review, 74
Brakes, 13–14
Burble point, 22, 42

Calibrated Airspeed, 34
Carburetor, 15
    heat, use of, 15
    ice, 15
Cardinal headings, 28
Category, class, type, aircraft, 73
Center of Gravity, 44
Certificates, aircraft, 8
    airworthiness, 8
    registration, 8
Certification requirements, pilot, 4
Checklist, 10, 14
    and engine start, 10–12
Clearance delivery, 19, 95–96
Climb airspeeds, 37
Climbs, 36–37
Cloud types, 171
Communication, 16–20
Compass correction card, 31
Compass rose, 28–29
Complex airplanes, 150–55
Coordination, 23–24
Cross-country
    flight–planning checklist, 132–39
    flying, the, 140–45
    summary outline, 139
Crosswind, 57–62
    component, 59–60
    landing, 60–62
    takeoff, 62
    track, 59

DF steer, 109–10
DME (Distance Measuring Equipment),
    103–4
Density altitude. *See* Altitude
Departing, controlled airport, 17–18
Descents, 37–38
Deviation error, 31

Emergency situations, 116–18
Engine
    care of, 25
    failure on takeoff, 56

181

fire, 12
prime, 12
shutdown, 11
start, 11
Extended traffic pattern, 54

FARs (*Federal Aviation Regulations*),
    71–86
    Part 61, 72–76
    Part 91, 76–86
Five-hour check, 49–50
Flight check, 175–77
    application for, 73
Flight computer, 6, 137
Flight plan, 106–8
Flight Service Station, 105–10
Flight Test Guide, 6, 96
Fog, 148, 172–74
Forward slips, 57–58
Fuel
    boost pump, 11–12
    flow and power percentage, 141–42
    fuel/air ratio, 15
    gauges, 8
    management, 143–44
    octane, 9
    selector, 14
    tanks, 10

G force limitations, category, 41
Glides, 37–38
Go, no go, 13, 16, 106, 174
Graveyard spiral, 41
Ground reference maneuvers, 46–48
    8s around pylons, 48
    rectangular course, 48
    S-turns across road, 48
    turns about point, 48
    wind circles, 47
Gust speed, 60
Gyroscopic
    effect, 24
    instruments, 27–30

Hemispheric rule, 68–69
Hood. *See* Under the hood

Indicated airspeed, 34
Inspection, 8
    walk-around, 7–10
Instrument flying, 122–28
    aircraft control, 123
    instrument cross-check, 123
    instrument interpretation, 123
    unusual attitudes, 125–28
Isogonic lines, 30–31

Kitchen simulator, 6–7

Landings
    accuracy, 121
    crosswind, 60–63

normal, 55–57
recoveries and other emergencies,
    54–57
short-field, 115–16
soft-field, 113–15
Lateral axis, 23
Lead compass heading, 31
Left-turning tendencies, 24
Local solo phase. *See* Solo
Logbook
    pilot, 5, 73
Longitudinal axis, 23

Magnetic compass, 30–31
Magnetic dip error, 31
Magneto, 10–15
Maintenance, 8
Medical certificate, 5
Microphone, 17
Minimum controllable airspeed, 44–46
Mixture control, 12, 141

Navigation plotter, 6, 132–39
Night operations, 147–50
Normal traffic pattern, 50–53
Northerly turn error, 31
Nosewheel steering, 13
NTSB (National Transportation Safety
    Board) Part 830, 5

Objectives, 3–6
Off-airport landings, 118–21
Oscillation error, 32
Owner's manual, 6, 8, 11, 15

Performance charts, 111–13
P-factor, 23
Pilotage and dead reckoning, 130–32
Pitot-static system, 32–36
Pitot tube, 9
Porpoising, 55
Precession, 28
Preflight, 7–10
Pressure altitude, 33
Primary flight instruments, 26–36
Primary flight maneuvers, 36–48
Private pilot – airplane, 177–79
Procedures, memorizing, 7, 36, 37, 38,
    43, 46, 52, 53, 61, 144

Radar, Stage III, 93–94
Radar summary chart, 168
Radio communication, 16–20
Radio frequencies, 19–20
Radio navigation, 99–105
Reciprocals, 29
Relative wind, 22
Reverse sensing, 103
Runup, 11–16

Short-field takeoffs and landings,
    115–16
Side slips, 58

Significant weather prognostic chart, 165
Simulator practice
  accelerated stall, 98
  approach to landing stall, 97
  cross-wind landing, 61
  cross-wind takeoff, 62
  ground reference maneuvers, 47–48
  minimum controllable airspeed, 44–46
  short-field takeoffs and landings, 115–16
  soft-field takeoffs and landings, 114–15
  takeoff and departure stall, 98
  traffic patterns, 52–53
  unusual attitudes, 128
Slips
  forward, side, 57–58
Soft-field takeoffs and landings, 113–15
Solo
  cross-country, flying the, 140–45
  first, 87–88
  local, 89–90
Spins, 43–44
Spiraling slipstream, 14
Stalls, 41–43
  accelerated, 98
  approach to landing, 97
  full, 42
  imminent, 42
  power-off, 37
  power-on, 42
  takeoff and departure, 98
  warning, 9
Standard atmosphere values, 32
Standard barometric pressure, 33
Standard rate turn, 30
Static source, 9
Steep spirals, 120
Steep turns, 40
Surface analysis, 162–63

Tachometer, 25–26
Takeoff, 20–21
  and departure stall, 98
  and landings, 50–62
Taxi, 13–14
TCAs, (Terminal Control Areas), 19
  Group I, 92
  Group II, 92
Throttle, 25, 38
Top of climb, 37
Torque, 14, 23, 36
Traffic pattern
  crosswind, 60
  extended, 54
  normal, 51
  off-airport emergency, 120

sharing, 53–54
Transponder, 11, 20, 90–91
Trim, 16, 123
Trim and throttle, 24–26
TRSAs (Terminal Radar Service Area), 93–94
  and Stage III Radar, 94
True airspeed, 34–35
True altitude, 33
True course, 131
Turn and bank, 29–30
Turns, 39–41
  climbing, 36–37
  gliding, 36–37
  to headings, 40
  steep, 40

Uncontrolled airports, 19–20
Under the hood, 28, 29, 30, 35, 36, 123
Unusual attitudes, 125–28

Vacuum gauge, 27
Vacuum pump, 27
Variation, 31
Vertical axis, 23
Vertical lift component, 40
Vertical speed indicator, 35–36
VOR (Very High Frequency Omnirange)
  intersection, 144
  receiver, 100–102
  reception, 100
  tracking, 102–3
  transmitter, 99–100
V speeds, 34
  V_a, 112, 159
  V_r, 53
  V_{so}, 37
  V_x, 37, 42–43, 53
  V_y, 37

Wake turbulence, 92
Walk-around inspection. *See* Inspection
Weather, 155–74
  in AIM, 156–61
  charts, 165–67
  definitions, 147–48
  judgment, 155
  in written exam, 161–74
Weather depiction chart, 166–67
Weather vaning, 14, 61, 62
Weight and balance, 111–13
Wheelbarrowing, 62
Winds aloft forecast, 137, 169
Wind shear, 60
Written examination, 5, 145–47
Written Test Guide, 6, 146–47